Mike Kalina's Travelin' Gourmet Cookbook

Mike Kalina's Travelin' Gourmet Cookbook

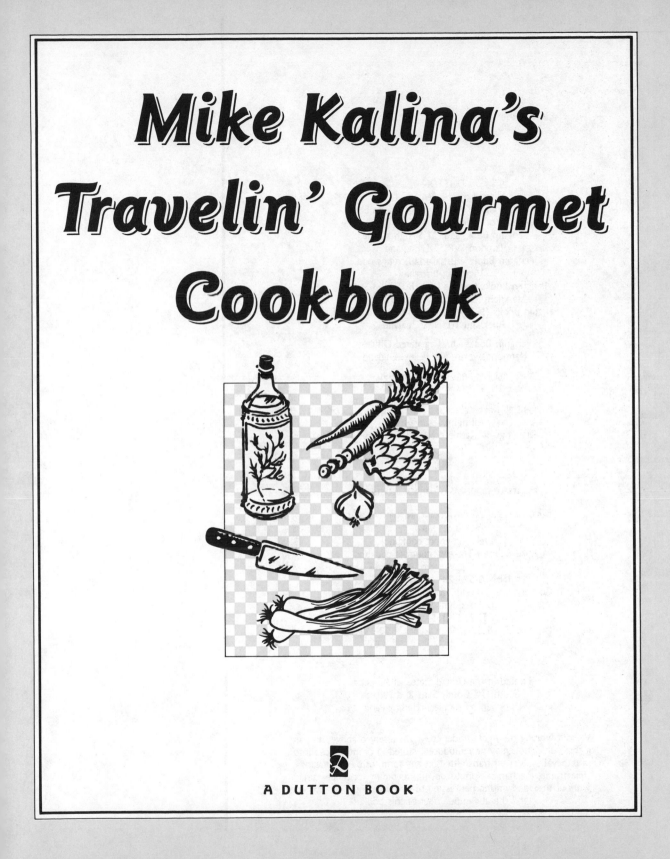

A DUTTON BOOK

DUTTON
Published by the Penguin Group
Penguin Books USA Inc., 375 Hudson Street,
New York, New York 10014, U.S.A.
Penguin Books Ltd, 27 Wrights Lane,
London W8 5TZ, England
Penguin Books Australia Ltd, Ringwood,
Victoria, Australia
Penguin Books Canada Ltd, 2801 John Street,
Markham, Ontario, Canada L3R 1B4
Penguin Books (N.Z.) Ltd, 182–190 Wairau Road,
Auckland 10, New Zealand

Penguin Books Ltd, Registered Offices:
Harmondsworth, Middlesex, England

First Printing, November 1990
10 9 8 7 6 5 4 3 2 1

REGISTERED TRADEMARK — MARCA REGISTRADA

LIBRARY OF CONGRESS CATALOGING IN PUBLICATION DATA:
Kalina, Mike.
[Travelin' gourmet cookbook]
Mike Kalina's Travelin' gourmet cookbook.
p.   cm.
ISBN 0-525-24916-8 : $18.95
1. Cookery. 2. Travelin' gourmet. I. Title. II. Title:
Travelin' gourmet cookbook.
TX714.K355   1990
641.5 — dc20   90-3578
CIP

Printed in the United States of America
Set in ITC Goudy Sans and Futura
Designed by Kathleen Herlihy-Paoli

To Doris, the spice of my life,
and to the one in the oven . . .

ACKNOWLEDGMENTS

My wife, Doris, was more than just an inspiration — she was a hands-on assistant, who helped test many of the recipes, contributed several of her own, made delicious suggestions, and did more than her share of copyreading. Her eager palate and unbridled joy at table also made my myriad dining experiences around the world more memorable. Rebecca West once said that she wrote to find out what she thought. Doris eats to find out what she likes (and she likes most everything). And what food writer could NOT love a woman who once commented how great it was that so many cities in Europe were named after cheese or wine?

Many thanks also to the man behind the scenes of "The Travelin' Gourmet" PBS series, executive producer John Swartz, Jr., who believed in me at the height of my obscurity. Other Pittsburghers who helped with the show include video editor Manny Politis, audio editor Danny Ferraro, and consultant Glenn Przyborski.

Thanks also to Bill Block, publisher of the *Pittsburgh Post-Gazette*, where my position as travel editor and food critic brought me the experience that made "The Travelin' Gourmet" series (and this cookbook) possible.

I also appreciate the guidance and support of George Anderson and his entertainment department of the *Post-Gazette*, of which I am proud to be a part. It was where my writing about food and travel took root and was honed. I'd also like to thank KDKA-TV, which opened the door to the world of television for me.

Many thanks also to my team of recipe-testers in Pittsburgh, who took the time to test and fine-tune many of the recipes: Melanie Casey, Joyce Renne, Tony D'Imperio, owner of D'Imperio's Restaurant, and his chef, Joe Schilling; Chef Dave McKinney, of Jake's Above the Square, and partner, Jake Hickton; Chef Robert Zelesko and brothers Bill and Eddie, of Tramp's Restaurant; Executive Chef Norbert Bomm, of the Pittsburgh Vista International Hotel, Vista general manager Paul Kelly, and Iga Gaj, public relations director of that hotel, who also helped me gather other recipes from Vista hotels throughout the world.

Also: Patty Tascarella, my long-time assistant; Doug Zimmerman of Christopher's Restaurant and owner Chris Passodelis; Chefs David Watson, Tim Tain, Larry Brudy, Joe Parrotto, Tony Mannella, and Ron Herbinko, of the International Culinary Academy, as well as the students at the school. Thanks also to Al Maglin, Larry Grotstein, and Ed Boyd, the behind-the-scenes men at the academy.

Other Pittsburghers who were helpful include restaurant consultant Lou Adams, who guided me in my early days as a food critic and assisted in the research for this book; Mike Alioto, of Alioto's Produce; Byron Bardy, of Heinz Corp.; Chef Nick Coletti; attorney Chris Copetas; producer Arthur Greenwald; photographer Roy Englebrecht; Paul and Jackie Busang, of Gulliver's Travels; Phil and Dorothy Petrulli, of Holiday Travel; Roy Davis, of Royal Travel Corp.; friends Tom and Susan Kapner; artist Girts Purins; Chris Schafer, of MicroAge Electronics; Mike Palamone and Mary Alice Polyak, of Graphics Plus; and Barry ("Norton") Paris and wife, Myrna, who are among my favorite dining companions.

Also kind enough to help me with this book and my TV series were countless individuals throughout the U.S. and Europe.

In New York, Morris Silver, of M. Silver Associates, not only helped coordinate many of the ground arrangements abroad and in New York for my crew and me as we filmed the series, but he and his wonderful public relations staff also helped gather many of the recipes herein.

I also appreciate his encouragement about "The Travelin' Gourmet" from the beginning. Quite frankly, without his help the project might never have gotten off the ground.

Thanks, too, to Susan Bang, of Lou Hammond Associates, who helped garner recipes from the Greenbriar and other noted resorts, as well as offered suggestions, supplied background information, and offered lots of encouragement; to publicist Ruth Epstein, for contributing recipes from the fine restaurants at Rockefeller Center; to Jessica Miller not only for opening up doors for me with the Vista organization but also for coordinating arrangements at such fabulous restaurants as Windows on the World and the Rainbow Room at Rockefeller Center.

Other New Yorkers who helped include my agent, the aptly named Nancy Love; Molly Allen, my compassionate and supportive editor at E. P. Dutton, who spearheaded this book; the ever bubbly and effusive Merry Clark of King Features; and publicist Tim Benford.

Also: Jack MacBean of the New York Convention and Visitors Bureau, who personally led me on glorious taste-tests of many New York restaurants through the years; owner George Briquet and Chef Antoine Bouterin of the famed Le Périgord Restaurant, who supplied background information on French cuisine (not to mention fabulous meals); the staff at the Maurice Hotel, for introducing me to Alain Senderens, who shared some of his magic with me; dining companion and friend Barbara Zitwer; Joan Bloom, of Hill and Knowlton; the publicity people with the Cunard Line; John Lampl, of British Airways; restaurant publicist Lee Canaan; the public relations staff of the wonderful Stanhope Hotel, and Jean Vergnes, the hotel's culinary consultant.

Also helpful were the staff of the Master Chefs Institute and public relations executive Suzanne Palmerick, of Porter/Novelli public relations, who helped in recipe research; and the crew at Middleburg, Middleton, Picower publicists, who provided introductions to countless chefs around the world.

In Los Angeles, I received delicious research assistance from Polly Dugas, Peggy Armstrong, and Larry Mayran; advisory aid and moral support from Stella Zadeh; musical aid from Marty Wereski, who wrote the music for my theme song and scored my PBS series; legal assistance from Ron herisko. I'd also like to thank the staffs of the Four Seasons Beverly Hills Hotel, the Beverly-Wilshire Regent, and L'Ermitage, where I enjoyed many comfortable stays while doing my research.

Two individuals in Philadelphia who helped me considerably were Chef Oliver de St. Martin of Atop the Bellevue, and writer Jack Smith.

Among the many people in Paris who assisted were Claude Terrail of La Tour d'Argent; restaurant consultant Robert Noah, writer Patricia Wells, and the staffs of the Plaza-Athénée and George V. I'm also appreciative for the aid of the Trusthouse-Forte Hotel Groups and Hilton International, which not only were gracious enough to house my crew in their lush environs but also contributed many recipes.

I know I may have inadvertently left out some of those who helped me. But you know who you are, and thanks a lot too!

CONTENTS

BORN TO EAT
The Travelin' Gourmet Theme Song*

LYRICS BY M. KALINA

Packin' my bags, 'cause I'm goin' to places,
To find new food, new sights, new faces!
Goin' wherever my palate may lead me,
Searchin' this whole world for great chefs to feed me!

This life can't be beat!
'Cause I was born to eat!

Salmon in Scotland, Alfredo in Rome.
Pastries in Vienna beat the donuts back home.
Pâté in Paree, so good that it's scary!
And how could I go "wong" with the dim-sum in Hong Kong?

This life can't be beat!
'Cause I was born to eat!

(Spoken)

I'll take one of those, and one of those
And two of those, hey, I'll try anything twice!
And I'd like the chef's special, but only if he's on a roll!
And the chef's surprise, too. But break it to me gently. I scare easily.
And bring the soup du jour. If you're out of it, hey!
Bring the soup of the day!

Caviar and champagne. Tapas in Madrid, Spain.
And nothin' could be finer than Peking Duck in China!

All such a treat for a man born to eat!

APERITIF

 I don't know about you, but I've been eating for as long as I can remember, and I've always felt that dining well was the best revenge. Little did I know when I started my career as a newspaperman at the Harrisburg (Pa.) *Evening News* in the mid-'60s that I'd end up not only as a career "eater" but also as a professional tourist. Nice work if you can get it, and that's what happened when I landed the dream job of covering food and travel after joining the staff of the Pittsburgh (Pa.) *Post-Gazette* in 1971.

I subsequently found myself in the enviable position of being paid to savor the pleasures of the world and to share my joy with my readers. I quickly became the Melba toast of the cocktail-party circuit in Pittsburgh, sort of a poor man's Lucius Beebe, weaving tales of travel and dining to an ever-changing audience constantly shouting "Bravo!" (But maybe it was the hors d'oeuvres that I brought.)

I had the opportunity to share my love of travel and food with a wider audience when my PBS series, "The Travelin' Gourmet," started airing in September, 1989, in the United States and a dozen foreign countries. I'm pleased to report that the concept worked. As I had hoped, the public was ready for a food show that combined food and travel with fun.

Once the contract was signed to film my series, I had *carte blanche* to the finest restaurants in Europe. I not only had the opportunity to dine in them but also to interview their illustrious owner/chefs and

work in their kitchens. I garnered countless recipes along the way, which I simplified, adapted for the American kitchen, and in many cases have included in this book. I think they prove that even the most inexperienced cook can turn out the kind of wonderful dishes that have made European chefs famous. If not, I'll eat my words.

And there are a lot of recipes from people and places here at home too. Whenever possible, I have also tried to utilize every shortcut known to man in the pursuit of good taste, from using frozen puff pastry, now available in most supermarkets, to bringing into play basic kitchen helpers like the blender and food processor.

I suspect the fact that I am from Pittsburgh has made it easier for viewers from Middle America to relate to me than to someone raised near a truffle thicket in France. My geographic location has also provided a plus for the recipes herein. My philosophy in adapting them for this book was to use only those ingredients I could find in Pittsburgh. I think it's an accurate assumption that if you can find it in Pittsburgh, you can probably find it anywhere. Rest assured, you won't have to send out a search party to find exotic ingredients that other cookbooks may call for. And I think you'll find it a welcome surprise that you can fashion an amazing array of exciting dishes with ingredients that are available in your local supermarket.

In addition to the recipes from the TV series, this book includes many of my favorite dishes from chefs at home and around the world, many of which I have discovered in my journeys as travel writer and food critic. The book also is larded with cooking tips, a cross-section of savory quotes, and some tasty bits of trivia, which I hope you find as fascinating as I did.

Yours in good taste. . .
and may the forcemeat be with you!

Mike Kalina
The Travelin' Gourmet
Pittsburgh, Pennsylvania
November, 1990

P.S. When I think back on the countless gastronomic experiences that resulted in much of the raw material for this book, I recall what my wife, Doris, one of the world's happiest eaters, said to me at 90 Park Lane, in London's Grosvenor House, after the captain had literally smothered our table with a sample of every dessert in the house. After staring lasciviously at the acres of confections spread out before us, she looked at me with mist in her eyes, and purred: "We can't go on eating like this!" Somehow, we managed.

P.P.S.: If you would like to write to me regarding the recipes, the show, or to suggest a restaurant or a city that you think I should cover in future episodes, kindly send them to me, ℅ Pittsburgh Post-Gazette, 50 Boulevard of Allies, Pittsburgh, Pa. 15222. I'll also send you information about the "Travelin' Gourmet Newsletter" and other items related to the series.

APPETIZERS

"**G**razers,'' those diners with promiscuous palates who like to sample a variety of dishes at one sitting — more or less how you and I act at a Sunday brunch — can be found in every country in the world. But "grazing" didn't really become trendy in this country until Spanish tapas were introduced at a New York restaurant called The Ballroom back in 1983.

Tapas, literally "little plates of little things," became fashionable in Madrid and other Spanish cities because most restaurants there don't take their first dinner customers until after 9 p.m. Noshing on a tapa or three is a great way to take the edge off the ol' appetite until dinnertime. The problem I always have is that I like tapas so much that dinner usually ends up being redundant.

Tapas bars are rampant in Old Madrid, one of the city's most colorful sections. They dispense everything from plump, delicious marinated Spanish shrimp to finger sandwiches. By the way, a well-littered floor is the sign of a good tapas bar. Customers are encouraged to throw the toothpicks used to hold them, as well as napkins and other debris, on the floor. The thinking is that a prospective customer poking his head in the door and seeing the delicious mess on the floor will be inspired to walk in.

The best tapas bar in Madrid, in my book, is Meson Puerto Cerrada, a.k.a. Rey de Pimiento, literally "The King of Peppers," 4 Plaza Puerta Cerrada. Peppers of all sizes, shapes, and colors are everywhere. My favorites include the marinated and braised peppers, mild jalapeños deep-fried in oil and served with sea salt, and the big, roasted red peppers bathed in olive oil offered on thick slices of crusty Spanish bread layered with a slice of wonderful Spanish ham, known as *jabugo*, which is even better than prosciutto. The pigs feed on acorns, and their unique diet results in a succulent, delicious ham that's one of the best things I've ever eaten. From tiny acorns great hams grow!

By the way, try to use Spanish olive oil, which is carried by many specialty stores. It's more fruity in flavor than Italian olive oil and gives dishes a unique Spanish "accent." Incidentally, many women in Madrid told me that they owed their wonderful skin to the consumption of Spanish olive oil. Two of the finest brands of Spanish olive oil available in the United States are Sierra de Segura and Lerida. Olive oil, in case you haven't heard, contains no cholesterol and some nutritionists feel that it actually helps to *lower* cholesterol.

Let's begin with a great peppery recipe inspired by the "King of Peppers." It's a bit unorthodox because I'm using puff pastry as the base, but it works beautifully, and buying frozen puff pastry takes the pain out of making it yourself. It can serve either as a one-dish meal or as an appetizer. It's filled with flavors, spark, and personality and is not that difficult to make. It freezes well, too. It's one of the most requested recipes from *The Travelin' Gourmet* series.

Or if you're in a hurry, you can try the Hot Banana Pepper Tapas recipe that follows — so easy it's embarrassing.

"Never eat more than you can lift."
—MISS PIGGY

TRAVELIN' GOURMET EMPANADA

2 tablespoons paprika
9 tablespoons olive oil, preferably Spanish
1 teaspoon crushed red pepper flakes
1 tablespoon minced fresh parsley
2 medium-sized garlic cloves, minced
pinch or two salt
3/4 pound pork loin, cut into julienne strips about 2 inches long
    × 1/8 inch thick
1 green pepper, cut into thin strips
1 red pepper, cut into thin strips
1 tablespoon water
3 medium-sized onions, thinly sliced
1/4 cup white wine
1/2 pound frozen puff pastry dough (1 sheet), thawed
1 egg, beaten with 1 teaspoon ice water

In a large bowl, combine the paprika, 5 tablespoons of the olive oil, and the red pepper flakes, parsley, garlic, salt, and meat. Mix well and refrigerate overnight. Heat 3 tablespoons of the remaining olive oil in a large skillet over medium heat. Add the peppers; stir-fry about a minute. Lower the heat; add the water. Simmer about 12 to 15 minutes, until the peppers are tender but not too soft.

Remove the peppers to a bowl. In the same skillet, add the last tablespoon of olive oil and sauté the onions over medium-high heat until they start to get golden (don't brown). Put the onions in the same bowl as the peppers.

Raise the heat to high; add the marinated meat and stir-fry until it begins losing its color and starts to become tender. Lower the heat a bit, and add the wine. Cook for another two minutes. Add the pepper/onion mixture and stir well. Cook for another 2 to 3 minutes, stirring all the while, then remove from the heat.

Roll the thawed puff-pastry sheet into a ball, then separate into two even parts. Refrigerate one part while you're rolling the other. Working as fast as possible, roll it into a thin sheet, about 12 inches in diameter. Put that into the refrigerator as you roll out the other about a half inch wider (this will be the top sheet).

Preheat the oven to 350°.

OFF THE EATEN PATH:
Spanish Olive Oil

Olive oil is nearly as old as civilization itself. It was so prized in ancient Greece that winners of athletic competitions were awarded jugs of it. Today, Spain is the leading producer of olive oil, with Italy second and Greece third.

When you've finished using olive oil, screw the cap on tightly and put the bottle in a cool, dark place—not in the refrigerator, where the condensation will make it cloudy.

Put the smaller crust on a buttered cookie sheet or on parchment paper. Mound it carefully with the pork/pepper mixture, leaving about a half-inch edge. Cover with the remaining pastry sheet. Rim the edges of the bottom crust with water and pull up to join the top crust, pressing to seal the two as tightly as possible. Brush the top crust with the egg/water mixture.

Cut a few slits in the top. Bake until the crust has become golden (30 to 40 minutes). Let cool a bit and serve.

SERVES 8 AS APPETIZER; 4 AS MAIN COURSE

HOT BANANA PEPPER TAPAS

Most supermarkets carry hot banana peppers, so named because they're shaped like bananas.

12–15 banana peppers
8-ounce package cream cheese
4¼-ounce can deviled ham

Cut the stems off the peppers, remove the seeds, and core. Blend the cream cheese thoroughly with the deviled ham. Fill each pepper with the mixture (I use a cake bag), then spear with a toothpick and serve.

NOTE: Be careful not to rub your eyes after handling the banana peppers. I did one time — that's why I'm warning you.

SERVES 12–15

❝Only mediocre restaurants are always at their best.❞

—M.K.

My second favorite tapas bar in Madrid is Meson Champinon, in the heart of Old Madrid, which boasts an awesome selection of mushrooms of all shapes, sizes, flavors, and textures. In addition to the aroma of mushrooms sizzling on the grill, the first things you notice when you enter are ceramic mushrooms on the ceiling and in cases behind the bar.

The specialty is mushrooms stuffed with diced peppers and Spanish ham, which are then sizzled in olive oil on the grill. They're delivered to your spot at the bustling bar along with ice-cold mugs of lusty Spanish beer.

These next four mushroom recipes are based on ones from Meson Champinon.

STUFFED MUSHROOMS MESON CHAMPINON

Look for chorizo, a Spanish sausage heavily scented with paprika and garlic, in specialty stores for this easy recipe. If unavailable, substitute a spicy, Italian sausage (loose or removed from its casings).

½ cup finely chopped walnuts
½ pound chorizo, finely chopped
½ pound cleaned mushroom caps

Preheat the oven to 350°. Mix the walnuts with the sausage. Stuff the caps with the mixture and place in a greased pan. Bake for about 45 to 50 minutes, or until the sausage is cooked through. Serve immediately.

SERVES 4–6

The "Ninja Method" of Peeling Garlic

The only thing about garlic I didn't like was peeling it. Until I discovered the "Ninja Method," that is. All you do is put a little salt on a cutting board, put the clove on top, and, with the back of a wide knife, give it a good whack, screaming like a Ninja warrior as you do. Then just pull off the skin and chop it with abandon.

"A gourmet is just a glutton with brains."
—PHILIP W. HABERMAN JR.

SHERRY MUSHROOMS

3½ tablespoons olive oil (Spanish preferably)
½ pound large mushroom caps, cleaned
4 garlic cloves, minced
3 tablespoons dry sherry (Spanish, such as Tio Pepe, if
    possible)
¼ cup beef broth
2 teaspoons lemon juice
½ teaspoon paprika
salt and freshly ground black pepper to taste
¼ teaspoon cayenne
3 teaspoons minced fresh parsley

Heat the oil in a large skillet over a high flame and add the mushrooms and garlic. Stir-fry for 2 to 3 minutes. Lower the heat and stir in the sherry, broth, lemon juice, paprika, salt, pepper, and cayenne. Simmer two minutes. Top with the parsley and serve.

SERVES 6–8

MUSHROOMS IN GARLIC SAUCE

⅓ cup olive oil (Spanish, preferably)
1 whole garlic clove, peeled
1 pound mushroom caps, cleaned
2 garlic cloves, finely chopped
2 teaspoons finely chopped fresh parsley
salt and freshly ground black pepper to taste

Heat the oil in a large skillet until hot (just under a sizzle). Add the whole garlic clove and the mushrooms and sauté, stirring all the while, until the mushroom juice evaporates (about 1 to 2 minutes). Add the chopped garlic and parsley, blend well, and cook for another minute or two. Season to taste with salt and pepper and serve right away.

SERVES 6

There is no such thing as a little garlic.

—ARTHUR BAER

OFF THE EATEN PATH:
Nailing Down a Connection

The word *clove* comes from the Latin word *clovis*, meaning "nail," which garlic cloves resemble—at least to some people. Incidentally, in some parts of the United States and overseas, they're known as "toes" of garlic. Guess why.

SPICY MUSHROOMS

Make this at least two days ahead.

1 pound small-to-medium mushroom caps, cleaned
white wine vinegar (enough to cover the mushrooms)
1 bay leaf
3 whole cloves
2 minced scallions (including green parts)
2 garlic cloves, minced
½ teaspoon Tabasco
salt and freshly ground black pepper to taste
about ½ cup vegetable oil

Put the mushrooms in a bowl, cover with wine vinegar, and refrigerate for 2 hours. After draining, transfer the mushrooms to a jar. Add the bay leaf, cloves, scallions, garlic, Tabasco, salt, and pepper. Add enough vegetable oil to just cover the mushrooms. Seal the jar tightly, shake a few times, and refrigerate for at least two days.

SERVES 6–8

Strange to see how a good dinner reconciles everybody.
—SAMUEL PEPYS

SOUTH SIDE TAPAS

On the South Side of Pittsburgh, where I live, all the bars have tapas. But they call them beer nuts. These "tapas" are in honor of my neighborhood.

1 egg white
2 tablespoons water
2 cups unsalted pecans
½ cup sugar
½ teaspoon salt
¼ teaspoon nutmeg
¼ teaspoon ground cloves
½ teaspoon cayenne pepper
1 teaspoon cinnamon

Preheat the oven to 300°.

Using an electric mixer, beat the egg white with the water until soft peaks form; stir in the nuts. In another bowl, mix the rest of the ingredients. Sprinkle the mixture over the nuts; mix all of the ingredients thoroughly.

Transfer the nuts to a buttered cookie sheet; bake for 30 to 40 minutes, or until the pecans are dry, stirring every 10 minutes or so. Cool, then serve.

SERVES 8

OFF THE EATEN PATH:
A Sticky Situation

Philadelphia was the birthplace of bubble gum in 1928 and the brown paper bag in 1883.

They use Spanish beer in Madrid when they make the batter for this next dish; if you can't find any, substitute a robust imported beer, such as Heineken or Amstel. By the way, if you like shrimp, you'll love the humongous ones you find in Spain. You can also buy them in the United States, but they're pretty pricey. This dish works well with the kind of shrimp you find in your local supermarket. However, if you can find (and afford) Spanish shrimp, which are carried in some fish markets, use them instead. And invite me over!

DEEP-FRIED SHRIMP

1 cup pre-sifted all-purpose flour
1 cup beer
1 tablespoon olive oil (Spanish preferably)
½ teaspoon salt
oil, for deep-frying
1 pound large raw shrimp, shelled, deveined, tails left on

Mix the flour and beer together in a bowl, then blend in the olive oil and salt. In order to get rid of any lumps, push the batter through a sieve. Then let it rest for 4 to 5 hours. Heat the oil in a deep-fryer to 365°. When ready to nosh, hold the shrimp by the tail and dip into the batter, shaking off any excess. Plunge into the deep-fryer until the batter is golden in color. Drain on paper towels and serve immediately.

SERVES 8

SHRIMP WITH VERMOUTH

A simple recipe from the Ritz Hotel in Madrid.

3 tablespoons Spanish olive oil (Italian can be substituted)
2 dozen large raw shrimp, shelled, deveined, tail left on
1/4 cup unsalted butter
1/4 teaspoon salt
1/4 teaspoon freshly ground black pepper
1 garlic clove, crushed
3 tablespoons lemon juice
1/4 cup vermouth

Put the olive oil in a large skillet over medium heat and add the shrimp; cook until golden. Turn them over and reduce the heat a bit. Add the butter, salt, pepper, and garlic; blend well. Raise the heat to high; add the lemon juice and vermouth. Stir constantly for about a minute; crack on some more black pepper if desired, and serve immediately.

SERVES 6–8

TRAVELIN' GOURMET TIP:
"A-peeling" Advice

Peeling onions can be a cryin' shame, but not if you know the cold facts; i.e., chill your onions in the freezer for about a half hour before you use them and you can become a kitchen cutup without tears! Also, a great way to take onion odor from your hands or other parts of the body is to rub them with the cut end of a celery rib. It works! It will remove garlic odor, too.

BROILED MARINATED SHRIMP

This is one of my favorite treatments for broiling shrimp. Although I think the accompanying dip works quite well with the shrimp, you may want to substitute your favorite dipping sauce.

1 pound raw shrimp, shelled and deveined
1 large onion, sliced
1 medium carrot, sliced
1 celery rib, sliced
5 sprigs parsley
2 tablespoons salad oil
juice of ½ lemon
salt and freshly ground black pepper
unseasoned bread crumbs
salad oil
paprika
Horseradish Sauce (recipe follows; optional)

In a deep bowl, combine the shrimp, onion, carrot, celery, parsley, salad oil, and lemon juice. Mix well. Store in the refrigerator overnight, covered. When ready to use, remove the shrimp from the vegetables. Preheat the broiler. Sprinkle the shrimp with salt and pepper to taste, then dip into the bread crumbs, coating thoroughly.

Place in a shallow metal pan, sprinkle lightly with a little salad oil and paprika, and broil 3 to 5 minutes on each side, or until brown. Offer with Horseradish Sauce.

SERVES 6–8

Horseradish Sauce

¼ cup mayonnaise
2 tablespoons sour cream
2 teaspoons horseradish

Combine all 3 ingredients and blend well. Serve on the side.

MAKES ABOUT ⅜ CUP

TUNISIAN SHRIMP KABOBS

A unique appetizer from the colorful country that extends from the Mediterranean into the Sahara. Incidentally, the dipping sauce also goes nicely on pasta.

DIPPING SAUCE:

2 tomatoes, peeled and chopped
¼ cup good-quality olive oil
¼ cup finely chopped fresh parsley
2½ tablespoons minced scallions (white parts only)
1 large garlic clove, minced
1 teaspoon salt
½ teaspoon freshly ground black pepper
⅓–½ teaspoon crushed red pepper flakes
¼ teaspoon sugar

SHRIMP:

2½–3 pounds large raw shrimp, shelled (with tails left on), deveined
good-quality olive oil
salt and freshly ground black pepper
lemon and lime wedges, for garnish

Put the sauce ingredients into a bowl and mix together well. Refrigerate until ready to use.

Preheat the oven to broil. Prepare the shrimp by dipping them into olive oil and seasoning with salt and pepper to taste. Thread them onto 6 to 8 skewers and broil on each side until they turn pink (4 to 5 minutes). Transfer to 6 to 8 plates, with a little bowl of sauce in the center of each; garnish with lemon and lime wedges; serve immediately.

SERVES 6–8

> ❝We may live without friends;
> we may live without books.
> But civilized man cannot live
> without cooks.❞
>
> —OWEN MERIDITH

OFF THE EATEN PATH:
A Wee Bit o' Scottish Culinary Terminology

Arbroath Smokies: Tiny smoked haddock usually presented with a butter-and-cream sauce.

Baps: Similar to a hamburger roll but a bit more floury.

Hatted Kit: A rich cream dessert flavored with nutmeg.

Haggis: A sausage with a thyroid condition. Specifically, a sheep's stomach stuffed with the organ meats of a lamb (or deer) along with oatmeal and a whole bunch of spices. I tried it once. Once is more than enough.

Neeps: Turnips.

Partan Bree: Crab soup popular in the Lowlands.

Scotch Broth: A soup made with turnips, carrots, onions, barley, and mutton.

Scotch Collops: Thin slices of lamb, venison, or beef fried with butter and onions.

Sweet Marag: A boiled pudding popular in the Outer Hebrides.

If there's a more unspoiled country in Europe than Scotland, I am not aware of it. You bump along its narrow roads in your generic rental for hours and all you see are fields greener than a billiard table, sheep standing like statues in verdant glens, and any number of the country's 1185 castles (you can get a great deal on one; castle-brokers are *dying* for buyers).

Scotland, of course, is salmon country. And the way they prepare "the king of fish" in the Scottish Highlands is a delicious exercise in simplicity. Mrs. Ann Nicol, chef at the Dunain Park Hotel near Loch Ness, brought me into her kitchen one Scottish morn' to show me how Highlanders prepare salmon. The twenty-five-pound salmon was so fresh that it still had the hook in its mouth.

"The old Highland way of poaching salmon is simply to cover the fish with water and add about three-quarters of a cup of vinegar," she said as she put it over a high flame. "After it comes to a boil, you remove it from the heat and let it rest until the water's cold. Then it's ready." You peel off the skin and serve it at room temperature with an appropriate sauce.

Mrs. Nicol made a silken hollandaise with eggs from free-range hens. They made eggs from the imprisoned U.S. chickens practically inedible by comparison.

SALMON PÂTÉ

One of the world's easiest pâtés.

8-ounce package cream cheese, softened
½ pound canned salmon, drained, cartilage removed
1 tablespoon vodka
1 tablespoon fresh lemon juice
2 drops red food coloring (optional)

Place all the ingredients in a mixing bowl and whip at low speed until well blended. Refrigerate for 30 minutes. Scoop, mold, or shape by hand and serve with good-quality crackers or toast points, if desired.

SERVES 6–8

SMOKED SALMON PÂTÉ

Some of the finest smoked salmon in the world comes from Scotland. Here's an easy smoked salmon pâté recipe.

1 tablespoon vegetable oil
1/4 cup unsalted butter, softened
8 ounces smoked salmon, minced
3 1/2 tablespoons whipping cream
1 tablespoon lemon juice
pinch nutmeg
freshly ground white pepper

   Beat the oil and the butter together until the butter is soft. Slowly beat in the minced fish until the mixture thickens. Mix in the cream, lemon juice, and nutmeg. Season to taste with the white pepper. Pour the pâté into greased ramekins or a small dish and chill in the refrigerator about an hour before serving with toast points or ''gourmet'' crackers.

   SERVES 4–6

SALMON CROQUETTES

Although they use fresh salmon in Scotland to make this pub snack, the canned variety works well, too.

CREAM SAUCE:

2 tablespoons unsalted butter, softened
2 tablespoons all-purpose flour
1/2 cup whole milk
pinch salt

CROQUETTES:

16-ounce can pink salmon, drained, cartilage removed
1/4 cup chopped onions, sautéed until translucent
1/2 teaspoon white pepper
1 tablespoon mayonnaise
2 tablespoons heavy cream
2 beaten eggs
1/2 cup white bread crumbs
vegetable oil, for deep-frying

"Salmon are like men, too soft a life isn't good for them."
—SCOTTISH PROVERB

OFF THE EATEN PATH:
Nova Salmon

   In the United States, particularly on the East Coast, smoked salmon often is called nova. The term comes from Nova Scotia, where much of the salmon that's sold on the East Coast comes from.

• Always work with small amounts, lest you clog the blades. You can fill up the blender to about a quarter of the way from the top when working with liquids. However, with denser, semiliquid ingredients, fill to about half or, to be even safer, a third capacity. Before adding solids, break them into pieces.

• A blender can clean itself! Just put some warm water and a little detergent into the container and turn it on. Rinse thoroughly and wipe dry before putting it away. Also, always wipe off the base with a damp cloth after using.

• One use of the blender that you may not have considered is to grind coffee beans.

Make the cream sauce by blending the butter, flour, milk, and salt. Put the sauce into a bowl and add all the croquette ingredients but the egg, bread crumbs, and oil. Shape the mixture into small balls or pyramids. Dip each first into the egg, then the bread crumbs. Let stand for 15 minutes, then repeat the battering process. Let stand for 15 more minutes. Heat the oil in a deep-fryer (or in a wok or deep, heavy saucepan) to 365 to 375°. Deep-fry the croquettes until golden brown, drain, and serve immediately.

SERVES 6–8

BLENDER SALMON MOUSSE

Here's an easy-to-make salmon mousse recipe I had in London.

3 tablespoons fresh lemon juice
3 tablespoons chopped raw onion
1 envelope gelatin
½ cup boiling water
½ cup mayonnaise
½ teaspoon paprika
1 pound canned salmon, drained, cartilage removed
1 tablespoon crushed dill seed*
1 cup heavy cream

Put the first 4 ingredients into a blender and mix on high speed for 1 minute. Add the mayonnaise, paprika, salmon, and dill seed. Blend on high while slowly adding the cream until all the ingredients are well incorporated and smooth. Pour into a mold and refrigerate for 3 to 4 hours before serving as a dip.

SERVES 6–8

*Crush the dill seed with a mortar and pestle or by putting it into a tablespoon and using the back of another tablespoon to crush it

CHICKEN LIVER PISTACHIO PÂTÉ

If you'd rather make a pâté with chicken livers, this is a best bet.

1 pound chicken livers
2 cups canned chicken broth
8-ounce package cream cheese, softened
1 onion, grated
1 tart apple, peeled and grated
3 teaspoons apple jack brandy
½ cup shelled and chopped pistachios
freshly ground black pepper

In a medium skillet, cook the livers in the broth for about 20 minutes over medium heat; drain. Process in a food processor until smooth. Add the cream cheese, onion, apple, and brandy. Process until smooth. Stir in the pistachios and season to taste with pepper. Chill in the refrigerator for several hours. Serve with toasted slices of sourdough bread, toast points, or gourmet crackers.

SERVES 8

ROQUEFORT GRAPES

This easy appetizer utilizing "the king of cheese" is from Chef Robert Zelesko of Tramp's Restaurant in Pittsburgh.

1 pound sliced almonds
8-ounce package cream cheese, softened
⅛ pound Roquefort cheese
2 tablespoons heavy cream
1 pound seedless green or red grapes

Toast the almonds in the oven until nicely browned, then chop finely. Combine the cream cheese, Roquefort, and cream and beat until smooth. Drop the grapes into the cheese mixture and stir by hand to coat them. Roll the coated grapes in the toasted nuts and place on a tray covered with waxed paper. Chill until ready to serve.

SERVES 6–8

OFF THE EATEN PATH:

The first microwave oven made its debut in 1952. It's an American innovation.

“After a good dinner, one can forgive any-body, even one's own relatives.”

—OSCAR WILDE

POACHED EGGS WITH LEEK SAUCE

The unique combination of eggs and a satiny leek sauce is from the accomplished kitchen of the chic Dorchester Hotel in London. The sauce also works with fish.

1 tablespoon unsalted butter
1 leek (white and light green parts), cleaned (see page 182)
    and julienned
salt and freshly ground black pepper to taste
3 tablespoons white wine
½ teaspoon salt
2 tablespoons white-wine vinegar
4 eggs, at room temperature
½ stick unsalted butter, cubed and chilled
4 slices toasted white bread, cut into small squares, for garnish
4 cherry tomatoes, for garnish
4 basil leaves, for garnish (optional)

Melt the butter over low heat in a small, heavy skillet; add the leek and season to taste with salt and pepper. Cover and cook over low heat about 3 to 4 minutes, turning once or twice. Add the wine and simmer, uncovered, until the leek is tender but still crisp (3 to 4 minutes).

Bring water seasoned with salt and vinegar to a simmer. Carefully crack the eggs to avoid breaking the yolk; add to the water and poach until set. With a slotted spoon, transfer the eggs to a bowl filled with warm water. Strain the leek-cooking liquid into a small saucepan and bring to a boil. Remove from heat; whisk in the cubed butter, a cube at a time; mix in the leeks and correct the seasonings.

Arrange the poached eggs on a warmed platter and spoon the leek sauce over them. Garnish with toast, tomatoes, and if available, basil.

SERVES 4

PUB-STYLE DEVILED EGGS

The reason they called deviled eggs "deviled" is because they're supposed to be hot! However, most renditions of the snack are bland beyond belief. Not so with this spicy offering from London's Black Friar Pub. However, if you want to tone it down a bit, substitute diced green pepper for the jalapeño or hot banana pepper.

8 hard-boiled eggs, shelled
¼ cup mayonnaise
1½ tablespoons finely diced onion
1½ tablespoons finely diced jalapeño or hot banana pepper
2 teaspoons vinegar
1 teaspoon Dijon mustard
1½ teaspoons curry powder
1 teaspoon minced fresh parsley
½ teaspoon cayenne
paprika

Cut the eggs in half lengthwise, remove the yolks, and reserve the whites. Mash the yolks with the mayonnaise and combine with the onion, pepper, vinegar, mustard, curry powder, parsley, and cayenne. Fill the egg halves with the yolk mixture;* sprinkle each egg with paprika.

SERVES 8

SCOTCH EGGS

This is a fun appetizer as well as a nice snack. Its name, however, is a misnomer. It actually was invented in England, where it is a popular pub snack.

vegetable oil for deep-frying
5 hard-boiled eggs, shelled
flour, for dusting
1 pound loose sausage meat (your favorite)
1 large egg, beaten
about ½ cup dry bread crumbs (plain or seasoned)

*Deviled egg filling can be spooned into a pastry bag, then piped decoratively into the waiting egg whites.

66Plain cooking cannot be entrusted to plain cooks.99

—COUNTESS MORPHY

• To determine if an egg is fresh, put it in water. If it sinks and rolls on its side, it's fresh. If it stands on its tapered end, it's not. If it floats to the top, you've got problems.

• To make a hard-boiled egg, cover it with water and bring to a boil. Reduce to a simmer; cook for 14 minutes.

• It's easier to peel a hard-boiled egg when it's hot, because the shell doesn't stick, as it does when it's cold. Also, if you want to slice a hard-boiled egg, refrigerate it for about 20 minutes or so, and the yolk won't be as apt to come apart when you slice it.

• If you've forgotten which eggs are hard-boiled and which are not, the way to determine which is which is to spin them. If an egg spins, it's hard-boiled.

Fill a deep-fryer halfway with vegetable oil; heat the oil to 365–375°. Lightly coat each egg with flour. On a floured surface, divide the sausage meat into 5 oval-shaped portions. Put each egg in the center of a mound of sausage meat and shape the meat around the egg, sealing as tightly as possible. Put the beaten egg into a shallow dish, and the bread crumbs into another. Dip each sausage-coated egg first into the beaten egg, then into the bread crumbs.

Lower the sausage-coated eggs into the deep-fryer and cook until meat is cooked through (about 5 to 7 minutes). Drain, cool, and eat, or serve sliced on top of lettuce as a lunch snack or picnic dish.

SERVES 4–6

EGGS WITH SHRIMP

This recipe from Madrid makes a nice buffet item as well as a delicious appetizer.

1 pound cooked, shelled, and deveined shrimp
1½ tablespoons lemon juice
1 tablespoon good-quality olive oil
¼ teaspoon Tabasco
1 cup mayonnaise
8 hard-boiled eggs, thinly sliced
lemon wedges, for garnish (optional)
fresh parsley, for garnish (optional)

Puree half the shrimp in a food processor with the lemon juice, olive oil, and Tabasco. Put the mayonnaise in a medium-sized bowl and add the shrimp mixture; blend well. Arrange the egg slices creatively on a platter and cover with the shrimp mixture. Garnish with the remaining whole shrimp and, if desired, lemon wedges and parsley.

SERVES 4–6

Whenever I get the chance, I travel to Crisfield, Maryland, for its annual crab festival, which includes a recipe contest judged by the crab-crazed citizenry. The next two appetizers are among my favorites of the prize-winning recipes.

CRAB CHEESECAKE

Can be served cold as a canapé for 12 or more, or hot as a brunch course for about 6.

1 cup crushed Ritz crackers
3 tablespoons melted butter
2 8-ounce packages cream cheese, softened
3 eggs
¼ cup sour cream
1 teaspoon fresh lemon juice
2 teaspoons grated onion
½ teaspoon Old Bay seasoning (or any chowder seasoning)
2 drops Tabasco
⅛ teaspoon freshly ground black pepper
1 cup canned lump crabmeat
½ cup sour cream

Preheat the oven to 350°. Mix together the crackers and butter and use the mixture to line a 9-inch springform pan. Bake for about 10 minutes. Set aside to cool. Reduce the oven to 325°.

With an electric mixer, beat together until fluffy the cream cheese, eggs, and ¼ cup sour cream. Add the lemon juice, onion, Old Bay seasoning, Tabasco, and black pepper. Stir in the crabmeat and mix well. Pour into the cooled crust and bake 50 minutes until the cake sets. Remove from the oven. Run a knife around the edge of the cake, loosening it from the pan. Cool on a wire rack. Remove the sides of the pan. Spread the cake with the sour cream.

SERVES 12

"God sends meat but the devil sends cooks."

—THOMAS DELONEY

HOT CRAB DIP

8-ounce package cream cheese, softened
1 tablespoon milk
1 pound canned lump crabmeat
2 tablespoons chopped onion
1 teaspoon prepared horseradish
1/8 teaspoon freshly ground black pepper
1/2 cup toasted almonds

Preheat the oven to 375°. Combine the cream cheese and milk; add the crabmeat, onion, horseradish, and pepper. Blend well. Spoon into an ovenproof dish; sprinkle with toasted almonds. Bake at 375° for 15 minutes. Serve hot, atop party rye.

SERVES 8–12

CRABMEAT HOELZEL

This appetizer was invented at the Duquesne Club in Pittsburgh, one of the nation's most exclusive. It once was a bastion for the barons of industry who forged their fortunes in Pittsburgh—men with last names like Mellon and Carnegie. Like Groucho Marx, I've always had a lot of respect for the Duquesne Club because it would never have me as a member.

1/3 cup tarragon vinegar
1/4 cup cider vinegar
2/3 cup olive oil
dash of salt
freshly ground black pepper to taste
1 pound fresh crabmeat

Combine all the ingredients except the crabmeat in a small bowl. Whisk vigorously to form an emulsion (the oil and vinegar should not separate). Refrigerate, covered, for two days.

Place the crabmeat in a shallow dish, spoon the dressing over it and serve immediately.

SERVES 8

RÉMOULADE DIP

This is great with crudités or crackers as well as with cold cooked lobster, shrimp, or crayfish. It is, of course, New Orleans-inspired.

1 cup mayonnaise
1 cup sour cream
¼ cup chopped chives
½ cup grainy mustard
pepper to taste

Mix the mayonnaise, sour cream, chives, mustard, and pepper together until incorporated. Chill for about an hour before serving.

SERVES 8–12

PARMESAN CHICKEN WINGS

Here's an interesting, easy-to-make snack or buffet dish that utilizes the classic Italian cheese, Parmesan, with chicken wings to set them aflutter with flavor. Don't overcoat the chicken with the butter. Just dip it in real quick and shake off the excess before coating the chicken with the mixture. Otherwise, it will become too greasy.

5 pounds chicken wings
1 cup freshly grated Parmesan cheese (or more if desired)
2 tablespoons paprika
2 tablespoons minced fresh parsley
1 tablespoon dried oregano
1 teaspoon salt
½ teaspoon freshly ground black pepper
½ cup melted unsalted butter, seasoned to taste with garlic salt

Preheat the oven to 350°. Cut the wings at each joint and discard the tips. Combine the cheese, paprika, parsley, oregano, salt, and pepper in a bowl. Quickly dip the chicken into the seasoned butter, shake off excess, then dip into the cheese/spice mix. Layer a cookie sheet(s) with parchment paper and put the wings on top. Bake for about 1 hour and 15 minutes, turning twice.

SERVES 12

OFF THE EATEN PATH:
Parmesan Cheese

The finest, Parmigiano-Reggiano, comes from a section of Italy that includes Parma, Reggio Emila (where most of the cheese actually is made), Modena, and parts of Bologna. All of the milk used to produce it is uniform, and cheese-making occurs from mid-April to about the middle of November (cheese made in the winter months is not as good as that produced during other months of the year). Aged Parmesan, which is pale yellow, is more flavorful than the younger variety, which is whiter.

Sake It to Me!

Although it may seem stronger, that popular Japanese elixir called sake, which is made of distilled rice wine, has about the same alcoholic content as sherry. In Japan, it is traditional for guests to pour for each other. It is considered rude to pour sake for yourself.

JAPANESE CHICKEN WINGS

You might consider "winging" it the Japanese way. These can be made in the oven, but they're even better on a grill. By the way, Japanese farmers used to grill meat and fish on spades, called *suki*, which is where we get the name *suki-yaki*.

14–18 chicken wings
1 cup pancake syrup
1 cup light soy sauce
1 cup sherry
2½ tablespoons lemon juice
1 large shallot, minced
1 garlic clove, minced
1 teaspoon shredded fresh ginger
1 teaspoon red pepper flakes

Cut each wing into 2 pieces by separating at the joint; discard tips. Put the wings in a large glass baking dish. Combine the remaining ingredients and pour over the wings. Cover and marinate in the refrigerator overnight.

Preheat the oven to 400°. Place the wings on a greased rack or broiler pan; reserve the marinade. Bake 45 minutes, or until tender, turning and brushing with marinade every 15 minutes.

NOTE: If you'd like to grill them outdoors, put the marinated wings on the greased rack of an outdoor grill and baste with the reserved marinade. Cook over glowing red coals about a half hour, or until tender, turning the wings and brushing with the marinade every 10 minutes.

SERVES 6–8

CHICKEN WINGS WITH OYSTER SAUCE

This recipe from London's Chinatown is well worth trying if you can find oyster sauce in your local supermarket or ethnic grocery store.

1 dozen chicken wings
2–3 thin slices fresh ginger
vegetable oil
4 tablespoons oyster sauce
1 tablespoon dry sherry
½ teaspoon sugar
2½ tablespoons soy sauce
1 cup water

Cut each wing into two pieces by separating at the joint; discard the tips. Heat the ginger slices in the oil in a wok; add a third of the wings at a time and brown. When the wings are browned, drain the oil and remove the ginger slices from the wok. Add the oyster sauce, sherry, sugar, soy sauce, and water. Place the browned wings in the wok and simmer, covered, for 10 to 12 minutes. Cook another 12 to 15 minutes with the lid off, basting frequently with the sauce. When wings are tender and nicely glazed, they are ready to be eaten.

SERVES 4

TRAVELIN' GOURMET TIP:
Wok It Up

Get more use out of your wok: It makes a good soup kettle, especially for bouillabaisse, and serves up chili or stew in a buffet situation.

So you thought the grilled-cheese sandwich was an American phenomenon? Actually, it's enjoyed, albeit in slightly different forms, in other countries of the world, including Italy and France.

MOZZARELLA IN CAROZZA

This Italian version of the grilled cheese sandwich makes not only a nice appetizer but also a great luncheon snack. "In Carozza" actually means "in a carriage."

3 slices good bread (homemade Italian or French), thinly sliced, crusts removed
1 cup milk
3 slices mozzarella cheese
1 cup all-purpose flour
1 egg, beaten
olive oil

Soak the bread in the milk briefly (be careful not to oversoak it because it may fall apart). Place 1 slice of cheese on top of each bread slice. Dip each piece gently into flour, then into the beaten egg. Put ¾ to 1 inch of oil in a heavy skillet and bring it to a boil. Lower the bread/cheese combinations into it and fry, turning once; brown each side as evenly as possible.

SERVES 3

CROQUE-MADAME

And here's how the French make it.

4 slices Swiss cheese, each about ¼ inch thick
1 cup all-purpose flour
½ cup unsalted butter
French bread
coarsely ground black pepper to taste

Cut the cheese into triangles and dredge in the flour. Melt the butter in a skillet and fry the cheese until golden. Serve on slices of good French bread. Top each slice liberally with the black pepper. Serve immediately.

SERVES 4

TRAVELIN' GOURMET TIP:
The Cold Facts

Mozzarella cheese can be grated and frozen. Measure out the portion size that you prefer for pizza, then place in plastic containers before freezing.

"Without butter, without eggs, there is no reason to come to France."
—PAUL BOCUSE

In this recipe, I have slightly modified a recipe for miniature spring rolls from the repertoire of the great innovative Parisian chef Alain Senderens (of L'Archestrate fame), and united it with a banana sauce I concocted.

It may be an unorthodox combination, but it sure makes for some interesting eating (the spring rolls also work without the sauce, but I like the two in concert). When I first tried this dish out on a friend, he described it as an "Indian burrito." You can find egg-roll wrappers in many supermarkets or gourmet groceries.

CURRIED SPRING ROLLS WITH BANANA-YOGURT SAUCE

1 tablespoon unsalted butter
3 tablespoons finely chopped onion
3 tablespoons finely chopped apples
2 teaspoons curry powder
1 teaspoon tomato paste
¾ pound boneless chicken breasts, finely chopped
4 tablespoons dry white wine
salt and freshly ground black pepper
1 package egg roll wrappers
4–5 tablespoons vegetable oil
Banana-Yogurt Sauce (recipe follows), optional

Melt the butter in a saucepan, then add the onion and apple. Cook over moderate heat about a minute. Stir in the curry powder and cook about 30 to 45 seconds. Add the tomato paste; lower the heat and cook about a minute. Add the chicken and white wine and season to taste with the salt and pepper. Cook very slowly (heat should be not quite a simmer) for 20 to 25 minutes, stirring often.

Spread a large, slightly damp towel on a table; separate the egg roll wrappers and spread them over half of the towel; fold the other half of the towel over them. Let them rest until the wrappers are softened and pliable (about 5 minutes). Cut each wrapper in half lengthwise, then cut off two inches from the long end, resulting in a wrapper about five by three inches. Cover with a damp towel until ready to use.

Spread 1 tablespoon of the filling about 1 inch from the end of the wrapper closest to you. With the index and third fingers of each hand, fold up the sides a bit and roll up the egg rolls with your thumbs to make a neat bundle. It may take a little practice at first, but you'll find it fairly easy once you develop the knack. Do the same with the rest of the wrappers. Put the finished wrappers on a lightly floured tray and cover with a damp towel until ready to use.

TO COOK: Heat 3 to 4 tablespoons vegetable oil in a large frying pan; place about half the spring rolls in the pan and brown over moderate heat for 2 to 3 minutes. Turn over and brown 2 to 3 minutes on the other side. Remove and drain on paper towels. Add another tablespoon oil to the pan and put in the rest of the egg rolls. Repeat the cooking procedure and drain on paper towels. Serve with the Banana-Yogurt Sauce if desired.

SERVES 6–8

Banana-Yogurt Sauce

½ teaspoon ground cumin
⅓ teaspoon ground coriander
1 cup plain yogurt
2 bananas, chopped
¼ teaspoon cayenne pepper
pinch salt

Put all the ingredients in a food processor and process briefly. Don't overprocess; it's all right to have little chunks of banana in the sauce.

MAKES ABOUT 1½ CUPS OF SAUCE

OFF THE EATEN PATH:

While food processors took America by storm in the 1970s, the product actually was invented in France in 1947. However, they didn't really start to catch on in France until the early 1960s.

One of the most delicious aspects of the culinary scene in wild and crazy Amsterdam is *rijsttafel*, an Indonesian specialty with Chinese, Indian, Portuguese, British, Dutch, and even Arab overtones. *Rijsttafel* actually means "rice table," because an assortment of a dozen or more dishes surrounds a bowl of rice at these Indonesian repasts. You address the feast by holding a fork in the left hand and a spoon in the right. You scoop the rice onto the plate with the spoon, and surround it with other dishes you pick up with a fork.

According to Sebo Woldringh, owner of the Sama Sebo, one of the most famous Indonesian restaurants in Amsterdam, *rijsttafel* was started by the Dutch in Indonesia centuries ago. "They wanted to sample a little of this and a little of that," he said. "So, the Indonesians decided to 'package' an assortment of the specialties." The idea caught on.

Now most Indonesian restaurants in Amsterdam offer rice table (from a dozen to three dozen dishes) in addition to à la carte dishes. One of its staples is saté (also satay), actually marinated, skewered meat that you broil, then grace with a spicy peanut sauce. By the way, the term *saté* is actually a corruption of the word *steak*, which Indonesians have difficulty pronouncing.

PORK SATÉ WITH PEANUT SAUCE

Look for coconut milk in your local supermarket or gourmet grocery, or in Asian markets.

4 shallots, minced
2 garlic cloves, minced
3 teaspoons brown sugar
1 teaspoon salt
½ teaspoon ground coriander seeds
½ teaspoon ground black pepper
½ teaspoon grated ginger
2 tablespoons lemon juice
2 tablespoons unsweetened coconut milk
1½ pounds pork, cubed into ¾-inch squares
Peanut Sauce (recipe page 29)

Combine all the ingredients except the pork and the peanut sauce and mix in a large bowl. Add the pork and mix well. Let sit overnight, turning occasionally. Remove pork from the marinade, thread on skewers, and grill over charcoal (or in a broiler) to desired doneness. Offer with Peanut Sauce.

SERVES 8 AS APPETIZER; 4 AS MAIN COURSE

Peanut Sauce

2 tablespoons butter
1 medium-sized onion, chopped
4 tablespoons chunky peanut butter
1 tablespoon light soy sauce
1 teaspoon fresh lemon juice
1 teaspoon peanut oil
1½ teaspoons hot red pepper flakes
½ cup unsweetened coconut milk

Heat the butter in a saucepan and add the onions. Sauté until the onions become limp and honey-colored. Add the peanut butter, soy sauce, lemon juice, peanut oil, and red pepper flakes and blend. Raise the heat and slowly add the coconut milk; bring to a boil, stirring all the while, until the mixture becomes creamy and thickened. Serve immediately.

MAKES 1 CUP

"**G**razers" in Amsterdam have their *rijsttafel*, but those in London can partake of delectable dumplings at *dim sum* spreads at the countless restaurants in that city's Chinatown. This first recipe, which is spiked with curry, was influenced by the myriad Indian restaurants in London. I urge you to try it.

The only thing difficult about making it is assembling the ingredients. You can cook the dumplings by steaming, frying, or deep-frying them. I usually use a bamboo steamer, but I also like them fried. Sometimes I steam them first, then put them into a hot skillet layered with a little oil and fry them until they're crunchy on the bottom. This gives nice textural overtones.

If you don't like your dishes spicy, you can eliminate the hot red pepper flakes in the dipping sauce, as well as substitute a teaspoon of additional soy sauce for the hot red pepper sauce. However, the dish was meant to be hot, and that's the way I recommend you prepare it. Also, a little bit of the dipping sauce is all you need. However, if you want to be a bit more "saucy," double the amount of ingredients in making the dip.

CURRIED BEEF DUMPLINGS

The dumplings can be either steamed or boiled. Won ton wrappers, Chinese chili sauce, and chili oil can be found in most supermarkets and in specialty stores.

DUMPLINGS:

8 ounces good-quality ground beef (preferably sirloin)
1 tablespoon minced ginger
1 medium-sized onion, minced
2 medium-sized carrots, minced
1 egg, slightly whipped
1 teaspoon Chinese chili sauce
1 tablespoon light soy sauce
1 teaspoon Chinese chili oil
1 teaspoon curry powder
1 tablespoon sugar
½ teaspoon salt
1 package won ton wrappers, thawed

SAUCE:

3–4 tablespoons finely chopped scallions (white parts only)
2 teaspoons sesame oil
I teaspoon hot red pepper flakes
2–3 tablespoons light soy sauce
I teaspoon Chinese chili oil
I teaspoon dry cooking sherry (or wine or even vodka)

THE FINAL TOUCH:

flour, for dusting
water, for sealing dumplings

TO MAKE THE FILLING: Combine all the dumpling ingredients except the won ton skins in a bowl and mix together very thoroughly. Refrigerate for about an hour.

TO MAKE THE SAUCE: Place all of the sauce ingredients into a bowl and mix together thoroughly. Refrigerate until ready to use.

TO MAKE THE DUMPLINGS: Spread a large, slightly damp towel on a table; separate the won ton skins and spread them over half of the towel; fold the other half of the towel over them. Let them rest until the wrappers are softened and pliable (about 5 minutes).

Dust your work area with a little flour and take one of the won ton skins from under the damp towel and onto your work surface, leaving the rest of the wrappers covered until ready to use. Take about 1½ tablespoons of the filling and place it in the center of the won ton skin. Coat the edges of the skin with water and fold over each dumpling either in a triangular fashion or into a rectangle, making sure that you seal it tightly all the way around.

Put the completed dumpling onto a baking sheet lightly dusted with flour, or atop parchment paper, and cover with a towel until ready to cook. Repeat the procedure with the rest of the dumplings until you've used up all of the filling (you should have 15 to 20 dumplings).

TO STEAM OR STEAM/FRY: Steam the dumplings for about 20 minutes in a bamboo or other steamer until they're cooked (use one or two dumplings as "test" dumplings to make certain they're cooked all the way through).

If desired, when all of the dumplings are steamed, put them into a hot skillet layered with about 2 tablespoons corn or peanut oil and fry just the bottoms. (Don't crowd them in the skillet; it's okay if they just touch each other. The togetherness makes for happy dumplings.) Serve hot, with the sauce on the side.

TO BOIL: Put about 3 to 4 pints of water in a pot or a wok and bring to a boil. Put in about a half-dozen dumplings; stir (so they don't stick together). Put the lid on until the water returns to a boil. Add the rest of the dumplings, put the lid back on until the water boils again. Stir the dumplings once again, lower the heat, and cover.

Gently simmer for about 10 minutes, or until the dumplings have floated to the top, which means they are ready for the plate and, pretty soon, your palate! Drain and serve hot, with the sauce on the side. Or you can fry the bottoms of the dumplings before serving.

SERVES 4–8 AS APPETIZER OR FIRST COURSE; 2–4 AS MAIN COURSE

SURF 'N' TURF CLUBS

Unless I'm mistaken, "Surf 'n' Turf," a.k.a.: "Reef and Beef," is an American invention. Here's a variation on that theme that makes an interesting appetizer or very ritzy picnic fare.

FOR EACH SANDWICH:

garlic butter*
3 slices sourdough, French, or Italian bread
2 large lettuce leaves
⅛ pound roast beef
1 cup crab or lobster meat, tossed with ¼ cup Rémoulade Dip
    (recipe page 22)
4 thin slices very ripe tomato

Spread the garlic butter on the bread and grill until lightly browned on both sides. On the first slice of bread, layer a lettuce leaf, half the seafood, 2 tomato slices, and half the roast beef. Top with a slice of bread and repeat the stacking. Top with a final slice of bread and secure with a sandwich pick. Cut each sandwich into quarters and secure each quarter with a toothpick.

SERVES 2

*To make garlic butter, simply mix 1 pressed garlic clove with 1 stick (¼ pound) of softened butter. Keep refrigerated.

> **Nouvelle cuisine, roughly translated, means, 'I can't believe I paid $96 and I'm still hungry.'**
>
> —M.K.

BUNG BUNG CHICKEN

This dish, based on one from Lion City, an Asian restaurant in London, is rich with flavor and texture. It is meant to be served at room temperature or slightly chilled, making it a perfect dish to offer as part of a party buffet. You can add (to taste) more than the ⅓ cup soy sauce called for, if you desire. Make it the night before and let it relax in the refrigerator, covered, until you're ready to serve.

1 whole chicken, boiled until cooked through
1 cup sliced scallions
½ cup coarsely chopped unsalted peanuts
⅓ cup soy sauce (or more, if desired)
2 teaspoons vinegar
1 teaspoon hot pepper oil
1 teaspoon sugar
½ teaspoon MSG (optional)
1 teaspoon sesame oil
3 teaspoons sesame seeds

Remove the meat from the chicken, cut into bite-sized chunks, and place in a medium-sized bowl. Add all the rest of the ingredients except the sesame seeds, and mix well. Top with the sesame seeds and refrigerate overnight, mixing occasionally. Serve chilled, and to be official, offer chopsticks.

SERVES 8

VARIATION: You might also consider serving this dish with Mandarin pancakes, which you can buy in your local supermarket or gourmet groceries. Diners simply layer each pancake with the chicken, roll it up, and eat it like an egg roll.

TRAVELIN' GOURMET TRIVIA:

Chopsticks

The term *chopsticks* comes from the pidgin English word "chop," which means "fast." Chopsticks preceded the fork by many centuries. By the way, prior to the fork, Europeans used knives to carry food to the mouth. I remember a story from an ancient book in which an Asian visitor to Paris, seeing the knife technique, exclaimed: "Those barbarians who eat with their swords!" Incidentally, the word *hash* comes from the French word *hacher*, which means "to chop." And while on the subject of hash, when I was filming the Dutch episodes of *The Travelin' Gourmet* in Amsterdam, I happened onto a house of hash—not the kind you eat but smoke. The manager asked me to sign the "register." He passed me a book filled with the stoned musings of the hash house's buzzed clientele. I wrote: "And I thought I could get *corned-beef* hash here!"

ALGERIAN MEATBALLS

You've heard of Italian and Swedish meatballs. But Algerian ones? Yes!

2 slices dry bread
½ cup milk
1 pound ground lamb or beef
½ cup finely chopped onion
½ teaspoon dried dill weed
½ cup chopped fresh parsley
½ teaspoon dried mint leaves
1 egg, slightly beaten
¾ teaspoon salt
½ teaspoon freshly ground black pepper
oil, for deep-frying

Soften the bread in the milk, then squeeze out the excess liquid. Put the bread in a medium-size bowl; add all the remaining ingredients except the oil and mix thoroughly. Refrigerate, covered, overnight. Shape the mixture into 1½-inch balls. In oil heated to 365–375°, deep-fry the balls, about 4 at a time, until nicely browned. Incidentally, if you don't have a thermometer, you can test if the oil is hot enough by putting a few drops of water into it. If it "pops," the oil is ready. (Be careful not to get too close to the fat when doing this.)

SERVES 8–12

All things require skill but an appetite.
—GEORGE HERBERT

HOT CHEESE CANAPÉS

1 cup chopped onions
3–4 tablespoons vegetable oil
1 pound Cheddar cheese, shredded
2 tablespoons Worcestershire sauce
½ cup mayonnaise
1 pound bacon, cooked extra-crisp and crumbled
crackers or wedges of rye bread

Sauté the onions in the vegetable oil until tender. In a medium bowl, combine the onions with the rest of the ingredients. Spread on crackers or rye bread. Broil until the cheese is bubbly (about 8 to 10 minutes). Serve hot.

SERVES 12–16

AVOCADO TOREY

A recipe from Le Ruth's, one of the finest restaurants in the New Orleans area, which has been fashioning wonderful meals since 1963.

2 avocados
romaine lettuce leaves
1 teaspoon salt
½ teaspoon white pepper
½ teaspoon dried oregano
1 garlic clove, minced
1 sprig fresh thyme (optional)
⅔ cup olive oil
1 tablespoon red wine
1 tablespoon vinegar

Cut the avocados in half and discard the pit. Scoop out the avocado meat with an ice-cream dipper, and shape into little balls. Place them on two plates lined with lettuce leaves. In a small bowl, whisk together the rest of the ingredients, pour over the avocados, and serve.

SERVES 2

DANISH SAUSAGES

You can get more personality into sausage by folding in the beaten egg whites, as they do in Denmark. You'll be surprised how light these are.

2 large eggs, separated
½ pound hot bulk sausage
½ pound mild bulk sausage
1 ½ teaspoons ground ginger
½ cup finely chopped dill pickles
⅛ teaspoon freshly ground black pepper
pinch of salt
vegetable oil, for frying

Whip the egg yolks until frothy and mix with the sausage, ginger, pickles, pepper, and salt. Whip the egg whites until stiff and fold into the sausage mixture. Fashion the mixture into bite-sized sausages; put a light coating of oil in a medium skillet and fry the sausages until cooked through and browned nicely. Drain on paper towels and serve immediately.

SERVES 4–6

TRAVELIN' GOURMET TIP:
Save Leftover Egg Whites

Leftover egg whites can be frozen. Just store in a tightly lidded container and mark how many whites are contained within.

TAPENADE PIZZA

This makes a great appetizer or a fun entrée.

1 lemon
1 pound pitted black olives
2 tablespoons capers
9-ounce tin anchovies
¼ cup olive oil
1 pound frozen white bread dough, thawed
1 pound mozzarella cheese, sliced thin or shredded

Peel the lemon and shred the peel; squeeze the juice. Combine the peel and juice in a food processor with the olives, capers, anchovies, and lemon peel and process until smooth. With the motor running, add the oil gradually.

Preheat the oven to 350°. Roll out the dough into a circle or oval shape and spread with the mixture (the "tapenade"). Top with the cheese and bake until the crust is browned (about 20 minutes).

SERVES 8 AS APPETIZER; 4 AS ENTRÉE

CHILI PORK SPARERIBS

A recipe from *A La Carte*, the late, great food magazine from London. You can find the yellow bean sauce in most Asian grocery stores and gourmet emporia.

1 pint vegetable oil, for deep-frying
1½ pounds pork spareribs, cut into individual ribs
1½ pints chicken stock
1 tablespoon chili powder
2 teaspoons sugar
5 tablespoons dry sherry
1 tablespoon dark soy sauce
1 tablespoon light soy sauce
2 teaspoons finely chopped garlic
1 tablespoon chopped scallion
1 tablespoon whole yellow bean sauce
1½ tablespoons hoisin sauce
1 scallion (white and green parts), chopped, for garnish

Heat the oil in a deep-fryer, heavy saucepan, or large wok to 365–375° and deep-fry the spareribs until crisp and brown. Do this in batches, draining each batch. In a large pot, combine and bring to a boil the chicken stock, chili powder, sugar, dry sherry, dark and light soy sauce, garlic, scallion, yellow bean sauce, and hoisin sauce. Add the deep-fried spareribs and simmer, covered, for about 40 minutes. Drain off the sauce; remove the fat and reserve.

Preheat the oven to 350°. Place the spareribs on a rack in a roasting pan and roast for 15 to 20 minutes, basting occasionally with the reserved sauce. Serve the ribs whole or chopped into 2- to 3-inch pieces, garnished with the chopped scallion.

SERVES 4

COQUILLES ST. JACQUES WITH VERMOUTH AND LEMON-BUTTER SAUCE

A gorgeous dish from the fabled Homestead in Hot Springs, Virginia. Be careful not to oversauté the scallops or they'll get tough.

1 pound fresh sea scallops
⅛ teaspoon salt
2 tablespoons clarified unsalted butter*
1 tablespoon minced shallots
1 teaspoon freshly crushed white peppercorns†
juice of ½ lemon
1 cup dry vermouth
8 tablespoons unsalted butter, softened
1 cup whipping cream
1½ teaspoons finely cut fresh chives
fresh dill or parsley, for garnish

Rinse the scallops under cold running water in a colander. Drain, halve them crosswise, and season with the salt. Preheat the sauté pan over high heat; add the clarified butter, then the scallops, and sauté for about 1½ minutes on each side.

Remove the scallops with a slotted spoon to a side dish and reserve. Add the shallots to the sauté pan and cook over medium heat for 1 minute. Add the crushed pepper to the sauté pan with the lemon juice and vermouth. Increase the heat and cook until the liquid is reduced to about 1½ tablespoons (this will take approximately 4 to 5 minutes).

Remove the pan from direct heat and let it cool slightly. Use a whisk to whip in the softened butter, a tablespoon at a time, blending completely before each addition. Strain the sauce through a sieve into a double boiler; keep the sauce warm over simmering water.

*"Clarified butter" means that the milky solids, which burn at high temperatures, have been removed. An easy way to clarify butter is to chop it and put it into a small saucepan; heat it gently until it melts. Skim the fat off the top with a spatula; pour the melted butter into a container, leaving the milky solids behind. Clean the saucepan and put the butter back into it until ready to use.

†Crush the peppercorns with a mortar and pestle or by putting into a tablespoon and using the back of another tablespoon to crush them.

In a saucepan, reduce the whipping cream over medium-high heat to ⅓ cup; whisk it into the butter sauce and add the chives.

Preheat the broiler. Divide the scallops into 4 individual ramekins or put into a heatproof serving dish. Broil for 30 seconds to warm the scallops; spread the sauce evenly over the scallops, decorate with a sprig of fresh dill or parsley, and serve immediately.

SERVES 4

MINCED MEAT KABOBS

This interesting appetizer is from the kitchen of the Hilton Hotel in Istanbul.

1 pound ground round steak
½ cup cooked rice
1 tablespoon minced onion
1 tablespoon minced fresh parsley
1 tablespoon minced fresh mint
1 teaspoon salt
⅛ teaspoon ground allspice
⅛ teaspoon ground cinnamon
¼ teaspoon freshly ground black pepper
3 small zucchini, cut into 1-inch pieces
1 sweet red pepper, cut into 1-inch pieces
2 tablespoons good-quality olive oil
1 tablespoon lemon juice
1 teaspoon minced fresh mint

In a large bowl, combine the first 9 ingredients and mix vigorously with your hands until smooth (5 to 6 minutes). Shape into about a dozen meatballs. Thread them onto 4 skewers, alternating with the zucchini and red pepper. Preheat the oven to broil.

In a glass jar, combine the olive oil, lemon juice, and the 1 teaspoon mint; cover and shake well. Brush the kabobs with the oil mixture and broil 4 inches from heat; turn the kabobs occasionally and brush with the remaining oil mixture until meatballs are brown (about 10 to 12 minutes).

SERVES 6–8

CHICKEN ELIZABETH "SANDWICHES"

This dish is from the repertoire of Tony D'Imperio, owner of D'Imperio's in Monroeville, near Pittsburgh, one of my favorite restaurants.

4 boneless chicken breasts
½ pound broccoli, cooked al dente and diced
salt, white pepper, and ground ginger to taste
8 slices mozzarella cheese
1 cup all-purpose flour
6 eggs, well-beaten
1 cup garlic-flavored or "Italian" bread crumbs
¼ pound unsalted butter
½ cup dry white wine
2 tablespoons brandy
½ cup chicken broth
lemon wedges, for garnish

Cut the boned breasts in half lengthwise and pound flat. Season the broccoli to taste with the salt, white pepper, and ground ginger. Make "sandwiches" by stacking 1 piece of chicken, 1 slice of mozzarella, about 2 ounces of broccoli, another slice of cheese, and another piece of chicken. Crimp the edges.

Repeat 3 times to make 4 sandwiches. Dredge both sides of each sandwich in the flour, dip in the egg, and roll in the bread crumbs. Heat the butter in a medium-sized skillet. Add the "sandwiches" and sauté on both sides until browned. Drain the butter and discard. Preheat the oven to 350°.

Make a sauce by combining the wine, brandy, and chicken broth in the same skillet and reducing it by about half. Lightly glaze each sandwich with the sauce. Place the sandwiches, uncovered, in the oven for 15 minutes (if your skillet has any wooden or plastic parts, transfer contents into any container suitable for an oven). Serve on warmed plates with lemon wedges and any remaining sauce.

SERVES 4 AS FIRST COURSE

TRAVELIN' GOURMET TIPS:
How to Cook Artichokes

We have Thomas Jefferson to thank for introducing America to the artichoke. He discovered those globes of goodness on a visit to Italy. To prep them for cooking, wash them, then snip off the pointy tips, which can jab your fingers when you're turning over a new leaf. Then you even up the bottom with a sharp knife so it can stand alone.

You then can boil or steam them, which can take up to an hour, but I've found the easiest way to cook artichokes is to nuke 'em. Simply wrap one in wax paper and pop it into the microwave for 5 to 7 minutes on high (a bit longer if you're cooking a bunch of them).

After they're cooked, let them stand for 5 minutes, then they're ready to be eaten. The meat on the end is delicious and you can dip it into melted butter, a rémoulade sauce, or mayonnaise. Then you pull the end through the teeth to remove the meaty part. Be careful not to eat the leaf itself.

When you get to the fuzzy inside, pull it off so you can get to the best part, the heart. Cut it out and use it as described in the recipe here. Or you can simply dip it into the sauce of your choice or just melted butter and eat your heart out, which is where that expression may have come from.

CROSTINI MISTO

This unique, delicious appetizer is from the kitchen of Il Focolare, one of Rome's most famous trattorias. The menu includes many peasant dishes from the Latium region of Italy as well as more sophisticated offerings.

12 slices French bread ("crostini"), cut about ¾ inch thick
1 pound mozzarella cheese, cut into 2-inch squares
2 canned artichoke hearts, halved
1 garlic clove, minced
1 teaspoon chopped fresh parsley
olive oil
4 anchovy fillets
1 tablespoon unsalted butter, softened
4 thin slices smoked salmon

Preheat the oven to 300°. Layer a greased baking pan with the bread, and cover each slice with squares of mozzarella. Bake until the cheese has melted. Meanwhile, sauté the artichoke hearts with the garlic and parsley in olive oil for 3 to 4 minutes. In a small bowl, mix the anchovies with the tablespoon of butter to form a paste.

When the cheese has melted, remove the bread from the oven and top 4 slices with the artichoke mixture, 4 slices with the anchovy mixture, and 4 slices with the salmon. Serve immediately.

SERVES 6

A LA CARTE:
The Palate Guard

 The French don't care any more or any less about astrology than Americans, but every spring a significant number of them look to the stars to find gastronomic nirvana: the stars in the Michelin Guide. There may be no other book on earth that wields so much power. It can turn a young, unknown chef into a millionaire, or change a sleepy hamlet into a tourist mecca.

Every year before the red-covered 1300-page compendium of good taste is published, Paris is abuzz with rumors. Which new restaurants have been added? Which ones have been demoted? Which have ascended into culinary heaven by being awarded three stars? The rumors are confirmed or put to rest every March when the Red Guide hits the streets — something it has been doing every year since 1900, when it was launched by André Michelin, founder of the tire company that bears his name.

And when Michelin hath given and when it hath taken away, intense reactions have been known to result. In 1966, Alain Zick, a Parisian restaurateur, killed himself after the Michelin men stripped away the single star that his restaurant once boasted. The French preoccupation with food notwithstanding, most restaurateurs snubbed by *le guide* don't react as drastically as M. Zick. But losing a star can be traumatic and something a restaurateur never forgets.

In addition to its senior *inspecteurs*, Michelin editors rely on opinions from a European staff of some three hundred salesmen. They're in the enviable position of being able to dine wherever their palates lead them — and bill it to their expense account. In return, they have to report back to Paris headquarters at 46 Avenue de Breteuil in Paris on new finds, or if a once-heralded spot has slipped.

The editors also consider recommendations from travelers. However, gushing letters don't carry nearly as much weight as staff reports, particularly those of the *inspecteurs*, who visit as many as a dozen restaurants and hotels a day. They have a checklist that covers everything from cleanliness to the comfort of the chairs. Decor is important in the overall rating of a restaurant, although not as much as it was, say, twenty years ago.

There are certain unwritten rules the guide's editors follow. For example, a restaurant cannot earn two stars until it has had one. And it cannot be honored with three until it has earned two. Without question, the longest gap of time is between two and three stars. A decade is not an inordinate amount of time before a two-star restaurant is elevated to three-star status. René Lasserre, owner of the prestigious Lasserre in Paris, said earning three stars is "like getting a field marshal's baton or the Grand Cordon of the Legion d'Honneur. It can only be done with absolute honesty toward food: Buy only the best. Prepare it only in the classic tradition. Treat every individual dish as though it were the only thing that matters in the world at the moment. Do all this. Then wait ten years."

Not as much as you might expect has changed in the guide since it made its debut ninety years ago. It's fatter (about 1300 pages today as compared with 900 in 1900). The modern guide rates restaurants separately (in the beginning, just hotels were scrutinized). And it's no longer given away, as it once was, to gas and repair stations along the roads of France.

The modern Red Guide, like its ancestor, is still a stew of symbols above the type. They include everything from whether or not dogs are allowed in the restaurant, or if it has a garden or terrace. The symbol system, Michelin executives are quick to note, is used in order to pack as much information as possible into the book. Without question, the most important symbols are its food stars. One star signifies "good cooking in its class"; two, "excellent cooking worthy of a detour"; and three, "here one will find the best cooking in France, worthy of a special journey."

Although one might jump to the incorrect conclusion that the Michelin Guide was the first in the world to rate restaurants, it actually was preceded by Grimond de la Reynière's *Almanach des Gourmands*, which was published in Paris in 1803. Because M. Reynière was the only game in town he, too, wielded considerable power, able to make or break a restaurant with the stroke of a pen, just as the Michelin writers can today.

SOUPS

Sobrino de Botin, 17 Calle de Cuchilleros, Old Madrid, owes much of its international reputation to the fact that Ernest Hemingway wrote about it in glowing terms in *The Sun Also Rises* and *Death in the Afternoon*. Papa once called it "the best restaurant in the world." It's good, that's for sure, but Hemingway had a tendency to get carried away every now and then. In fact, if the stories are correct, he also had a tendency to get carried *out* of the restaurant after knocking back too many Spanish cocktails.

The restaurant's specialty is suckling pig. The little critters are roasted in wood-fired ovens dating back to 1725. They emerge from the 700° ovens with crisp, brown skin encasing the juicy, unbelievably tender meat inside. Since most of you aren't about to attempt finding a suckling pig to roast, I offer a Botin recipe for gazpacho, which originated in a colorful section of Spain called Andalusia. Although it's a great summer soup, it can be served year-round.

GAZPACHO À LA BOTIN

6 thin slices bread, diced
3 very ripe tomatoes, chopped (the riper the better)
1 cucumber, chopped
3 teaspoons olive oil
1 quart water
2 garlic cloves, minced
2 teaspoons wine vinegar
2 teaspoons salt
1½ teaspoons lime juice
1 teaspoon ground cumin
4 ice cubes
2 slices bread, browned in unsalted butter then diced, for
    garnish
1 diced red or green pepper, for garnish
1 large, diced ripe tomato, for garnish
1 small diced cucumber, for garnish

In a mixing bowl, put the first 6 slices of bread and the chopped tomatoes, chopped cucumber, olive oil, and water. Let soak for an hour, then puree in a food mill or blend in two batches on high speed in an electric blender for 10 seconds. Strain through a coarse sieve into a large soup bowl. Add the garlic, vinegar, salt, lime juice, cumin, and ice cubes and mix well. Chill in the refrigerator for at least half an hour.

To serve, pour the gazpacho into well-chilled bowls. Accompany in small bowls with the browned, diced bread, diced red or green pepper, tomato, and cucumber and let each person help himself to the diced garnishes, sprinkling some of each into his soup bowl.

SERVES 4–6

"Cold soup is a tricky thing and it is a rare hostess who can carry it off. More often than not, the dinner guest is left with the impression that had he only come a little bit earlier he could have gotten it while it was still hot."
—FRAN LEBOWITZ

"Cooking is not chemistry. It requires instinct and taste rather than exact measurements."

—X. MARCEL BOULESTIN

VICHYSSOISE

Louis Diat, former chef of the late, great Ritz Hotel in New York City, is credited for inventing vichyssoise, which he originally called "Cream Vichyssoise Glacée." He named it after the town in France, not too far from where he was born. This is a slight variation of his original recipe.

1 tablespoon unsalted butter
4 leeks (white parts only), cleaned (see page 182) and thinly sliced
1 medium onion, thinly sliced
5 medium potatoes, peeled and thinly sliced
1 quart chicken broth
2 teaspoons salt
2 cups milk
2 cups regular cream
salt and freshly ground white pepper
1 cup heavy cream
2 tablespoons chives

Melt the butter in a heavy saucepan and lightly sauté the leeks and onions; add the potatoes, broth, and the salt and bring to a boil. Continue boiling for about 35 minutes. Remove from the heat and puree in a blender. Return the liquid to the heat and add the milk and regular cream. Season to taste with salt and white pepper and return to a boil. Cool, then rub through a sieve. Chill. When cold, add the heavy cream. Serve thoroughly chilled, with a light topping of chives.

SERVES 8

CHILLED AVOCADO SOUP

An avocado soup from Madrid that will curry the favor of your guests. A snap to make! The salsa can be found in most supermarkets.

4 ripe avocados, peeled, pits removed and cubed
4 cups very cold whole milk
¾ teaspoon curry powder dissolved in 1½ teaspoons warm
    water
salt and freshly ground pepper
salsa (optional)

Puree the avocado meat in a blender; chill for 2 hours. Stir the curry powder into the milk, then blend with the avocado until well incorporated. Season with salt and pepper to taste. Serve right away in chilled soup bowls. Garnish with a dollop of salsa, if desired.

SERVES 4

COLD CREAM OF ZUCCHINI SOUP

A nice, cooling summer soup from Italy.

¼ pound unsalted butter
2 tablespoons minced sweet onion
1 medium-size zucchini, grated
1 heaping tablespoon flour
2 cups chicken stock
1 quart half-and-half
salt and white pepper

Melt the butter in a large pot. Add the onions and cook until transparent (don't brown). Add the zucchini and the flour; whisk until thoroughly incorporated. Simmer 5 minutes, then stir in the stock and bring to a boil. Reduce the heat and stir in the half-and-half. Season with salt and white pepper to taste and let simmer without boiling for about 20 minutes. Refrigerate overnight. Serve cold.

SERVES 4–6

OFF THE EATEN PATH:
Avocados

The Spaniards discovered the avocado. The name is derived from the Indian word *ahuacatl*. It turns up in a variety of different Spanish dishes, from salads to desserts, as well as in a dressing for fish.

TRAVELIN' GOURMET TIP:
Taking Stock of Fat Removal

Trying to get all the fat skimmed from your stock? Refrigerate it; the fat hardens on top and you can practically lift it off.

There are many ways to love a vegetable. The most sensible way is to love it well-treated.

—M. F. K. FISHER

COLD BLUEBERRY SOUP

Try this interesting soup if you can put your hands on fresh blueberries. It is from the late Colosseum Restaurant, Pittsburgh.

1 pint blueberries
2 cups water
½ cup maple syrup
½ teaspoon ground cinnamon
pinch cardamom
1 cup sour cream

Wash the blueberries and discard any that don't look appetizing. Put them in a saucepan with the water, maple syrup, cinnamon, and cardamom. Cook over a low flame for 10–15 minutes. Remove from the heat and cool. Stir in the sour cream. Chill at least 4 hours before serving.

SERVES 4–6

COLD CUCUMBER-YOGURT SOUP

This Greek soup is quite filling, so I suggest you serve it as a first course in cups rather than bowls. A little goes a long way!

3 medium-size cucumbers, peeled, seeded, and shredded
2 garlic cloves, minced
1 teaspoon crushed dried leaf mint (2 teaspoons fresh)
2 cups plain yogurt
2 cups buttermilk
salt
1 tablespoon olive oil

Mix the first 4 ingredients in a large bowl. Stir in the buttermilk, then add salt to taste. Sprinkle the top with the olive oil. Chill before serving.

SERVES 4

PEANUT SOUP

If you're nuts about peanuts, you'll love this Dutch recipe.

1 medium onion, chopped
1 celery rib, diced
3 tablespoons clarified unsalted butter (see page 38)
1½ tablespoons all-purpose flour
4 cups chicken broth
¼ cup water
1 cup smooth peanut butter
1 cup half-and-half
½ cup chopped peanuts, preferably unsalted, for garnish

Over low to medium heat, sauté the onions and celery in butter until the onions are limp (don't let them brown). Add the flour slowly, stirring constantly until it's well blended. Slowly add the chicken broth, stirring all the while. After it is all added, turn the heat to high and bring to a boil. Reduce the heat and simmer 5 minutes. Remove from heat and push through a sieve. Put what remains in the sieve into a blender with the water. Blend to a liquid, then add the strained liquid.

Put the peanut butter into a bowl and slowly add the liquid; blend with a whisk until the mixture is very smooth. Whisk in the half-and-half. Pour into a saucepan over low to medium heat and heat gently for about 5 minutes. Pour into 6 bowls and garnish each with an equal amount of chopped peanuts.

SERVES 6

COCK-A-LEEKIE-SOUP

One of the most famous Scottish soups is cock-a-leekie, made with chicken broth and leeks — hence the name.

1 stewing chicken (2–3 pounds) with giblets
4 pints water
2 bay leaves
1 pound leeks (white part only), slit, cleaned (see page 182), and chopped
salt and freshly ground black pepper
⅔ cup dried pitted prunes, soaked overnight in water to cover
3 tablespoons uncooked long-grain rice

TRAVELIN' GOURMET TRIVIA:

A Rosa Is a Rosa Is a Rosa

The ancient Romans not only had an affinity for fine food and flagrant partying but also for gossip. The sign of a thoughtful host was to place a rose on the plate of each of his guests. That meant that nothing said at the meal would be repeated afterward. Well, at least that was the idea. This is where the expression "sub rosa" comes from.

Put the chicken and giblets (except the liver) into a large pot with the water, bay leaves, and chopped leeks; season liberally with salt and pepper. Bring to a boil. Skim the surface, and reduce heat to a simmer. Cover and simmer for 2 to 3 hours, or until the chicken is tender.

Remove the chicken, bay leaves, and giblets; skim off the fat. Drain the prunes, dice, and add to the pot with the uncooked rice. Simmer for 30 to 40 more minutes. Adjust the seasonings and serve immediately. (If you like, you can add some of the chicken to the soup before serving. In Scotland, they generally present it as the next course, serving the chicken with an egg or caper sauce.)

ZUCCHINI-HAM SOUP

A robust soup, perfect on a cold wintry day. Your butcher probably will have the shanks on hand, or will be able to get them for you with little problem. From Chef Robert Zelesko, Pittsburgh.

2 pounds ham shanks
2½ quarts water
1 medium onion, chopped
2 celery ribs, chopped
4 carrots, sliced
2 tablespoons olive oil
1 cup chicken broth (optional)
1½ pounds zucchini, diced
salt and freshly ground black pepper

Boil the shanks in the water for 1 hour. Remove the shanks and reserve the stock. Allow the stock to cool enough to remove the layer of fat. Remove the ham from the shank and set the meat aside.

In a large pot, sauté the onion, celery, and carrots in the olive oil. Add the reserved ham stock to the sautéed vegetables (if stock seems weak, add the chicken broth). Add the zucchini to the stock. Bring to a full boil, then reduce heat and add the ham pieces. Simmer 30 to 40 minutes. Season to taste with salt and pepper before serving.

SERVES 4–6

MANHATTAN CLAM CHOWDER

I'm told that this was once the most popular soup among English passengers on the *QE II*.

½ dozen large clams
1 large onion, diced
1 leek, chopped (white part only)
6 tablespoons unsalted butter
2 medium potatoes, peeled and chopped
1 green pepper, seeded and diced
4 tomatoes, blanched, seeded, and chopped
1 bay leaf
1 celery rib, diced
⅛ teaspoon powdered thyme
2½ pints water
salt and freshly ground black pepper to taste
½ teaspoon caraway seeds

Steam the clams until the shells are wide open; reserve and strain the liquid. Dice the clams and set aside. Sauté the onion and leek in the butter until lightly browned. Add the potatoes, green pepper, tomatoes, bay leaf, celery, thyme, water, and the reserved clam liquid. Season with salt and pepper, cover, and bring to a boil; lower heat and simmer for 30 minutes.

Add the chopped clams and caraway seed; continue to cook another 5 minutes. Serve immediately.

SERVES 6–8

DUTCH PEA SOUP

From Amsterdam's famous Dorrius' Restaurant.

½ pound lean bacon
2 quarts water
1 pound split peas, rinsed and picked over
1 cup sliced leeks (white parts only), cleaned (see page 182)
    and cut into ½-inch rounds
1 cup chopped celery
1 medium onion, sliced
salt and freshly ground black pepper to taste
½ cup dry sherry

Put the bacon in the water and bring to a boil; let boil for 5 minutes. Remove the bacon with a slotted spoon and skim off the fat from the cooking water. Add the split peas to the water in which the bacon cooked and bring to a boil. Reduce to a high simmer and cook with the lid partially on for about 90 minutes. In another pot, cover the leeks, celery, and onion with salted water and bring to a boil. Cook until tender (about 5 to 8 minutes).

Drain the vegetables and add to the split pea soup. Mix well and season with salt and pepper. Heat to a boil once again and continue to boil for 5 minutes. Reduce the heat and cook for about 30 minutes, or until the soup has reduced by about 25 percent. Stir in the sherry and serve immediately.

SERVES 8

LOUISIANA CAJUN OYSTER STEW

From the delicious repertoire of Certified Master Chef Byron Bardy of Pittsburgh.

6½ tablespoons unsalted butter
1 teaspoon finely minced shallots
1 pound fresh oysters with the "liquor"*
3 teaspoons Cajun spice (available in most supermarkets)†
3½ tablespoons dry sherry
2 cups heavy cream

Melt 4½ tablespoons of the butter in a heavy sauté pan; sauté until it turns light brown. Add the shallots and quickly sauté them, being careful not to let them brown (or they'll get bitter). Add the oysters, liquor, and Cajun spice. Cook until the mixture reduces by half. Add the sherry and cook it for 1 minute. Add the cream and bring the mixture to a boil. Remove from the heat and stir in the rest of the butter. Serve immediately.

SERVES 4

*The natural juices of an oyster are known as its liquor.

†You can make your own Cajun spice mix by combining 1 teaspoon garlic powder, 1 teaspoon onion powder, ½ teaspoon dried oregano, 1 tablespoon sweet paprika, 1 teaspoon freshly ground black pepper, 1 teaspoon cayenne, ¾ teaspoon white pepper, 2 teaspoons salt, and ¾ teaspoon dried thyme.

Beautiful soup! Who cares for fish, game or any other dish?
—LEWIS CARROLL

If a great hotel is measured in part by the quality of its restaurant, the Windsor Court is the *crème de la crème* of hotels in New Orleans. But the sleek property has far more going for it than its magnificent restaurant, the Grill Room — namely a subdued aura of European elegance, more than the usual share of amenities, and a staff that gives new meaning to the word *motivated*.

Here's a recipe from the Grill Room. If you can find andouille sausage in your local specialty store, I urge you to try it. Andouille (from the French word for sausage) is usually made with the stomach and the neck meat of the pig. The stock may be made the day before making the gumbo.

TURKEY AND ANDOUILLE GUMBO

THE STOCK:
4 turkey legs
1 tablespoon vegetable oil
1 gallon water
1 large onion, quartered
2 ribs celery
2 carrots
2 bay leaves
3 teaspoons salt
1 teaspoon black pepper

THE GUMBO:
¾ cup flour
⅔ cup vegetable oil
2 garlic cloves, minced
1 cup finely chopped onion
½ cup finely chopped celery
1 cup finely chopped green bell pepper
1 pound andouille sausage
4 tablespoons filé powder (available in specialty stores)
¼ cup chopped fresh parsley
2 teaspoons salt
½ teaspoon black pepper
2 cups hot cooked rice

TO MAKE THE STOCK: Brown the turkey legs in the vegetable oil in a stock pot. Add the water and simmer with the onion, celery, carrots, bay leaves, salt, and pepper. Strain; skim off all grease and reserve 3 quarts of the stock. Remove the skin from the turkey legs and discard it. Remove the meat from the bone and cut into bite-sized pieces; return to the stock.

TO MAKE THE GUMBO: In a large Dutch oven or pot, make a dark brown *roux* with the flour and oil. Add the garlic, onion, celery, and green pepper; sauté, uncovered, on medium heat or until the onions are transparent (about 30 minutes). In a separate, large stock pot, warm the turkey stock and slowly stir in the roux and the vegetable mixture. Simmer for 1 hour and skim foam from the top.

Cut the sausage lengthwise and then into ½-inch slices. In a separate skillet, sauté the sausage slowly for about 5 minutes in order to get rid of the fat. With a slotted spoon, remove the sausage from the pan and add to the pot with the stock mixture. Whisk in the filé powder and cook for an additional 5 minutes. Stir in the parsley and salt and pepper and remove from the heat. Adjust seasonings and serve over hot, fluffy rice.

SERVES 8–12

CORN AND LOBSTER SOUP

From the Four Seasons Hotel, Boston, comes this rich, wonderful soup.

1 pound cooked lobster meat, cut into 2-inch cubes
1 tablespoon Jack Daniel's whiskey
⅛ pound bacon, chopped
2 leeks (white parts only), split, cleaned (see page 182), and
    cut into slices
vegetable oil
1 pound frozen corn
½ cup dry white wine
1 quart heavy cream
salt and white pepper
1 tablespoon snipped chives, finely minced

Marinate the lobster in the whiskey for an hour. In a medium-size soup pot, sauté the bacon and leeks in a little oil over medium heat until the leeks color slightly. Add the corn and sauté gently (about 5 to 6 minutes). Add the wine and simmer for about 2 minutes. Add the cream and bring the soup to a simmer; cook 20 minutes.

Remove the soup from the heat and puree in a blender or food processor until very fine. Return to heat; bring to a boil and season to taste with salt and pepper. Arrange the lobster in the bottom of 6 soup bowls. Pour the soup over the lobster meat, sprinkle with chives, and serve right away.

SERVES 6

OFF THE EATEN PATH:
How to Hypnotize a Lobster

If you're like me, you hate to sentence the lobster, that cardinal of the seas, to his doom by throwing the poor critter into a pot of boiling water. However, there's a more civilized way to cook a lobster—by hypnotizing him so he feels no pain when getting his final steam bath. All you do is balance the lobster on his front claws with his tail up in the air. Rub the front of his tail a few seconds and before you know it, he'll be asleep. When he hits the boiling water not only will it be painless, but he won't go into shock and secrete enzymes that cut down on the sweetness of the meat.

MOROCCAN SOUP

The late Lee Foster, an editor in *The New York Times* travel department who shaped many of my articles for that august publication, was a great food-lover and edited a cookbook of some of the favorite recipes of *New York Times* correspondents. This soup from Morocco was one of Lee's favorites.

¾ *pound lamb, cut into 1-inch julienne strips*
3 *tablespoons good-quality olive oil*
½ *teaspoon ground ginger*
⅓ *teaspoon turmeric*
2 *medium, ripe tomatoes, cubed*
½ *cup chopped onions*
1 *cup canned (or cooked) chick-peas, drained*
½ *teaspoon dried coriander seed*
2 *quarts chicken broth*
⅛ *teaspoon salt*
⅛ *teaspoon freshly ground black pepper*
2 *eggs, well beaten*
1½ *tablespoons lemon juice*
ground cinnamon to taste

In a large pot, over medium-high heat, brown the lamb in olive oil with the ginger and turmeric. Raise the heat to high and add the tomatoes, onions, chick-peas, coriander, broth, salt, and pepper. Bring to a boil, then cover the pot and reduce the heat to low. Simmer until the meat is very tender (about an hour).

Remove from the heat. Slowly add the eggs, stirring all the while. Gently stir in the lemon juice and cinnamon. Serve right away.

SERVES 6–8

In an era when many Caribbean islands are so commercialized that they seem nothing more than shopping centers surrounded by the sea, it's nice to know islands like St. Kitts still exist. When you set foot on the sixty-eight-square-mile rhapsody in green in the northern Leeward Islands, it's as if you've been catapulted back to the Caribbean of yore. Rather than a landscape verdant with hotels and fast-food stands, St. Kitts looks pretty much like it did when Christopher Columbus discovered it in 1493. It's a land of emerald-green hillsides, towering peaks embraced by clouds, and acres of sugarcane amid the benign chimneys of ancient sugar plantations.

In an age when some travel writers deem any island without a McDonald's as "unspoiled," I feel I can pronounce St. Kitts as precisely that without fear of equivocation. Its population of 45,000 also is unspoiled. The natives aren't restless as they try to foist straw baskets on you, nor do they rush up to you brandishing fake Rolexes. Fact is, tourists are so relatively few in St. Kitts that locals still look upon them with curiosity. In more than one sector of town I was gazed at by Kittians as if I were some new species of exotic fauna that stumbled into town.

There really isn't much to do in St. Kitts but laze on the beach or scamper into its azure waters like a sandpiper bent on destruction. That's exactly why it's so attractive to travelers who more or less have to be "forced" into submission, among whom I number myself. To me, St. Kitts is Valium-by-the-Sea.

If you're well-heeled enough to demand nothing more than plain old excellence, without a doubt *the* place to stay is the whimsically named Golden Lemon. Built in 1690, the sixteen-room posh inn rests regally on a palm-fringed, black-sand beach on the northern end of the island. It attracts a cross-section of well-to-dos, including, I am told, some well-to-dos who got that way being ne'er-do-wells. If you're a people-watcher, lunch at the Golden Lemon can be an eye-opening experience.

In addition to being a hideaway for an international cast of characters, the Golden Lemon, not surprisingly, has a kitchen to match its appealing ambiance. Here is a variation of one of its easiest soup recipes.

CREAM OF PUMPKIN SOUP

The Amaretto adds "zing" to the proceedings.

2 small onions, minced
2 tablespoons unsalted butter
2 cups pumpkin pie mix
1 cup canned chicken broth
1 cup heavy cream
dash Tabasco sauce
salt and freshly ground black pepper
3 tablespoons Amaretto (optional)
freshly grated nutmeg, for garnish

In a large saucepan over moderate heat, cook the onions in the butter until softened. Add the pumpkin and broth and bring to a boil, still over moderate heat. Stir in the cream and simmer, covered, for 15 minutes.

Let the mixture cool slightly, then puree in batches in a blender or food processor. Transfer the puree to the pan, season to taste with Tabasco, salt, and pepper, and heat over moderately low heat, stirring occasionally, until the soup is hot. Stir in the Amaretto (if desired). Divide the soup among heated bowls and garnish with freshly grated nutmeg.

SERVES 6–8

OFF THE EATEN PATH:
The Dishwasher

That almighty kitchen device known as the dishwasher was invented by Josephine Cochrane, an Illinois housewife, back in 1886. Ironically, Mrs. Cochrane was married to a wealthy politician and had a house full of servants.

FRENCH ONION SOUP

The easiest recipe I know for the French classic.

6 large onions, thinly sliced
1 tablespoon olive oil
3 tablespoons unsalted butter
6 cups beef broth
salt and freshly ground black pepper
¼ cup sherry
½ cup diced Gruyère cheese
6 slices French bread, toasted
½ cup shredded Swiss cheese
½ cup shredded Parmesan cheese

Cook the onions in the olive oil and butter over low heat until limp (15 to 20 minutes), stirring occasionally. Add the beef broth, turn the heat to high, and bring to a boil. Reduce the heat, cover, and let simmer for 30 minutes. Season with salt and pepper to taste. Stir in the sherry. Simmer another 5 minutes.

Preheat the oven to 425°.

Pour the soup into 6 ovenproof soup bowls. Distribute the diced Gruyère cheese evenly into each of the bowls. Top with the French bread. Sprinkle shredded Swiss and Parmesan on the bread. Put the soup in the oven until the cheese melts. Let it cool a bit before serving. Additional untoasted French bread is the perfect complement.

SERVES 6

TRAVELIN' GOURMET TIP:
How to Eat Onion Soup the Easy Way

French onion soup is delicious, but a lot of people find it difficult to eat. I've seen grown men make fools of themselves at fancy dinner parties twirling cheese around a spoon. But it's easy, if you know how. And you'll never have to be intimidated by it again. All you need is some bread in a plate at the side. Then you delicately lift off the cheese and fashion some mini-cheese sandwiches, and you alternate sips of the soup and bites of the bread and cheese.

CHICKEN AVGOLEMONO SOUP

If you can't find rosemarie, a pasta carried by many specialty shops, you can substitute rice in this recipe from Greece.

¾ cup rosemarie (or rice)
2 quarts chicken broth
salt and white pepper
4 eggs
juice of 1 lemon, mixed with ¼ cup water

Simmer the rosemarie (or rice) in the chicken broth for 25 to 30 minutes. Season to taste with salt and pepper. Beat the eggs vigorously in a large bowl with an electric beater, then slowly add the lemon-juice mixture. Continue beating while slowly adding 4 to 5 cups of the simmering broth to the egg mixture. Pour back into the pot and stir well. Leave on low heat 2 to 3 minutes before serving.

SERVES 6

WATERCRESS AND PEAR SOUP

From the kitchen of the Bath Hotel, Bath, England.

1 large onion, chopped
1 leek (white part only), cleaned (see page 182) and sliced
1 small celery heart, sliced
½ cup unsalted butter
½ cup all-purpose flour
1 quart chicken broth
8-ounce can pear halves in syrup (reserve the pears for garnish)
3 bunches watercress (2 bunches chopped, leaves of the third
    reserved for garnish)
½ teaspoon minced fresh parsley
pinch dried thyme
¼ teaspoon dried basil, or ½ teaspoon fresh
salt and white pepper to taste

Sauté the onion, leek, and celery heart in the butter until tender (be careful not to brown). Slowly add the flour and whisk until very smooth (don't brown). Add all but about ¼ cup of the chicken broth, the syrup from the pears, and the chopped watercress. Reduce the heat, cover, and simmer for about an hour.

Transfer the mixture to the container of a blender and puree, adding the rest of the chicken broth if necessary. Add the parsley, thyme, and basil; season with salt and white pepper. Put into 4 to 6 bowls, and garnish with the reserved pears and the watercress leaves. Serve immediately.

SERVES 4–6

TRAVELIN' GOURMET TIP:
Taking Stock of Things

Chicken or beef stock, lemon juice, and pureed tomatoes can be frozen in ice cube trays, then plopped into soups or sauces as needed.

MINESTRONE WITH TORTELLINI

This recipe won a top prize in a recipe contest sponsored by the Heinz Corporation, which is based not far from my home in Pittsburgh.

1½ pounds bulk Italian sausage
1 cup chopped onions
6 cups beef broth
½ cup dry red wine
16-ounce can tomatoes, with liquid
2 cups thinly sliced carrots
1 cup thinly sliced celery
1 cup tomato ketchup
1 teaspoon Italian seasoning
2 garlic cloves, minced
2 cups sliced zucchini (about two small)
½ pound meat- or cheese-filled tortellini (frozen)
1 medium green pepper, diced
¼ cup chopped fresh parsley
salt and freshly ground black pepper
grated Parmesan cheese to taste

Brown the sausage in a 5-quart Dutch oven; drain off the excess fat. Add the onions and sauté until tender. Add the beef broth, wine, tomatoes, carrots, celery, ketchup, Italian seasoning, and garlic. Bring to a boil and simmer for 30 minutes. Skim away the fat from the soup. Stir in the zucchini, tortellini, green pepper, and parsley. Simmer, covered, until the tortellini are tender (about 30 to 40 minutes). Season to taste with salt and pepper. Sprinkle with cheese before serving.

SERVES 8

OFF THE EATEN PATH:
One Nation Divided by a Common Language

We say biscuit, the English say scone. We say cookie, they say biscuit. We say molasses, they say black treacle. We say turnips, they say Swedes. We say squash, they say vegetable marrow. We say soda cracker, they say water cracker. We say cornmeal, they say Indian meal.

The Brits call a T-bone steak a porterhouse, a rib steak a rump steak, the shank the shin, the bottom round the silverside, and a sirloin tip a top rump.

Last but far from least, here are some English translations of British dishes:

Bangers and mash: Sausages with mashed potatoes.

Bubble and squeak: Leftover roast beef, potatoes, and cabbage fried together.

Howtowdie with drappit: Roasted hen rimmed with spinach and poached eggs.

Chip butty: A french-fry sandwich, would you believe? Popular in Liverpool.

ALMOND-CREAM SOUP

Roger Vergé is one of the world's few "superstar" chefs. His restaurant, Le Moulin de Mougins, in Mougins, France, has earned the highest rating in the revered Michelin Guide. This is a slight variation of one of his famous soup recipes.

1 leek (white part only), cleaned (see page 182) and cut into thin rounds
1 tablespoon unsalted butter
1 tablespoon water
4 cups water
2 chicken bouillon cubes
¾ tablespoon washed, drained, uncooked Carolina rice
¾ cup ground almonds
1¼ cups whipping cream
2 egg yolks
salt
2 tablespoons slivered almonds (optional)

Cook the leeks gently in the butter and the 1 tablespoon water until softened (about 5 minutes). Add the water and bring to a boil. Add the bouillon cubes, rice, and ground almonds. Cover and cook over low heat for about a half hour.

Puree the soup in a blender. In a large bowl, whisk together the cream and the egg yolks. Add the soup to the cream mixture, whisking all the while. Return the mixture to a saucepan and cook gently until bubbles start to appear on the surface (don't boil). Season to taste with salt and strain through a fine sieve. Transfer to 4 soup bowls and top each with slivered almonds, if desired.

SERVES 4

GERMAN WINE SOUP

An unusual soup from Deutschland.

3 medium-sized onions, thinly sliced
4½ tablespoons unsalted butter
1 tablespoon cornstarch
1½ quarts beef broth
2 yolks from extra-large eggs
½ cup dry white wine
½ cup heavy cream
salt and freshly ground black pepper
4 slices white bread (crusts removed), cut into cubes
4 tablespoons unsalted butter
2 teaspoons chopped chives, for garnish
1½ teaspoons chopped fresh dill, for garnish

In a large saucepan, cook the onions in the 4½ tablespoons butter until limp and translucent. Sprinkle in the cornstarch; cook 1 to 2 minutes, stirring all the while. Add the broth; cook over medium-high heat for 20 minutes. Meanwhile, put the egg yolks into a bowl and add the wine, cream, salt, and pepper and beat well.

Make croutons by browning the bread cubes in the remaining butter. Remove the soup from the heat and quickly stir in the egg mixture. Transfer to 4 bowls, and top each with a quarter of the croutons, chives, and dill.

SERVES 4

MUSHROOM BISQUE

This recipe from France is even better if you use wild mushrooms. But it's also eminently edible with domestic ones.

3 cups chicken stock (the richer the better)
salt and freshly ground black pepper to taste
1 pound mushroom stems and caps, cleaned and chopped
4½ tablespoons unsalted butter
1 pound mushroom caps, sliced
3 tablespoons flour
⅓ teaspoon dry mustard
¼ cup cream sherry
½ cup whipping cream

In a large pot, season the stock with salt and pepper. Add the chopped mushrooms and simmer 25 to 35 minutes. Strain out the mushrooms and discard; reserve the stock.

Melt the butter in a sauté pan. Add the sliced mushrooms and sauté lightly. Add the flour and cook for 2 to 3 minutes, whisking all the while. Add the sliced mushrooms and the dry mustard to the reserved chicken stock. Cook over medium-high heat until the mixture starts to thicken, stirring all the while. Add the cream sherry.

When the mixture begins to boil, remove from heat and add the whipping cream. Reduce the heat and simmer for a few minutes. Serve immediately.

SERVES 4–6

MEXICAN LIME SOUP

The lime juice makes this soup uniquely refreshing.

3-pound broiler chicken, cut up
2½ quarts water
6 sprigs parsley
10 peppercorns
1 rib celery, chopped
1 medium onion, quartered
1½ teaspoons salt
½ teaspoon dried thyme, or 1 teaspoon fresh
2½ tablespoons vegetable oil
2 small onions, chopped
1 green pepper, seeded and chopped
2 cups tomatoes (about three small), peeled, seeded, and
    chopped
4 carrots, chopped
2 limes, halved
3 tablespoons minced fresh parsley
salt and freshly ground black pepper to taste
4 dozen unsalted tortilla chips
8 lime slices, for garnish

In a Dutch oven, combine the chicken, water, parsley, peppercorns, celery, onion, salt, and thyme. Bring to a boil, then simmer, uncovered, until the chicken is tender (this will take about an hour and a half). Occasionally skim the fat off the top. Remove the chicken to cool, then cut the meat from the bones; strain the broth and reserve.

Meanwhile, heat the vegetable oil in a Dutch oven and sauté the onions and green pepper about 4 to 5 minutes, or until tender. Add the tomatoes and carrots and cook, uncovered, for 5 minutes. Add the reserved broth; squeeze in the juice from the limes; add 2 of the lime halves to the soup mixture. Stir in the parsley, season with salt and pepper, and simmer 45 minutes. Add the chicken meat; heat until the mixture starts to bubble (about 10 to 12 minutes). Adjust seasonings if necessary. Arrange 6 tortilla chips in the bottom of each of 8 soup bowls and pour in the soup. Garnish the top of each with a thin slice of lime; serve immediately.

SERVES 8

FISHERMAN'S CHOWDER

A robust soup from Newfoundland sent to me by a *Pittsburgh Post-Gazette* reader.

1 tablespoon diced salt pork
1 onion, cut into thin slices
5 small potatoes, pared and cut into thin slices
½ cup water
½ teaspoon salt
pinch white pepper
1 pound cod fillets, cut into strips about 1½ inches wide
1½ tablespoons unsalted butter
2 cups milk

In a Dutch oven, cook the salt pork over moderate heat until it starts to turn golden. Stir in the onion and cook until the onion is limp and tender (12 to 15 minutes). Add the potatoes, water, salt, and pepper. Bring to a boil. Reduce heat to a simmer and cook for 10 to 12 minutes, covered.

Add the cod to the soup mixture; cook over moderate heat until the potatoes and fish are tender (15 to 20 minutes). Stir in the butter and milk and continue cooking until the chowder is very hot. Serve right away.

SERVES 4

A LA CARTE:
A Super Supermarket in Munich

 There was a time when Munich was more noted for the quantity rather than quality of its food — a stereotype spawned by countless photos of beer-swilling, sausage-downing, pretzel-munching locals reveling it up at the city's famed *Oktoberfest*. Make no mistake about it, many of the locals still think more is better, which culinary historians attribute to the aftereffect of near-starvation of much of the populace during World War II. But today München's gastronomic side has more sophisticated overtones, most notably two of the finest restaurants in Europe: Aubergine and Tantris. Each has earned the highest rating in the revered Michelin Guide.

Munich also is the site of Dallmayr, a paradise for the palate that is one of the greatest food markets on earth. One visit and you'll find it not surprising to learn that it's been a purveyor to sixteen royal houses of Europe in its three-hundred-year history. From the outside, it looks like a chic German department store. At any hour of the day, window-shoppers can be seen salivating as they gaze into the arched windows at samples from Dallmayr's vast larder. When you step inside, you enter what looks like the baronial manse of some eccentric foodie. There's something intriguing about shopping for food under high, vaulted ceilings braced by marble columns. The focal point is a fountain filled with live crayfish, that frolic in water spewing from mouths of marble fish.

Dallmayr is in the enviable position of having customers who demand the finest to flatter their palates — and are willing to pay for it. That's a merchant's dream. It's also a supplier's dream to be welcomed into Dallmayr's inner sanctum.

"We sell nothing that has not been meticulously put to the test," said Georg Randkofer, managing partner of the family enterprise that owns the store, in business since 1895. "That applies to everything from homemade rolls to Bavarian-broiled chicken, guaranteed to have scratched the ground under the blue-white sky before we grill it in pure butter. Suppliers must be prepared to work to our specifications. In the case of jams and marmalades, for example, we accept only the best hand-picked fruits, and the sugar content is lower than usual."

Dallmayr also is internationally known for its "edible bouquets," actually candies made to look like flowers that are fashioned into delicious bouquets. Incidentally, six hundred different types of candies are made on the premises.

Dallmayr is the leading importer of coffee from Ethiopia, where coffee originated. Its twenty-four different blends are stored in porcelain urns so gorgeous that a clerk told me some tourists come in just to see the priceless containers, which are from Munich's rococo Nymphenburg castle.

What separates Dallmayr from most other chic food emporia are the wines in its "treasure chamber." Although some of its wines and liqueurs can be purchased for under $100, its classic bottles are very pricey — some cost over $2000. The crown jewel in the collection had been a 1789 Grande Fine Champagne, a cognac dating back to the French Revolution, which was sold to an anonymous customer for $2500.

But Dallmayr is most noted for its food, and its buyers will go anywhere to get it, Randkofer said. I was curious to learn where it found the best of everything. Randkofer shared some of Dallmayr's secrets with me. Some of his answers were surprising, including the fact that Dallmayr prefers smoked salmon from Norway rather than Scotland (but in the case of fresh salmon, it opts for the Scottish variety). Another surprise was that Dallmayr bought *foie gras* from the Perigord region of France rather than from Strasbourg, long synonymous with the silken delicacy made of the livers of specially fattened geese. Here are his other answers:

For caviar, it's Russia; for poultry, Bresse, France; duck, southwest France; lobsters, Maine; beef, U.S. Midwest; wine,

France; oysters, the Netherlands. And for truffles, it's France for the black variety, Italy for the white.

Dallmayr also stocks 250 varieties of cheese, 20 kinds of smoked fish (smoked on the premises in its master kitchen); 100 kinds of sausage, 60 varieties of bread, 15 varieties of herring, 50 different kinds of salads, as well as vegetables and fruits from around the world, including tomatoes from Morocco, papaya from Brazil, and carambola fruit from the Caribbean.

After your appetite is sufficiently whetted from browsing on the first floor, you might consider dining upstairs, where chefs fashion meals from the store's enviable inventory. The dining room is one of quiet elegance and everything is just perfect: from the subdued lighting to the crystal, the silver, and the tablecloths. The ceramic place settings are made exclusively for Dallmayr by Italian and French craftsmen.

One writer called Dallmayr a "gourmet's El Dorado." The Germans have a simpler word for it: *wunderbar*.

PASTA

A lot of people ask me where I first developed my passion for food. The answer is simple: at funerals. In the Italian neighborhood where I was raised, the sting of death was tempered by the great Italian feasts that followed most funerals. One of the indelible impressions I have from my youth is of my grandmother, all in black, in front of an open casket, her head bowed as she prayed silently, intermittently pounding her chest with a pair of steel-belted rosary beads. The next thing I knew, we were partaking of an incredible Italian feast.

Until I was twenty-seven, I thought the only way to secure a great Italian meal was to pound your chest with a pair of rosary beads.

One time my grandmother and I actually "crashed" a funeral. She read in the paper that a famous local chef had died and immediately realized what a great post-funeral banquet there would be. She and I showed up at the funeral parlor and patiently stood in line to issue sympathy to the widow, whom we'd never met. Later at the marvelous banquet that sent the late chef to that great larder in the sky, my grandmother patted my head as I happily swallowed a forkful of the most incredible *brasciole* I've ever had, and she whispered:

"Remember, as you go through life, whenever you get the chance, never pass up the funeral of a chef." It's been my credo ever since.

I learned to love pasta in Dunmore, Pennsylvania, not only at post-funeral bashes but also in my grandmother's aromatic kitchen. And that was long before pasta became so trendy that even French restaurants began offering it. I can only wonder what my grandmother would think about sampling some of the more eccentric renditions of pasta being served today, like Farfalle with Peanut Sauce. I think that you'll find the pairing of a classic Indonesian sauce with farfalle (a.k.a. "butterfly" or "bowtie" noodles) results in a unique, delicious dish.

FARFALLE WITH PEANUT SAUCE

¾ cup crunchy peanut butter
1½ cups unsweetened coconut milk (available in cans at Asian grocers, gourmet shops, and some supermarkets)
2 tablespoons soy sauce
2 teaspoons brown sugar
4 garlic cloves, minced
¼ cup lime juice
pinch salt
½ teaspoon cayenne pepper (or to taste)
¼ cup whipping cream
¼ cup chicken broth
¾ pound farfalle (bowtie noodles), cooked al dente
2 tablespoons unsalted butter
¼–½ cup sesame seeds

Mix together the first 8 ingredients in a medium saucepan over medium-low heat. Stir until the mixture becomes thick and satiny. Add the whipping cream and the chicken broth. Stir until smooth and well heated. Remove from the heat and set aside.

Put the noodles in a large bowl and toss with the peanut sauce. Before serving, sprinkle the sesame seeds on top.

SERVES 4 AS MAIN COURSE; 8 AS APPETIZER

TRAVELIN' GOURMET TIP:
How to Cook Pasta Perfect!

When I was growing up, my grandmother would test whether the pasta was properly cooked by throwing it against a wall. If it stuck, it was ready to be graced with one of her legendary sauces. Problem was, if I barged into her kitchen unannounced I might get splattered with an unidentified flying noodle. I've got pasta scars on my forehead to prove it. A cleaner and easier way to prepare pasta *al dente*, literally "to the tooth" (i.e., slightly firm to the bite), is to test it while it's cooking, but you risk barbecuing your chin while you raise the hot noodle to your mouth—if it doesn't slip off the fork.

Here's the easiest and safest way I know to cook pasta *al dente* every time. (The technique works with most pasta, except large types like lasagna and manicotti, which take a bit more time to cook.) In a large pot, bring 5 quarts of water to a boil, add about a teaspoon of salt and 1 pound of dried pasta. Let the pasta cook for exactly 2 minutes after you get it all into the pot. Stir it a bit as it's cooking. After the 2 minutes are up, remove the pot from the heat, drape a towel over the top, and put on the lid. Let the pasta steam for exactly 9 minutes. Bingo! *Al dente* every time.

All you do then is drain it immediately and toss it with your favorite sauce. By the way, don't drain it dry; if you do, the pasta may become sticky. If you drain it over a bowl, you can return a few tablespoons of the water to the pasta to prevent it from becoming too dry. For best results, serve pasta on heated plates.

PASTA CARBONARA

Not to be confused with "caponata," the Italian version of ratatouille. "Carbonara" is a classic Italian pasta dish that derives its name from the fact that the sauce looks as though it's flaked with carbon.

1 pound bacon, cut crosswise into 1/3-inch-wide strips
6 tablespoons unsalted butter
4 garlic cloves, minced
2 cups heavy cream
6 egg yolks
2 cups freshly grated Parmesan cheese
3/4 pound spaghetti, cooked al dente
1/3 cup minced fresh parsley
freshly ground black pepper to taste

In a large skillet, sauté the bacon in the butter until it's crisp. Drain off most of the fat but leave a little to sauté the garlic. Add the garlic and sauté it for exactly 1 minute, then remove the skillet from the heat.

In a bowl, beat the cream, egg yolks, and 1½ cups of the cheese. Add the cooked pasta to the skillet and add the cheese mixture. Toss it together over low heat until the sauce has thickened and all of the pasta is coated. Transfer to heated plates, sprinkle with the remaining cheese, parsley, and black pepper. Serve immediately.

SERVES 4

Around man with a moustache gone wild and a half-moon smile prances up to a nest of fettuccine writhing in steam on an ivory plate. He dusts the satiny noodles with a handful of young Parmesan cheese and starts twirling them like a madman with a solid gold fork and spoon. As the noodles dance on the plate, he does a sort of Italian rap-tune about the joys of eating the most famous pasta dish in the world — and one that bears his name.

Alfredo DiLelio III's gastronomic antics inevitably evoke smiles on the faces of the salivating diners waiting to taste his handiwork, which he offers with the panache of a playboy presenting his lady of the moment with a diamond ring.

And so it goes, day after day, year after year, decade after decade at Alfredo L'Originale, at Piazza Augusto Imperatore 30, right across from the tomb of Caesar Augustus in the heart of the Eternal City.

Today, Alfredo III carries on the tradition started about seventy-five years ago by his grandfather. Numero Uno Alfredo first fashioned the concoction of fettuccine, butter, and cheese for his pregnant wife, who was craving something "different." He came up with the dish that became known as Fettuccine Alfredo. She liked it so much, Alfredo I introduced it at his restaurant. It was an overnight sensation.

When Douglas Fairbanks and Mary Pickford honeymooned in Rome in the '20s, they were so impressed with the theatrics Alfredo employed while twirling noodles for them — as well as how wonderful they tasted — that they presented him with a solid gold fork and spoon with their names inscribed on them. The implements are still employed by Alfredo III as he goes about the never-ending task of slaking the appetites of the fettuccine-craving customers from around the world who stream into his restaurant every day. Many of the more famous ones — from John F. Kennedy to John Wayne — can be seen partaking of the noodles in photos blistering the walls of the restaurant.

Incidentally, there are at least two other restaurants in Rome that claim the paternity of Fettuccine Alfredo, but most culinary historians back up Alfredo III's claim that his grandfather was the originator.

This is a recipe for making Fettuccine Alfredo at home, modified for the American kitchen (in Rome, they used "triple butter," which is richer than what we can get in the States, so we have to add a little cream). It's important to crown the noodles with freshly grated Parmesan cheese (domestic Parmesan works nicely because it is not as sharp as imported) and coarsely ground black pepper. You'd be surprised what a nice effect this has on the dish. If possible, use homemade noodles, now available in many supermarkets. If using dried fettuccine noodles, use an imported brand such as DiCecco.

Fettuccine, incidentally, means "little ribbons" in Italian.

FETTUCCINE ALFREDO

Normally, a pound of regular pasta is enough to serve 4 people, unless it is being tossed with a rich sauce such as the one in this recipe, when ¾ of a pound is usually sufficient.

¾ pound fettuccine noodles, cooked al dente
1 stick unsalted butter
1 cup heavy cream
1 cup freshly grated domestic Parmesan cheese
freshly grated Parmesan cheese, for dusting
coarsely ground fresh black pepper

While the noodles are cooking, melt the butter in a saucepan large enough to accommodate the pasta with room to toss it without spilling. Over moderate heat, add the noodles and mix very well with the butter. Add half of the cream and toss with a fork and spoon. Add half of the cheese and toss to incorporate well, adding more cream a little at a time but never too much (the cream should hardly be noticeable when the dish is finished; use only enough to keep the noodles from sticking together). Keep tossing and add the rest of the cheese and, if needed, more cream. Toss until all of the cheese is melted. Remove to heated serving plates and top with freshly grated cheese and a few turns of the pepper mill on coarse grade. Serve immediately.

SERVES 4–6

Today, tortellini, those little rings of pasta usually filled with a cheese or a meat mixture, can be bought dried or frozen at many supermarkets and specialty stores. But when I was growing up, the Italian ladies in my neighborhood would get together periodically to make them. By the end of the day, their fingers would ache from pinching together hundreds of tortellini, but the smiles that would erupt on the faces of those who partook of the plump pasta helped ease their pain.

Here's a recipe that works well with store-bought tortellini.

TORTELLINI IN CREAM SAUCE

¾ pound cheese-filled tortellini, cooked al dente
4 tablespoons unsalted butter, softened
1 cup cooked peas or julienned carrots
½ cup heavy cream
½ cup freshly grated Parmesan cheese
salt, freshly grated nutmeg, and freshly ground black pepper to
    taste
1 teaspoon dried basil, or 3 teaspoons fresh

After cooking and draining the tortellini, return the pasta to the same pot. Add the butter to the pasta over low heat and mix with a wooden spoon (which is gentler on the pasta than metal) until the butter is melted. Add the peas (or carrots) and the cream; cook for 3 to 4 minutes, or until the cream has thickened slightly. Add the cheese, then season with the salt, nutmeg, and pepper; mix well. Sprinkle the basil on top and serve immediately.

SERVES 4

OFF THE EATEN PATH:
Basil Lore

In ancient Greece, if you slipped a sprig of basil into someone's hand, it warned him that an enemy was near. In Italy, if a young man wore a leaf of basil in his hair while squiring a young lady, it meant that his romantic intentions were serious. After a couple is married in India, basil is planted to ensure household happiness.

PASTA WITH AVOCADO SAUCE

I first had a version of this in the Jacuzzi capital of the world, Palm Springs. It's a great summer dish.

1 large, ripe avocado, cut in half, pit removed
2/3 cup regular cream
1 teaspoon sugar
juice of 1 lemon
1 teaspoon lime juice
1 garlic clove, chopped
salt and freshly ground black pepper to taste
6 scallions (white parts only), cut into tiny rounds
2½ tablespoons minced fresh parsley
¾ pound spiral pasta (fusilli),* cooked al dente

Scoop out the flesh from the avocado and puree in a blender with the cream, sugar, lemon and lime juice, garlic, salt, and pepper. Add the scallions and parsley to the noodles and toss with the sauce. Serve chilled.

SERVES 4–6

*Or you may substitute penne or ziti.

I'm really a fan of pesto sauce, but I always have trouble finding fresh basil in my local supermarket. And if I find it in Pittsburgh's produce yards, I usually end up paying the basil hucksters too much for what little they have. Then one magic day I learned how to simulate the flavor of a classic pesto sauce by using two ingredients found in every supermarket on earth: parsley and spinach. I also substitute sour cream for olive oil, which helps cut the pungency of the sauce, and use walnuts instead of the more traditional (and pricey) pine nuts.

With the aid of a food processor, you can whip up this unique, versatile sauce in a flash. In addition to pasta, the sauce works well atop a baked potato or on other vegetables. And you might consider using a dollop or two to enliven broiled, baked, or sautéed fish.

Here's a recipe for a unique pasta dish that you might consider for your next buffet.

OFF THE EATEN PATH:
Mortar and "Pesto"

Before blenders or food processors were invented, pesto sauce was made with a mortar, pestle, and a lot of elbow grease. The term *pesto* actually is a corruption of the word *pestle*.

PASTA WITH PRESTO PESTO

½ cup fresh parsley, cleaned, stems removed
2½ cups spinach leaves, cleaned, stems removed
½ cup grated Parmesan cheese
8 ounces sour cream
1½ teaspoons dried basil
2 garlic cloves, minced
½ teaspoon salt
4 tablespoons walnuts
dash freshly ground black pepper
1 tablespoon olive oil
½ stick unsalted butter
¾ pound ziti, bowtie, penne, or rigatoni pasta, cooked al dente
freshly grated Parmesan cheese, for dusting

Put the first 10 ingredients into a food processor or blender and process until almost smooth (1 to 2 minutes) but still left with some "chunk" from the walnuts (if too thick, stir in a tablespoon or two of warm water). In a large skillet, over medium heat, melt the butter. Add the noodles and coat with the butter. Add the sauce, about ½ cup at a time, and twirl until the noodles are coated. Top with the grated cheese and serve immediately, or at room temperature.

SERVES 4–6

LINGUINE WITH ARTICHOKES AND ONION

In Italy, they often toss pasta with ingredients you don't find with pasta in the United States, including rabbit, chicken livers, or artichoke hearts, as in this recipe from Milan.

⅓ cup olive oil
2 tablespoons minced onion
14-ounce can artichoke hearts, drained, quartered
salt and freshly ground black pepper to taste
½ cup chicken broth
3 large eggs
½ cup freshly grated Parmesan cheese
1 pound linguine, cooked al dente

In a saucepan that will be large enough to accommodate the pasta with room to toss it without spilling, heat the olive oil and sauté the onion until it becomes soft. Remove the onion with a slotted spoon and discard, reserving the oil. Add the artichoke hearts to the oil; lower the heat and season with salt and pepper. Add the broth to the saucepan and cook on low heat for 5 minutes, turning the artichokes gently.

Whisk the eggs with ¼ cup of the Parmesan cheese and stir it into the saucepan. Add the noodles to the saucepan and toss thoroughly, slowly adding the remaining cheese. Serve immediately, with freshly grated Parmesan on the side if desired.

SERVES 4–6

LINGUINE WITH ARTICHOKES AND BROCCOLI

Artichoke hearts also work nicely in this dish created by one of my former cooking-class assistants in Pittsburgh, Judy Collins (no, not the singer).

1 garlic clove, crushed
⅓ cup olive oil
1 bunch broccoli, stemmed, coarsely chopped, and cooked al dente
14-ounce can artichoke hearts, drained, halved
juice of 1 lemon
⅓ cup black olives, pitted and chopped
2 tablespoons chopped fresh parsley
salt and freshly ground black pepper
1 pound linguine, cooked al dente
1 cup freshly grated Parmesan cheese

Sauté the garlic in hot olive oil until golden, then remove as much of the garlic as you can. Add the cooked broccoli and the artichoke hearts. Sauté about 10 minutes, stirring to brown the pieces lightly. Add the lemon juice, olives, and parsley. Season to taste with salt and pepper. Toss with the hot linguine and Parmesan cheese and serve immediately.

SERVES 4–6

OFF THE EATEN PATH:
Some Sage Advice

At one time, sage was renowned as a medicinal plant and an aid to digestion. In fact, it comes from the Latin root *salvere*, to salve. Ancient Greeks and Romans recommended that old people consume sage to restore their memory, and some American Indians used it as an aid to dental hygiene, brushing their gums with sage twigs. Fresh sage can be found in many gourmet produce stores and in some supermarkets.

TRAVELIN' GOURMET TOMATO SAUCE

Don't let the number of ingredients scare you. This is a great tomato sauce and it takes less than two hours to make. It works wonders not only on your favorite pasta but also on fish and baked potatoes. It is one of the most requested recipes from *The Travelin' Gourmet* PBS series.

3 medium-sized onions (preferably white), quartered
1 medium-sized carrot, quartered
1 rib celery, quartered
3 garlic cloves, chopped
2 tablespoons olive oil
28-ounce can plum tomatoes
15-ounce can tomato sauce
1 teaspoon dried basil, or 2–3 teaspoons minced fresh
1 tablespoon minced fresh parsley
1 teaspoon dried oregano
½ teaspoon salt
2 teaspoons red pepper flakes
1 teaspoon freshly ground black pepper
1½ cups Italian red wine
1 cup freshly grated Parmesan cheese

Process the onions, carrot, celery, and garlic in a food processor until nearly minced (you can do this by hand, too). In a large sauté pan, over medium heat, add the olive oil, then the minced vegetables; sauté until the onions are limp. Transfer to a large pot. Add the plum tomatoes and break them into little chunks with a fork. Add the tomato sauce, then turn the heat to high in order to bring to a boil.

As the sauce is coming to a boil, add the basil, parsley, oregano, salt, red pepper flakes, black pepper, half the wine, and half the Parmesan cheese. Stir vigorously until the ingredients come to a boil. Let boil for about 2 minutes, then reduce the heat and cook uncovered just above a simmer for 45 minutes, stirring occasionally. Add the rest of the wine and cheese and stir well. Cover and cook over low heat for 45 minutes more, stirring occasionally.

This recipe makes enough sauce for 12 or more servings of pasta. Store what you don't use, covered, in the refrigerator. When ready to reuse, reheat, adding a little water or red wine to thin.

SERVES 12

BÉCHAMEL LASAGNE

Rather than using the more customary ricotta cheese, I layer the lasagne with a variation on the classic French sauce named after Louis de Béchameil, chef for Louis XIV.

12 lasagne noodles (about ½ pound), cooked al dente
¾ stick unsalted butter
4 tablespoons cornstarch
2 cups milk
½ cup Parmesan cheese
1 large egg, beaten
salt and freshly ground white pepper to taste
2–3 cups Travelin' Gourmet Tomato Sauce (page 81) or your
    favorite marinara sauce
1 cup thinly sliced mushrooms
¼ pound prosciutto

While cooking the lasagne noodles, melt the butter in a medium-sized sauté pan. Remove from the heat and whisk the cornstarch into the butter. Put the pan over moderate heat and whisk in the milk, one cup at a time, until it's well incorporated. Cook, whisking all the while, until the sauce starts to thicken. Remove from the heat and whisk in ¼ cup of the Parmesan cheese, then fold the beaten egg into the sauce. Season with salt and pepper.

Preheat the oven to 350°. Drain the lasagne noodles and put a layer of tomato sauce on the bottom of an 8 × 13-inch pan or one wide enough to comfortably accommodate 3 noodles across, and long enough to hold the noodles lengthwise. Put 3 noodles on top of the sauce, then coat each noodle with a thin layer of béchamel sauce (about a quarter of the sauce).

Put another layer of noodles over the béchamel sauce and cover with a thin layer of tomato sauce, then layer with the sliced mushrooms. Put 3 noodles on top of the mushroom layer, coat with the remaining béchamel sauce, and top with the prosciutto.

Put the remaining 3 noodles over the prosciutto, then cover with about a cup of tomato sauce (you can use more sauce if you like). Make sure that the curly edges of the lasagne are coated with the sauce. Dust with the remaining Parmesan cheese and bake until the sauce begins to bubble (20 to 25 minutes). Remove and let stand for about 5 minutes, then serve, with freshly grated Parmesan on the side.

SERVES 8–12

"To eat is a necessity, but to eat intelligently is an art."
—LA ROCHEFOUCAULD

PASTA IN HERB BUTTER

Many Romans keep pasta dishes as simple as possible, like this one, which you should consider if you can put your hands on fresh sage. Don't attempt it with dried sage — it's just not the same!

½ pound unsalted butter
1 tablespoon fresh whole-leaf sage, stems removed
1 pound tiny pasta shells, cooked al dente
2 cups lightly packed, freshly grated Parmesan cheese

Melt the butter in a skillet large enough to accommodate the pasta with room to toss it without spilling. Add the sage by rubbing it vigorously between the palms of your hands, letting the flakes drop into the butter. Stir and allow to cook over a low flame about 5 minutes (do not burn the butter). Add the pasta, being careful not to splash the hot butter, and toss well. Add the cheese and toss again. Serve immediately.

SERVES 4–6

Marriage is not merely sharing one's fettuccine, but sharing the burden of finding the fettuccine restaurant in the first place.

—CALVIN TRILLIN

LINGUINE WITH TUNA SAUCE

Something easy and delicious!

4 tablespoons unsalted butter
2 tablespoons flour
1 cup dry white wine
7-ounce can tuna fish in water, drained and flaked
¾ cup freshly grated Parmesan cheese
freshly ground black pepper to taste
1 pound spaghetti, cooked al dente
2 tablespoons olive oil

Melt the butter in a large saucepan over low heat. Stir in the flour and cook until it starts to brown. Slowly add the wine, stirring all the while. Simmer for 5 to 7 minutes. Remove from the heat and mix in the tuna, cheese, and pepper. Put the cooked pasta into a large bowl, toss first with the olive oil, then with the sauce. Transfer to separate heated plates and serve immediately.

SERVES 4–6

PASTA WITH SHRIMP AND TUNA

A variation on the preceding recipe, given a new dimension by the addition of the shrimp. If you can get your hands on crayfish, by all means substitute it for the shrimp.

2½ tablespoons olive oil
1 garlic clove, minced
1 medium-sized onion, peeled and chopped
⅓ pound uncooked shrimp, shelled and deveined
7-ounce can tuna fish in water, drained and flaked
1 cup heavy cream
salt and freshly ground black pepper to taste
grated rind of ½ lemon
¾ pound penne, shell, ziti, or similar pasta
¼ cup minced fresh parsley, for garnish

In a large saucepan, heat the oil and add the garlic and onion; sauté until the onion becomes limp. Stir in the shrimp and sauté until cooked; add the tuna, cream, salt, pepper, and lemon rind. Add the cooked, drained pasta to the sauce and toss. Serve immediately, garnished with parsley if desired.

SERVES 4–6

ENRAGED PASTA

This is a variation of "enraged" pasta (*arrabiata*) — a specialty of the Grand Hotel in Rome.

½ cup olive oil
4–5 garlic cloves, minced
4 red chili peppers, seeded and minced
¾ pound spaghetti, cooked al dente
salt and freshly ground black pepper
3 tablespoons chopped fresh parsley

Heat the oil in a skillet large enough to accommodate the pasta with room to toss it without spilling. Add the minced garlic and chili peppers, and sauté for about 2 minutes. Reduce the heat to practically nothing — just enough to keep the skillet warm —

OFF THE EATEN PATH:
Noodles in Ancient Rome

Although the original "Travelin' Gourmet," Marco Polo, is alleged to have introduced pasta to the Western world, ancient Romans enjoyed a noodle known as *laganum*, which is considered by many culinary historians as the forerunner of spaghetti. It was served with fish or meat sauces dusted with cheese.

while you cook the pasta. Drain the pasta well and unite it with the garlic and chili mixture in the skillet. Raise the heat to about medium and quickly toss the spaghetti with the sauce, seasoning to taste with salt and pepper. At the last minute, add the parsley and toss well. Serve immediately.

SERVES 4–6

LINGUINE WITH ANCHOVY SAUCE

If you like anchovies, you'll love this easy pasta dish, which I first enjoyed in Venice.

2 garlic cloves, minced
¼ cup olive oil
10–12 anchovy fillets, mashed to a paste
½ teaspoon red pepper flakes
1 pound linguine, cooked al dente
freshly grated Parmesan cheese

In a small skillet over medium heat sauté the garlic in the olive oil until it starts to brown. Stir in the anchovy fillets and cook for 2–3 minutes, stirring all the while. Stir in the red pepper flakes and lower the heat.

Put the pasta in a large bowl, add the sauce, and toss. Transfer to heated plates, dust with Parmesan, and serve immediately.

SERVES 6–8

LINGUINE WITH WHITE CLAM SAUCE

While linguine with clam sauce isn't nearly as popular in Rome as it is in American cities, some restaurants there do offer it. Here's the easiest recipe I know for it, using canned clams.

1 large white onion, minced
4 tablespoons unsalted butter, melted
4 tablespoons olive oil
2 garlic cloves, minced
2 4-ounce cans minced clams (1 can drained; juice from the
*   other can reserved)*
salt and freshly ground black pepper to taste
1 pound linguine, cooked al dente
⅓ cup minced fresh parsley
freshly grated Parmesan cheese (optional)

Sauté the onion in the butter and oil. Over medium heat, stir in the garlic. Add the clams and the juice from 1 can. Cook over medium heat for about 10 minutes, then season with salt and pepper. Add the sauce to the cooked pasta and toss well. Add the parsley and toss again. Top with freshly grated Parmesan if desired, and serve immediately.

SERVES 4–6

OFF THE EATEN PATH:
A Breath of Fresh Air

Parsley was originally used as a garnish not just because of its visual appeal but because it is a good antidote for bad breath.

What may be the most famous pasta dish in the whole of New York City is the Pasta Primavera offered at Le Cirque in the Mayfair-Regent Hotel. Chef Jean Vergnes, co-founder of the restaurant, got the idea for the dish while visiting a friend who served him a pasta dish that he tossed with vegetables from his garden.

The next day, Vergnes presented the idea to his chef, Jean Louis Todeschini, and his partner, Sirio Maccioni. They started experimenting with a variety of vegetables to see what combination would work the best in concert. Vergnes said that he had first suggested that grated Swiss be used instead of Parmesan, but, not surprisingly, that was vetoed by Todeschini, an Italian.

One of the elements of delicious luck that figured in the early history of pasta primavera was the fact that shortly after the dish was added to the menu at Le Cirque, *New York Times* food writer Craig Claiborne happened to be lunching there. He was so impressed that he wrote about it in *The New York Times* Magazine. Word was out. *House and Garden* was the next major publication to trumpet its praise. Then it seemed that every food writer in America who visited New York wanted to sample the dish and ended up writing about it (yours truly included).

The original recipe for the famous dish, which I've adjusted only slightly, appears on the next page. If you're in a hurry, I've included a simpler rendition of the dish (page 90).

LE CIRQUE'S PASTA PRIMAVERA

1 bunch broccoli, trimmed and broken into bite-sized
    flowerettes
1½ cups (about 2 small) unpeeled zucchini, ends trimmed,
    halved, and julienned
5 asparagus spears, each about 5 inches long, cut into thirds
1½ cups fresh green beans, trimmed and cut into 1-inch lengths
½ cup frozen peas, thawed
1 tablespoon peanut oil
2 cups thinly sliced fresh mushrooms
salt and freshly ground black pepper to taste
½ teaspoon red pepper flakes
⅓ cup finely chopped fresh parsley
6 tablespoons olive oil
3 cups ripe tomatoes, cut into 1-inch cubes
1 teaspoon finely chopped fresh garlic
1 teaspoon dried basil or ¼ cup finely chopped fresh basil
4 tablespoons unsalted butter
2 tablespoons chicken broth
½–¾ cup heavy cream
⅔ cup freshly grated Parmesan cheese
1 pound spaghetti, cooked al dente
⅓ cup toasted pine nuts

Separately cook the broccoli, zucchini, asparagus, and green beans in boiling salted water that just covers until *al dente* (about 5 minutes). Drain and chill under cold running water; drain again and transfer all to a medium bowl.

Cook the peas in lightly salted water for about 30 seconds. Drain and chill under cold running water; drain and combine with the rest of the vegetables.

In a medium skillet, heat the peanut oil over moderately high heat. Add the mushrooms, season with salt and pepper, and cook for 2 to 3 minutes. Drain and combine with the rest of the vegetables. Stir in the red pepper flakes and the parsley.

Heat 3 tablespoons of the olive oil over medium heat in a small skillet. Add the tomatoes and ½ teaspoon of the garlic; season with salt and pepper. Cook 4 to 5 minutes, stirring gently all the while (try not to break up the tomatoes any more than necessary). Stir in the basil, remove from the heat, drain, and set aside, reserving the juices.

In a large skillet, add the rest of the olive oil and the rest of the garlic. Add the vegetables and cook over medium heat, stirring all the while, until heated through.

In a pot large enough to hold the vegetables and the spaghetti, add the butter. Cook over low heat until it melts, then stir in the chicken broth, ½ cup of cream, and the cheese. Cook gently, moving on and off the heat, stirring all the while, until the mixture is smooth.

Add the spaghetti and toss. Over low heat, add half the vegetables and the liquid from the tomatoes, and toss. Add the rest of the vegetables. If the sauce is too dry, add about ¼ cup more cream (the sauce should not be soupy). Add the pine nuts and toss.

Transfer to plates and distribute equal amount of tomatoes over each plate. Serve immediately with additional freshly grated Parmesan on the side.

SERVES 8 AS AN APPETIZER; 4 AS AN ENTRÉE

OFF THE EATEN PATH:
A Long Story

The world's longest noodle was crafted in October 1988 by a baker in Thailand. It was 2900 feet long, according to Japan Air Lines. Some 120 pounds of flour, a gallon of oil, and 360 eggs went into it. A noodle-making machine had to be cranked around the clock for an entire day to produce it.

EASY PASTA PRIMAVERA

⅓ cup olive oil
½ pound broccoli, washed, trimmed, and chopped
1 pound zucchini, washed, trimmed, and chopped
½ pound fresh green beans, trimmed and chopped
6 shallots, chopped
1 garlic clove, minced
¼ cup chopped fresh Italian parsley
2 tablespoons minced fresh basil, or ¾–1 tablespoon dried
salt and freshly ground black pepper to taste
1 pound linguine, cooked al dente
⅓ cup freshly grated Parmesan cheese

In a large skillet, heat the oil and add the broccoli, zucchini, green beans, shallots, and garlic. Cover and steam for 5 to 6 minutes. Uncover, and stir the ingredients well before adding the parsley and basil. Re-cover and steam until the vegetables are cooked to your liking (they should still be slightly crisp and colorful). Season with salt and pepper. Put the pasta into a large bowl, add the vegetable mixture, and toss. Dust with Parmesan cheese and serve immediately.

SERVES 6

PASTA FRITTATA

Don't throw away that leftover pasta. Store it in the refrigerator until you're in the mood for a unique omelet that the Italians call a frittata. No matter what sauce you have on the pasta — tomato, cheese, or even pesto — it will work with this recipe.

2 green peppers, thinly sliced
2 onions, halved vertically, then thinly sliced
2 garlic cloves, minced
3 tablespoons olive oil
½ teaspoon freshly ground black pepper
leftover pasta with its sauce (a few cups at least)
¾ cup freshly grated Parmesan cheese
8 eggs, beaten

> **"The degree of civilization is often measured by the cuisine."**
> —MARY TODD LINCOLN

Preheat the oven to 350°. In a medium-sized skillet, sauté the peppers, onions, and garlic in the oil until soft (about 10 minutes), stirring occasionally. Season with the black pepper. Add the pasta with its sauce and mix together. Beat ½ cup of the cheese into the eggs and pour into the pan, mixing well with the pasta. Sprinkle the remaining cheese on the top and bake, uncovered, for about a half an hour, or until set.

SERVES 4

PASTA WITH MUSHROOMS

Mushrooms of all varieties have been mushrooming in popularity in recent years, from the traditional to the exotic. This recipe from Florence calls for the traditional variety, i.e., the ones you find in most supermarkets. However, if you can find (and afford) morels or chanterelles, use them instead.

1 medium onion, finely chopped
5 tablespoons unsalted butter
½ pound fresh mushrooms, cleaned and thinly sliced
½ cup Marsala wine
salt and freshly ground black pepper
½ cup half-and-half
1 pound spaghetti or linguine, cooked al dente
1 dozen stemmed parsley sprigs, finely chopped
freshly grated Parmesan cheese

In a heavy skillet large enough to accommodate the pasta with room to toss it without spilling, sauté the onion in the butter until limp and caramel-colored. Add the sliced mushrooms and cook until they begin to give up their natural juices. Add the wine and cook 2 to 3 minutes. Season to taste with salt and pepper. Lower the heat and slowly stir in the half-and-half; cook about 30 seconds. Add the pasta to the skillet and toss together. Transfer to heated plates; sprinkle with the parsley and grated Parmesan to taste. Serve immediately.

SERVES 4–6

PASTA PIE

No pie in the sky is this dish! It takes a bit of an effort, but the payoff is on the palate. This recipe is based on one from La Foresta, a wonderful restaurant not foo far from the papal summer residence outside of Rome.

½ pound egg noodles, broken into pieces
3 garlic cloves, minced
1 tablespoon unsalted butter
4 eggs
1 cup diced cooked ham
½ cup freshly grated Parmesan cheese
2 tablespoons minced fresh parsley
½ teaspoon dried thyme
½ teaspoon dried oregano
2½ teaspoons paprika
salt to taste
½ teaspoon cayenne pepper
1 teaspoon Tabasco sauce
⅛ teaspoon black pepper
pimientos, for garnish

Cook the noodles until they are not quite *al dente* (they will cook more in the oven). Drain, rinse well in cold water, and drain again. In a small saucepan, sauté the garlic in the butter over moderate heat until limp (do not brown) and reserve.

Preheat the oven to 350°. Beat the eggs well and add the reserved garlic and butter as well as the ham, cheese, parsley, thyme, oregano, paprika, salt, cayenne, Tabasco, and black pepper. Mix the noodles into the sauce, then pour into a buttered pie pan. Bake for 30 to 35 minutes, or until firm and nicely browned on top. Remove from the oven and cool. Cover with aluminum foil and refrigerate until well chilled. Cut into slices, garnish each slice with two pieces of pimiento, and serve cold.

SERVES 6–8

TRAVELIN' GOURMET TIP:
Making "Cents" of Pasta

To determine how much spaghetti (or linguine or fettuccine) to serve each person as an entrée, put a quarter on the table and grab a handful of the pasta. Cover the coin with the ends of the pasta; that is approximately the right amount for one serving.

LINGUINE LIGURIA

A recipe from Lou Adams, one of Pittsburgh's most noted restaurant consultants, who helped me tremendously when I was starting out as a food writer.

¾ pound linguine
4 tablespoons olive oil
1 stick unsalted butter, clarified (see page 38)
1 garlic clove, minced
¼ teaspoon dried oregano
¼ teaspoon dried basil
½ teaspoon salt
½ cup walnut halves
⅓ cup white raisins
1 cup plus 1 tablespoon grated Romano cheese
⅓ cup Italian-seasoned bread crumbs
freshly ground black pepper to taste

Put the pasta in boiling salted water and cook until *al dente*. When pasta has been cooking about 4 minutes, start the sauce by pouring the oil and butter into a saucepan that will be large enough to accommodate the pasta with room to toss it without spilling; cook over medium heat. When small bubbles appear, add the garlic, oregano, basil, salt, walnuts, and raisins. Stir until well blended and hot.

Remove from the heat. Drain the linguine. Return the sauce to low heat and add the pasta. Toss with a fork and a tablespoon until strands of the pasta are well covered with the sauce. Add ½ cup of the cheese and half of the bread crumbs and toss well. Add another ½ cup cheese and the remaining bread crumbs. Toss again, then transfer to heated plates. Top with the remaining cheese and freshly ground black pepper. Serve immediately.

SERVES 4 AS MAIN COURSE; 8 AS APPETIZER

TRAVELIN' GOURMET TIP:
Stick to This Advice

To keep pasta from sticking together before you add the sauce, add a little butter or olive oil after you drain it in a colander.

PASTA WITH FOUR CHEESES

A delicious, easy-to-prepare dish from Venice. Italians call the blend of four cheeses *quattro formaggi*.

½ cup unsalted butter
1 pound rigatoni, cooked al dente
½ cup shredded mozzarella cheese
½ cup shredded provolone cheese
½ cup Parmesan cheese
½ cup ricotta cheese, thinned with 3–4 teaspoons water
salt and freshly ground black pepper

Melt the butter in a saucepan large enough to accommodate the pasta with room to toss it without spilling. Add the rigatoni and toss in the butter over low heat until well coated. Add the mozzarella, provolone, Parmesan, and the ricotta and toss well. Season with salt and pepper and serve immediately.

SERVES 4–6

PASTA WITH CREAM, SPINACH, AND CHEESE

A tasty Tuscan dish.

¼ cup coarsely chopped cooked spinach
2 cups heavy cream
¾ cup ricotta cheese
½ pound ziti or rigatoni noodles, cooked al dente
freshly grated Parmesan cheese
freshly ground black pepper to taste

Squeeze out as much moisture from the spinach as possible, then mix it together with the cream and ricotta in a saucepan and bring to a boil. Add the noodles and continue cooking until the sauce begins to thicken. Distribute onto 4 heated plates and sprinkle liberally with grated Parmesan and a dusting of black pepper. Serve immediately.

SERVES 4

SCOTCH PASTA

No, this pasta dish isn't from Scotland. But the Scotch whiskey is.

2 shallots, finely chopped
3 tablespoons unsalted butter
4 ounces smoked salmon, chopped
1/8 teaspoon cayenne
1 cup heavy cream
1/4 cup Scotch whiskey
2 tablespoons lemon juice
1/2 pound penne (or spiral noodles, rigatoni, or shells), cooked
   al dente
salt and freshly ground black pepper to taste
2 tablespoons freshly grated Parmesan cheese
chopped fresh parsley

In a large skillet, sauté the shallots in the butter until tender (don't brown). Add the smoked salmon and cayenne and sauté for 2 to 3 minutes, stirring all the while. Whisk in the cream, Scotch, and lemon juice. Cook over medium heat 2 to 3 minutes to thicken, stirring gently all the while. Season with salt and pepper. Pour the sauce over the pasta and transfer to 2 serving plates (or 4 small plates if using as an appetizer). Sprinkle with Parmesan cheese and fresh parsley and serve immediately.

SERVES 2 AS MAIN COURSE; 4 AS APPETIZER

OFF THE EATEN PATH:
Putting Away the Pasta

Not surprisingly, Italians consume more pasta than any other nation, an average of sixty-five pounds per person annually, according to food researchers. Second in the pasta-consumption sweepstakes are the Japanese, who eat an average of thirty pounds per capita per year. That's about three times the pasta consumption of the typical American.

The following recipe actually is an adaptation of recipes from two famous restaurants. The lobster ravioli recipe is from the accomplished Windows on the World Restaurant in New York City, and the vanilla-butter sauce is from L'Archestrate, Alain Senderens's three-star establishment in Paris.

I first had the butter sauce at a dinner prepared by Senderens himself at the Parker Meridien Hotel in New York and found it whimsical and unique. I thought it might work with the wonderfully light lobster raviolis that I enjoyed at the Windows on the World. I put the two together and liked the results. I think you will, too!

LOBSTER RAVIOLI WITH VANILLA-BUTTER SAUCE

3 small cooked lobsters (about 1 1/4 pounds apiece), meat
    removed from shell
3/4 pound chanterelles or regular mushrooms
4 tablespoons unsalted butter
1 shallot, chopped
3 ounces crème fraîche*
salt and freshly ground white pepper
1 1/2 teaspoons chopped fresh chives
4 dozen thin won ton wrappers (available in most
    supermarkets)
2 egg yolks, lightly beaten
1/4 stick unsalted butter
Vanilla-Butter Sauce (page 97)

Dice the lobster meat into 1/2-inch cubes. Clean the chanterelles (or regular mushrooms) and sauté in the butter in a large sauce pan. Add the shallot. Mix in the crème fraîche and quickly bring to a boil. Season to taste with salt and pepper. Add the chives and lobster meat; gently blend. Simmer for about 5 minutes. Remove from heat and cool to room temperature.

TO ASSEMBLE THE RAVIOLI: Lay the won ton wrappers on a flat surface lightly dusted with flour. Brush the perimeter of each

*To make crème fraîche, mix together 1 cup heavy cream with 1/2 tablespoon buttermilk. Put into a jar, seal, shake, and store at room temperature for 24 hours, then in the refrigerator.

OFF THE EATEN PATH:

Ravioli is Italian for "little turnips."

(about ⅓ inch all the way around) with the egg yolk. Place about ½ tablespoon or so of the lobster mixture into the center, fold over the top, and seal tightly all the way around. (If you want to make them larger, use 2 won ton wrappers—one on top and one on the bottom with about a tablespoon or so of the filling. Seal with the egg yolk.) Let the raviolis "relax" on a lightly floured surface.

THE FINAL TOUCH: Put the ravioli into a large pot filled with lightly salted boiling water. They will cook pretty quickly, so be careful. When they come to the top, they are ready. Remove immediately and drain in a colander and stir in the ¼ stick butter. Gently warm the Vanilla-Butter Sauce, pour over the raviolis, and serve immediately.

Vanilla-Butter Sauce

2 teaspoons unsalted butter
5 shallots, diced
3 tablespoons white wine vinegar
1 cup dry white wine
1 stick unsalted butter, softened and cut into cubes
salt and white pepper
1 vanilla bean, split in half lengthwise

Melt the 2 teaspoons butter in a small saucepan. Add the shallots and simmer until soft. Add the vinegar and white wine; cook, uncovered, at a low boil until the mixture reduces to about 2 tablespoons (10 to 12 minutes).

Lower the heat to moderate and add a few cubes of butter; remove the pan from the heat and whisk vigorously until the butter is blended in. Continue to add the butter this way—i.e., putting the pan back on the heat, then lifting it off. (This is done in an effort to maintain the heat as evenly as possible. The sauce should be hot, but make sure it doesn't burn.) Season to taste with salt and pepper, then remove from the heat.

Use the tip of a small knife to scrape the pulp from the vanilla bean, then whisk it into the sauce. Strain the sauce into a clean saucepan, using pressure with a wooden spoon to make sure that as much of the vanilla and shallots goes through as possible.

MAKES ⅓ CUP

ZITI AU GRATIN

This is a terrific way to treat pasta, but be sure you have a gratin pan or ovenproof skillet.

½ pound ziti or penne, cooked al dente
2½ tablespoons unsalted butter
¾ cup loosely packed grated Parmesan cheese
¾ cup loosely packed grated Swiss cheese
⅛ teaspoon nutmeg
salt and freshly ground black pepper to taste
¾ cup heavy cream, heated
⅓ cup Italian bread crumbs

Preheat the broiler.

In a pan large enough to accommodate the pasta with room to toss it without spilling, add the drained, hot noodles; toss with the butter, half the Parmesan, and half the Swiss cheese. Add the nutmeg and season with salt and pepper.

Transfer to a buttered gratin pan, add the cream, and mix with the noodles. Dust with the remaining cheese and bread crumbs; brown under the broiler until the top bubbles and has a light brown crust. Let rest for 4–5 minutes before serving.

SERVES 4–6

RIGATONI CORNELIA

A rigatoni recipe from Taberna Dei Gracchi in the heart of Rome.

½ cup sliced fresh mushrooms
2 tablespoons olive oil
¼ cup chopped Italian salami
¼ cup chopped prosciutto
3 tablespoons unsalted butter
½ cup cooked peas (fresh or frozen)
2 tablespoons tomato paste
¾ pound rigatoni, cooked al dente
2 cups light cream
½ cup freshly grated Parmesan cheese
freshly ground black pepper to taste

In a small pan, sauté the mushrooms in the olive oil until tender. In another saucepan that will be large enough to accommodate the pasta with room to toss it without spilling, sauté the salami and prosciutto in the butter for 4 to 5 minutes. Add the reserved mushrooms, peas, and tomato paste. Cook on low heat for 5 to 6 minutes.

Raise the heat to moderate and add the cooked rigatoni, cream, and ¼ cup of the Parmesan cheese and toss well. Transfer to heated plates, dust with the rest of the Parmesan cheese, season with pepper, and serve immediately.

SERVES 4–6

ZITI WITH SALMON

This is an easy but delicious dish based on one I enjoyed at the chic Half Moon Club in Jamaica. There, however, they used smoked marlin. Since that's not easy to secure, I tried substitutes and discovered that smoked salmon works just as well. Use lightly salted salmon, if possible.

3 tablespoons unsalted butter
¼ pound smoked salmon
1 tablespoon finely chopped shallots
1 tablespoon lemon juice
1 cup heavy cream
2 ounces vodka
salt and white pepper to taste
¾ pound ziti noodles, cooked not quite al dente
freshly ground black pepper to taste

In a saucepan large enough to accommodate the pasta with room to toss without spilling, melt the butter and add the salmon and the shallots; cook 2 to 3 minutes. Add the lemon juice and mix thoroughly. Slowly stir in the cream and the vodka. Raise the heat to high and let the alcohol cook off (1 to 2 minutes).

Lower the heat and add the salt and white pepper. Add the very firmly cooked pasta to the saucepan, where it will cook to the *al dente* stage as you twirl it with the salmon mixture. Make sure that the noodles are well coated. You can add a bit of cream if the sauce gets too dry. Remove to warmed plates and dust with freshly ground black pepper. Serve immediately.

SERVES 6

SHRIMP AND SWEET CORN RAVIOLI

This is one of my all-time favorite ravioli recipes. It's adapted from one from the accomplished kitchen of the Park Hyatt in Washington, D.C.

RAVIOLI:

2 ears fresh corn, scraped of kernels
½ pound large raw shrimp, shelled and deveined
1 cup heavy cream
salt and white pepper
2 teaspoons fresh chopped chives
30 won ton wrappers
1 large egg, lightly whipped with 1 teaspoon water (egg wash)

SAUCE:

2 shallots, minced
½ bay leaf, crumbled
¼ teaspoon dried thyme
½ teaspoon white peppercorns
1 cup dry white wine
juice of 1 lemon
1 pound unsalted butter, softened and cut into chunks
salt and white pepper

GARNISH:

8 large shrimp, shelled and deveined
2 ears fresh corn, scraped of kernels
¼ cup freshly cracked black pepper

TO ASSEMBLE THE RAVIOLI: Put the corn, shrimp, and heavy cream into a food processor and puree. Season to taste with salt and white pepper, then mix in the chives. To make each ravioli, take about 1 teaspoon of the shrimp mixture and place it in the center of each won ton wrapper. Brush the edges with the egg wash, fold over the top, and seal very tightly all around. Place on a lightly floured surface and cover with a towel until ready to use.

TO MAKE THE SAUCE: Bring the shallots, bay leaf, thyme, peppercorns, wine, and lemon juice to boil in a medium-sized saucepan. Simmer until the mixture reduces to about ⅓ cup (6 to

OFF THE EATEN PATH:
More Than Just a Food

Once olive oil was appreciated only in the Mediterranean; in recent years its popularity has spread worldwide. But olive oil is not just for cooking. In many cultures it turns up in folk remedies. In fact there's an ancient proverb that promises, "Olive oil makes all your aches and pains go away."

Greek athletes actually rubbed their bodies with it to maintain the suppleness of their muscles and skin. For centuries, women have used it for curing disorders ranging from insomnia to boils.

One of the reasons for its renewed popularity in the United States is the fact that recent research indicates that olive oil helps to lower cholesterol. And, get this, olive oil also has been shown to prevent the wear and tear of age on the brain and the body.

10 minutes). Whisk in the butter, a chunk or two at a time, until it is all well incorporated. Season with salt and white pepper; strain. Keep warm.

THE FINAL TOUCH: Cook the raviolis in salted boiling water for 4 minutes. Meanwhile, prepare the garnish by simmering the shrimp and corn in salted water for about 3 minutes. Drain the raviolis well and place on heated plates. Spoon the sauce over the raviolis, garnish with the shrimp and corn, then dust with the black pepper and serve immediately.

SERVES 6–8

A LA CARTE:
The "King of Cheeses"

Although most Americans are familiar with it only as an integral part of a diluted dressing that bears little resemblance to the real thing, in France, Roquefort is the king of cheeses. This blue-veined product of sheep's milk — one of the oldest protected product names in the world — has tantalized the noses and palates of gourmets since the first century. It has also turned the tiny village of Roquefort sur Soulzon in southwest France, about four hundred miles from Paris, into one of the world's lesser known though charismatic tourist attractions.

Wedged against the rocky cliffs of the more than 2000-foot Combalou Plateau, Roquefort is connected to the outside world by only one road, making it one of France's most isolated villages. The fact that it's literally a treasure-trove of Roquefort cheese is apparent as soon as you set foot in town. The pungent aroma of the cheese that bears its name seems to waft up from the very earth. That's because below the streets of Roquefort, 6 million wheels of the fabled cheese are left to age each year in a warren of caves that are the product of a most fortunate seismic collision of clay and rock nearly 100,000 years ago.

The manufacture of Roquefort cheese became a veritable monopoly by official French edict in the year 1070 when the *Société Anonyme des Caves et Producteurs*

Réunis de Roquefort was formed. Although you might be able to find bastardized versions in the dairy case at some supermarkets, pedigreed "Roquefort" must be "ripened in the caves of the village of Roquefort according to local, honest and constant practice."

These practices have changed very little through the years, save for the use of electric sheep-milking machines and some man-made refrigeration. The size of the herds has also increased dramatically, from a few hundred five centuries ago to about 5000 today.

The first-time visitor to Roquefort may think for all the world that he happened onto a ghost town, for much of the activity is underground, in the cornucopia of caves that miraculously are the perfect environment for the proper ripening of the fabled cheese.

Amazingly, the other important ingredient for ripening is whole-wheat bread. Giant loaves are left near the mouths of the caves; Mother Nature does the rest. The result is a microscopic mushroom called *penicillium* (not related to penicillin) *roqueforti*, which erupts on the bread that is then ground into a powder and mixed into ewe's milk. It is left to curdle and superlative Roquefort is the result.

After about three months, the cheese is ripe, and if it passes a rigorous inspection, it's turned over to an army of women all clad in white, like an order of nuns.

They wrap each wheel in thick foil and apply the government's seal of approval — red silhouettes of sheep.

Incidentally, during World War II after the Germans occupied France, they converged on Roquefort not for the cheese, but for the tinfoil supplies they heard were plentiful there. Their intelligence was right. The Société did indeed have a five-year supply on hand, but it had been smart enough to spirit it away in one of the most remote and dank of the caves in town. The Germans never succeeded in unearthing it — a graphic case of "foiling" the Germans.

The biggest importer of Roquefort is the United States, which buys one in every thirty wheels, much of it ending up, alas, as salad dressing. In the Grand Hotel in Roquefort, however, it is fashioned into soufflés, dumplings, and crêpes, as well as being offered on a cheese tray along with a tiny cup of honey, an unexpectedly pleasing combination.

ENTRÉES

One of the few unsavory things about being a food critic is that your casual eating habits are scrutinized by your colleagues. If I get a craving, say, for a Big Mac, woe is me if I decide to eat it at my desk at the *Pittsburgh Post-Gazette*. Anyone spotting me munching on the Pittsburgh-invented sandwich invariably will make some kind of snide quip about "how the food critic eats when he's not on the expense account."

One time, however, I had the last laugh. The night before I was about to jet off to Paris, I visited a French chef based in Pittsburgh to get the names of some chefs he knew in Paris whom I planned to look up. As is the case with most chefs when a food critic enters their kitchen, he expected me to eat something. I wasn't hungry, I told him. He wasn't listening.

After hassling for about ten minutes, I agreed that I'd take something to go, just to make him happy. He ended up preparing a platter of poached chicken breasts graced with a homemade mayonnaise, a recipe based on one from the fabled Tour d'Argent in Paris (recipes for both follow). He garnished it attractively with sculpted vegetables and other goodies. When he was finished, I was presented with the prettiest takeout order I'd ever seen. The chef packed my *haute* snack in a box we found in the kitchen, which looked exactly like one for a small pizza. I chuckled silently at the incongruity of it all.

As luck would have it, as I was heading for my car, two sports writers from my paper spotted me toting what they thought was pizza. They made a big scene about how "Mr. Big Shot Food Critic" really has the palate of a copyboy. I stood there patiently as they had their little laugh. Then I slowly opened the box and when they saw what it contained, their smiles turned to stone.

They never teased me again.

"Before food was invented, cookbooks were unknown."

—FRED ALLEN

POACHED CHICKEN BREASTS WITH BLENDER MAYONNAISE

1½ pounds boned chicken breasts
salt and white pepper to taste
1 tablespoon fresh lemon juice
3 tablespoons unsalted butter
2 garlic cloves, minced
¾ cup dry white wine
Blender Mayonnaise (page 107)

Remove the skin from the breasts and pat dry. Rub both sides with a little salt and pepper, then sprinkle each side with the lemon juice. Melt the butter in a sauté pan, add the garlic, and cook for a few minutes (don't let the garlic brown). Add the chicken and sauté over medium heat for a few minutes on each side, occasionally pressing down gently.

Add about half of the wine and continue to sauté for 2 to 3 minutes on each side. Lower the heat a bit, then add the rest of the wine; cook for another minute or so, turning once. Lower the heat to a simmer and cook, covered, for about 5 minutes on each side, or until the chicken is cooked through. Remove the chicken from the pan and blot dry with paper towels (don't be too firm, or the paper will stick to the chicken).

Transfer the chicken to a casserole dish, daub on some of the blender mayonnaise, and store in the refrigerator until cold. Before serving, bring to room temperature and offer with the remaining mayonnaise on the side.

SERVES 4

Blender Mayonnaise

In addition to beautifully complementing the poached chicken breasts, this mayonnaise goes well with fish, slathered on a hamburger, or as a salad dressing.

¾ teaspoon Dijon mustard
1 large egg
1 tablespoon fresh lemon juice
salt and white pepper to taste
1 cup olive oil
1 tablespoon ketchup
1 teaspoon Tabasco
1 tablespoon cognac or brandy

Put the mustard, egg, and lemon juice into the container of a blender; season with salt and pepper and blend for 5 seconds. With the machine still running, slowly start adding the oil. Blend until smooth and satiny. Add the ketchup, Tabasco, and cognac or brandy. Blend another 10 to 15 seconds.

MAKES ABOUT 1 CUP

CHICKEN WITH JAVANESE SPICES

Poultry with personality! A recipe from the Peacock Café in the Hilton International in Jakarta. The lemon grass, Chinese chili sauce, and coconut milk can all be found at Asian groceries or gourmet shops.

6 medium chicken leg and thigh pieces (about 3 pounds total)
3 tablespoons vegetable oil
2 stalks lemon grass
4 shallots
4 garlic cloves
2-inch chunk fresh ginger
3 tablespoons ground coriander
2 teaspoons ground turmeric
4 bay leaves
¾ teaspoon salt
1½ cups unsweetened coconut milk
¼ cup Chinese chili sauce
3 tablespoons brown sugar
⅓ cup toasted macadamia nuts, chopped fine

Cut the chicken legs at the joint. In a skillet over moderate heat, brown the legs and thighs on both sides in the oil. Transfer to a dish and reserve all but about 2 tablespoons of the fat.

Prepare the lemon grass by trimming off the upper leaves; unwrap the dry green layers to get to the core. Cut in half lengthwise and trim into 2-inch slices. Transfer to a food processor; with the motor running add the shallots, garlic, and ginger to the lemon grass and process until very fine.

Over moderate heat, warm the reserved fat and add the lemongrass mixture. Cook for 2 minutes, stirring constantly. Add the coriander, turmeric, bay leaves, and salt; cook for 1 minute, stirring all the while. Stir in the coconut milk, making sure it is well blended into the mixture. Add the Chinese chili sauce, brown sugar, and macadamia nuts; cook 1 more minute, stirring all the while. Add the chicken, press into the thickened sauce; cook over low heat for 25 minutes, stirring often and moving the chicken to prevent it from sticking to the pan and to make sure it cooks evenly.

“Between the ages of twenty and fifty, a person spends some 20,000 hours chewing and swallowing food, more than 800 days and nights of steady eating.”

—M. F. K. FISHER

Preheat the broiler. Put the chicken, skin-side up, into a broiler pan. Remove the bay leaves and spoon off the fat from the sauce. Simmer the sauce, stirring, until it becomes pasty (about 5 minutes). Spoon off any more fat and liberally coat the chicken with the sauce. Broil the chicken until crisp (about 10 to 15 minutes).

SERVES 4

BREAST OF CHICKEN TANGERINE

A low-calorie recipe from Larry Brudy, one of the founders of the International Culinary Academy in Pittsburgh.

3 tablespoons vegetable oil
4 boneless chicken breasts (about 8 ounces each), skin removed
1 cup minced white onion
½ cup dry sherry
6 tablespoons orange juice concentrate
4 tablespoons brown sugar
1 teaspoon ground ginger
1½ cups chicken broth
1 tablespoon sweet paprika (preferably Hungarian)
freshly ground black pepper
4 small tangerines, peeled and sectioned

Heat the oil in a skillet large enough to comfortably hold the breasts; sauté the chicken until browned on both sides. Add the onions and cook over medium heat until they are translucent. Raise the heat to high and add the sherry; cook for 1 minute (to burn off some of the alcohol). Lower the heat to medium and add the orange juice concentrate, brown sugar, ginger, broth, and paprika. Cook until reduced by about half. Season to taste with pepper. Add the tangerines and cook until heated through (about 1 to 2 minutes). Serve immediately.

SERVES 4

TRAVELIN' GOURMET TIP:
Make Brown Sugar a Soft Touch

You can soften brown sugar that has hardened like a rock in the box by putting it into a microwave-safe bowl with an apple slice, covering it with microwave-safe cling-wrap, and nuking it on high for 20 seconds.

CHICKEN BREASTS WITH RED PEPPER SAUCE

A relatively easy but wonderful dish from La Grignotière Restaurant in the Hilton in Geneva, Switzerland, a food operation spearheaded by the charismatic Jean-Claude Bergeret. Not surprisingly, this vibrant dish is one of the best-sellers at the restaurant. The chef recommends that for a velvety sauce, you grill and peel the red bell peppers before simmering.

2 chicken breasts (with wings), cut in half
salt and white pepper to taste
3 tablespoons unsalted butter
1½ cups chicken broth
2 large red bell peppers, halved, seeded, and coarsely diced
2–3 tablespoons raspberry vinegar
2–3 teaspoons sugar
1 large green bell pepper, halved and seeded
¼ cup dry white wine

Preheat the oven to 350°. Trim the wing tip and attached joint from each piece of chicken and discard (or reserve for stock-making). Sprinkle the breasts with salt and pepper. In a wide ovenproof skillet, heat the butter until it foams, then add the chicken, skin-side down. Brown on one side over moderate heat (about 5 minutes). Turn over and cook for 1 minute, just to color slightly. Cover and roast in the oven until the meat is cooked through (about 15 minutes).

In a medium saucepan, combine the broth and red peppers and simmer until tender (10 to 12 minutes). Transfer to a blender or food processor and puree. Add the vinegar and sugar to taste; process to make a fine puree. Season with salt and pepper. Return to the saucepan over high heat and boil for 1 to 2 minutes. Remove from the heat.

Drop the green bell pepper into boiling, salted water; return to a boil. Remove and place in ice water for about 10 seconds; pat dry with paper towels, then cut into fine strips. Reserve as garnish.

Transfer the chicken to a platter (remove breast bones, if desired) and cover with aluminum foil. Bring the liquid left in the roasting pan to a boil, scraping up the particles on the bottom. Skim off any fat, add the wine, and cook until it boils again; lower the heat and simmer for 2 minutes. Add to the pepper puree, and heat the mixture until it starts to simmer.

Layer individual plates or a platter with the sauce and put the chicken on top, garnished with the green pepper. Serve immediately.

SERVES 4

CHICKEN CURRY IN A HURRY

The easiest curry recipe I know.

2 tablespoons unsalted butter
1 medium onion, sliced
2 garlic cloves, minced
2½ tablespoons curry powder
½ teaspoon cumin seeds
4 tablespoons flour
1½ cups beef broth
¾ cup water
1 whole chicken (2½–3 pounds), cooked, skinned, and cut into chunks
¾ cup chopped peanuts

In a large, heavy skillet, melt the butter and sauté the onion, garlic, curry powder, and cumin seeds until the onion turns golden in color. Put the flour and beef broth into a blender and add the onion mixture; blend until the mixture is pureed. Return the mixture to the skillet and add the water; simmer on low heat, uncovered, for 30 to 40 minutes, stirring occasionally. Raise the heat to high and stir in the cooked chicken; cook until the chicken is hot. Sprinkle the chopped peanuts on top and serve immediately.

SERVES 4–6

We never repent on having eaten too little.

—THOMAS JEFFERSON

When it comes to Indian cuisine, there's no city in Europe with a better selection than London. In fact, some people think London even outdoes India. There are more than 3000 restaurants in London specializing in the unique, aromatic cuisine of India. The heart of any good Indian restaurant is the tandoor, a clay oven that heats up to 700°, sealing in the juices of the specially marinated meats that are plunged inside.

It's hard to duplicate the results of a tandoor, but the recipe that follows will give you some indication. While it's fairly easy to make, you should start marinating the chicken a day in advance in order to get the proper flavor. Some of the spices used in London's Indian restaurants are a bit esoteric, but this recipe calls for ingredients available in most supermarkets and specialty stores in the United States.

CHICKEN TANDOOR

2½–3 pounds of chicken thighs and drumsticks
½ cup fresh lime juice
1 cup plain yogurt
¾ teaspoon ground fennel seed
1 tablespoon grated fresh ginger
1 tablespoon coriander powder
1½ teaspoons cayenne pepper
1 teaspoon red chili powder
¼ teaspoon salt
2 tablespoons paprika
½ teaspoon dry mustard
¼ teaspoon ground cumin seed
2 garlic cloves, minced
6 bay leaves, crumbled
1 teaspoon red food dye (optional)
¼ cup melted unsalted butter
¾ cup thinly sliced onion rings
3 tablespoons fresh lemon juice

Remove the skin from the chicken and thoroughly pat dry with paper towels. Cut a 2-inch slit on the smooth, meaty part of each thigh and drumstick about ½ inch deep. Distribute half of the lime juice into the slits and transfer thighs and drumsticks to a baking pan large enough to hold them comfortably; refrigerate for at least 2 hours.

In a medium-sized bowl, make the marinade by mixing together the remaining lime juice and the yogurt, fennel seed, ginger, coriander, cayenne, chili powder, salt, paprika, dry mustard, cumin seed, garlic, and bay leaves. Add the food dye if desired and mix well.

Remove the chicken from the baking pan and put a thin layer of marinade on the bottom of the pan. Layer the chicken on top of the marinade in the pan and pour the remaining marinade over it, turning a few times to coat the pieces well. Cover and refrigerate overnight, turning at least once.

Preheat the oven to 450°. Remove the chicken from the refrigerator and turn a few times in the marinade, ending with the meaty parts top-side up; discard excess marinade, and roast for 15 minutes. Lower the heat to 400°; baste the chicken with half of the melted butter and roast for another 15 minutes.

Lower the heat in the oven to 375°; baste the chicken with the remaining butter, and cook for 12 to 15 minutes more, or until the chicken is cooked thoroughly. Preheat the broiler. Meanwhile, soak the onion rings in the lemon juice. Put the chicken under the broiler until the top is nicely charred. Serve with the lemon-soaked onions rings sprinkled on the top.

SERVES 4–6

TRAVELIN' GOURMET TIP:
Save that Ginger!

Put pared fresh ginger in a glass jar and cover it with sherry. It will keep indefinitely with no alteration in flavor.

The best champagne bar in the world is in Paris. Le Montana is on the Left Bank, just a cork's pop away from the famed Café de Flore, where expatriates used to congregate. In addition to offering exquisite champagne by the glass, Le Montana is the first place I've ever found where you can nosh on either chili or *pâté de foie gras* between sips and listen to live jazz.

Besides offering everything from Pommery Brut Royal to Bollinger Spéciale Cuvée by the glass, it boasts an obscene selection of champagne cocktails, including one that Papa Hemingway was fond of. Called a Champernod, it's half champagne, half Pernod. After one of those, more than one person has been known to dance atop the glass-topped tables, several of which have been cracked by flying feet in the "whee" hours of the morning. They pay silent testimony to some of the more raucous times at Le Montana.

Owner Frederic Boissier is as effervescent an entrepreneur as you'll ever find. Although he looks like the kind of guy who walks around with a joy-buzzer in his hand, he's quite serious when it comes to his champagnes, which he drinks with as much *joie de vivre* as his best customers. He's particularly proud of the *Club des Sabreuers*, an august organization that meets at his place on special occasions and goes about opening huge bottles of champagne with sabers. They erupt like a volcano, spraying champagne on the ceiling, on the walls, and on most of the patrons, much to their unbridled glee. Here is an adaptation of a recipe from Le Montana.

CHICKEN IN CHAMPAGNE

1 frying chicken (2½–3 pounds), quartered
3 tablespoons olive oil
¾ cup champagne
1 teaspoon dried tarragon, or 2 teaspoons fresh
1 cup heavy cream
1 egg yolk, lightly beaten

In a large skillet, sauté the chicken in the oil until tender (this will take 25 to 30 minutes). Transfer the chicken to 4 serving platters and keep in a low oven. Add the champagne to the skillet and mix it well with the drippings. Mix in the tarragon, add ⅔ cup of the cream, and simmer until the sauce is reduced by a third.

Whisk the lightly beaten egg yolk with the remaining cream. Add 2 to 3 tablespoons of the champagne sauce to the egg-cream mixture, then quickly add it to the skillet. Raise the heat to moderate and cook until it thickens slightly, stirring constantly. Crown the chicken with the sauce and serve immediately.

SERVES 4

CHICKEN PAPRIKA

A recipe based on one from the kitchen at Dallmayr, Munich's fabled gourmet store (see A La Carte, page 68).

2 frying chickens (2–2½ pounds each), cut into serving pieces
salt and freshly ground black pepper to taste
¼ pound unsalted butter
2 small onions, diced
2½ teaspoons sweet paprika
½ tablespoon all-purpose flour
1 tablespoon heavy cream
2 cups chicken broth
1 cup sour cream

Season the chicken with salt and pepper. Refrigerate, covered, for 1 hour. In a Dutch oven, melt the butter; add the onions and cook over medium heat until they become limp. Stir in the paprika, lower the heat, and add the chicken; cook over low heat, covered, until the chicken is tender (25 to 30 minutes).

Sprinkle with flour and add the heavy cream and broth. Raise the heat to high, cover, and bring to a boil; continue boiling for about 15 minutes. Remove from the heat and keep the chicken warm by putting it into a low oven and covering with aluminum foil. Add the sour cream to the Dutch oven and stir well; bring to a boil, stirring often. Pour the sauce over the chicken and serve immediately.

SERVES 4–6

POLLO CAMPAGNOLE

This is a great Italian "peasant" dish, perfect for big eaters. You can speed up the cooking time by buying ready-made tomato sauce and brown gravy in your local supermarket or specialty store.

3½ tablespoons olive oil
1 red bell pepper, cored, seeded, and julienned
1 green bell pepper, cored, seeded, and julienned
1 medium onion, chopped
1 pound medium-hot Italian sausage links
2–2½ pounds chicken, cut up
2 garlic cloves, minced
1 teaspoon dried rosemary, or 3 teaspoons fresh
15-ounce jar or can tomato sauce, or just under 2 cups
    homemade
12-ounce jar or can brown gravy
½ pound peeled new potatoes, halved (optional)
¾ cup burgundy
¼ cup heavy cream
salt and freshly ground pepper to taste

In a large sauté pan, heat 1½ tablespoons of the olive oil and sauté the peppers and onion until the onions are limp. Remove the vegetables and set aside, but let the juices remain in the pan. Add the sausage to the pan and, over high heat, brown all sides; lower the heat and continue cooking until the sausage is about half done (it will finish cooking in the oven). Remove and set aside.

In a Dutch oven, put the remaining 2 tablespoons olive oil and sauté the chicken pieces until they are browned on all sides; drain off the fat. Add the garlic and rosemary and stir in the cooked peppers and onions, tomato sauce, brown gravy, potatoes (if desired), wine, and cream. Season with salt and pepper. Add the sausage and cover it as much as possible with the sauce. Cook, covered, over medium heat for 45 minutes.

SERVES 4

"Bad cooks, and the utter lack of reason in the kitchen, have delayed human development longest and impaired it most."
—NIETZSCHE

CHICKEN PASTIES

Using frozen puff pastry takes the pain out of making this dish, which is popular in London pubs.

3 tablespoons unsalted butter
6 strips cooked bacon, cut into small pieces
1 medium onion, chopped
¼ cup all-purpose flour
⅔ cup whole milk
1 cup cooked chicken (or turkey), diced
1-pound box frozen puff pastry, thawed
3 tablespoons water for sealing
1 egg, beaten with 1 teaspoon water

Melt the butter in a medium saucepan. Add the bacon pieces and onion and cook until the onion is soft and translucent. Remove from the heat, stir in the flour, and slowly blend in the milk. Return to the heat and bring to a boil, stirring all the while. Stir in the chicken and cook until it's heated through; remove from the heat and cool.

Roll out both sheets of the pastry into 2 rounds about ⅛ inch in thickness. Using a 3- to 4-inch pastry cutter, cut out about 20 circles (if you have any filling left, gather up the scraps, re-roll the pastry, and cut out a few more rounds). Divide the total number of circles in half (half of the circles will be used as the bottom layer, and the other half as the top). Transfer half the circles to a lightly floured surface; put about a tablespoon of the stuffing on top of each, leaving room around the edge to seal with the water.

Preheat the oven to 425°. After all of the bottom layers have been topped with the stuffing, moisten the outer edge of each circle with the water and cover with the top layers. Pull up and seal as tightly as possible. Brush the top of each with the egg wash. Cut a few small slits in the top of each with the tip of a paring knife (to let the steam escape). Place on a well-greased baking tray (or one lined with parchment paper). Bake for about 25 minutes, or until the pasties have puffed nicely and are golden brown in color. Serve warm.

SERVES 6–8

I love L.A. It's everything I've always thought it would be — and more. It's the only city in America where you can judge how good a restaurant is by the quality of the cars parked outside. I remember one night waiting for a valet to fetch my car from the lot at Spago, that fabled restaurant of the rich and famous (or those who appear to be). A hotshot-looking gent with young ladies in tow flipped the keys to one of the parking valets and chirped: "It's a convertible Rolls, kid." Without batting an eye, the valet countered, matter-of-factly, "What *color*?"

Only in Los Angeles.

I've been lucky on my many visits to have been put up in baronial splendor in such wonderful hotels as L'Ermitage, the Beverly-Wilshire, the Westwood Marquis, the Four Seasons, and the fabled Beverly Hills Hotel. Most recently I stayed at the Biltmore, among the grandest of them all. One of the hotel's most impressive sights is its hand-painted ceiling frescoes, the likes of which I haven't seen since meandering through the famed castles of Europe. They were the work of Giovanni Smeraldi, of Vatican and White House fame, who was imported specially for the task.

The hotel's first-rate restaurant, Bernard's, is headed by Chef Roger Pigozzi, a former Pittsburgher. This is one of the chef's simpler offerings.

BILTMORE FAJITAS WITH GUACAMOLE

The tortillas can be found in most supermarkets.

½ pound flank steak
4 tablespoons green chili picante sauce
2 tablespoons beer
salt and freshly ground black pepper to taste
4 corn or flour tortillas

GARNISH:
shredded Monterey Jack cheese
sour cream
shredded iceberg lettuce
chopped tomatoes
Guacamole (recipe below)

Marinate the steak overnight in a mixture of the picante sauce and the beer. Broil the steak to the degree of doneness you prefer; season with salt and pepper, then cut it into strips. Divide the meat among the corn or flour tortillas. Garnish each tortilla with the shredded cheese, sour cream, lettuce, tomatoes, and guacamole.

MAKES 4 SERVINGS

Guacamole

Although a lot of people use a blender or food processor to make guacamole, I've found doing it by hand is not only easy but also enables you to control the chunkiness of the dip (blender-made guacamole too often is runny). Also, cleaning a bowl is easier than cleaning the blades and container of a blender or food processor.

1 large, ripe avocado
1 small white onion, diced
1 ripe tomato, diced
2 teaspoons fresh lemon juice
2 tablespoons mayonnaise
salt and freshly ground black pepper to taste
1 chili pepper, seeded and diced (optional)

Remove the meat from the avocado; in a small bowl, mix it together with the onion, tomato, lemon juice, mayonnaise, salt, and pepper. If you'd like to spike it up a bit, mix in the chili pepper.

MAKES ABOUT 1 CUP

If you have a rotisserie, you must try the next dish. I use an old Farberware electric rotisserie, which cooks the chicken slowly (taking up to 90 minutes), but it also works fine on an outdoor rotisserie if you happen to have one on a grill. The recipe was inspired by my visit to Giggi Fazi, one of my favorite restaurants in Rome. In fact, if I were facing the gallows and had the opportunity to dine out for my last meal, I might well select Giggi's. It has one of the finest antipasto bars in the world, the pastas are sublime, and in the rear of the restaurant they lovingly roast meats on a wood-fired spit. It makes your mouth water just looking at it. Also, Giggi's is the only restaurant I've ever visited where the specials of the day are embroidered in the tablecloths.

SKEWERED HENS

1 cup olive oil (extra-virgin, if possible)
2 garlic cloves, crushed
4 Cornish game hens (legs, thighs only; reserve body for other use)
8 slices French bread, about ½ inch thick
1 cup melted unsalted butter

Put the oil into a large bowl with the garlic. Add the meat and mix well with the marinade. Refrigerate, covered, overnight, turning a few times.

Remove the meat and reserve the marinade. Thread the meat onto the rotisserie skewer, alternating with slices of French bread liberally brushed with the reserved marinade.* As the meat slowly turns on the rotisserie, periodically alternate brushing it with the melted butter and the marinade until it's cooked through (75 to 90 minutes). Serve with the bread.

SERVES 2

*You can also put potatoes and vegetables in between the bread and hens.

PUB STEW

The beauty of this stew recipe from Ireland is that you don't have to simmer it on the stove and keep checking it. All you do is put everything into a pot and pop it into the oven. You don't even have to stir it as it's cooking, but it wouldn't hurt.

1½ pounds top-quality beef, cut into chunks
¼ cup margarine
10–11-ounce can tomato soup, plus an equal amount of water
3 carrots, peeled and cut into chunks
4 medium potatoes, peeled and cut into chunks
1 rib celery, cut into chunks
4 onions, cut into chunks
2 teaspoons salt
½ teaspoon freshly ground black pepper
¼ cup minced fresh parsley
½ cup cooking sherry
2 bay leaves

Preheat oven to 275°. In a heavy skillet, brown the beef in the margarine over medium-high heat. Add the soup and water and stir well. Add the rest of the ingredients and cook for about 5 minutes, stirring once or twice. Transfer the mixture to an oven-proof pot and cook in the oven, covered, for 5 hours, stirring occasionally if desired.

SERVES 4–6

OFF THE EATEN PATH:
Spit Runners

When the spit was invented about 500 years ago, the problem was cranking it. In England they trained terriers to do the job. A rope-and-pulley led from the spit to a drum-shaped wooden cage attached to a wall. When the dog ran, the spit turned. The more hyperactive dogs were the most prized, and dogs were actually trained to be hyperactive so they could become better "spit runners."

London has one of the biggest Chinatowns in Europe — a paradise for foodies. Your appetite swells as you wander its colorful streets, which are lined with restaurants and food shops boasting everything from Peking ducks to scrumptious Asian pastries. You can almost taste the food with your eyes as you go on your culinary window-shopping jaunt.

I came to love Peking Duck in London, and I subsequently learned to make it at home. The only catch is you have to prepare it the day before and hang it in a window to dry. By the way, the first time I hung my duck up to dry, my neighbors thought I was practicing some weird form of witch-craft.

After the duck's ready, you present it with hoisin sauce and Mandarin pancakes, as well as scallions and cucumbers. If you can't put your hands on any Mandarin pancakes, you can substitute large blanched and dried iceberg lettuce leaves.

TRAVELIN' GOURMET PEKING DUCK

5-pound duck (fresh, if possible, or frozen and thawed)
½ cup corn syrup (or any type of pancake syrup)
2 tablespoons thick soy sauce
2 tablespoons wine
1 tablespoon vinegar
2 cups boiling water
hoisin sauce
6–8 Mandarin pancakes (available in some supermarkets and Asian groceries)
8 scallions (white parts only)
1 cucumber, diced

Clean the duck inside and out with warm water and pat dry. Remove as much fat as possible. In a wok or a bowl large enough to accommodate the duck, vigorously mix together the corn syrup, soy sauce, wine, and vinegar with the boiling water. Add the duck to the mixture; thoroughly coat it, basting for about 5 minutes.

OFF THE EATEN PATH:

One Man's Goose Is Another Man's Meal

I always wondered why the expression "your goose is cooked" meant something bad. To me, it would mean something good, because I happen to like roast goose. But French prisoners on death row often would request roast goose for their last meal. So when the gendarme arrived and said, "Your goose is cooked," it meant the prisoner was not too far away from facing the guillotine.

Marinate the duck, uncovered, in the refrigerator for 2 hours (turning it once or twice).

Tie a string around the neck and hang the duck to dry for an afternoon in a window (make sure to put something underneath it to catch the drippings). I blow-dry the duck periodically with a hair dryer to make it as dry as possible—this will help make the skin crispy.

When ready to cook, preheat the oven to 450°. Put an oiled rack over a large roasting pan. Take the duck from its hanging place, discard the string, and place the duck on the rack, breast-side up. Roast for 30 minutes; reduce the heat to 375° and roast until the skin becomes ebony-colored and crisp (45 to 55 more minutes). Remove from the oven and let rest for 10 minutes. Meanwhile, cut the scallions in half lengthwise, then in half crosswise. This should result in a bunch of thin strips about 2 to 3 inches long. Carefully remove the crisp outer skin from the duck, cut into pieces, and set it aside as you carve the rest of the bird. Put the meat on a platter and surround it with the skin.

TO SERVE: Slather each Mandarin pancake with a thin layer of hoisin sauce, leaving about a 2-inch border uncovered. Put some scallions and cucumbers on top of the hoisin sauce, followed by the inside meat of the duck. Finish with a topping of duck skin. Roll it up and eat it with your fingers. Enjoy!

MAKES 6–8 BUNDLES OF DUCKY FLAVOR; SERVES 4

A version of steak tartare fueled Genghis Khan when he led the ferocious Tartars into battle. The Somali tribes of the Nile consumed it as a prelude to performing incredible feats of strengths. In the latter part of the past century, it was the rage among proper British gentlemen, who enjoyed it as a mid-afternoon snack aimed at maintaining their masculine potency. And when the Germans occupied Paris during World War II, members of its military high command developed a passion for steak tartare, one of the world's oldest culinary specialties.

The name is derived from the Tartar tribes in the 13th century, who prided themselves on their masculinity, much of which they said they owed to eating raw meat. They kept that meat, incidentally, under the saddles of their horses as they galloped across Asia. Not only was it a convenient place to store the meat as they rode for days on end on their trusty steeds, but the friction of the saddle also tenderized it. They consumed it with a sauce made from mare's milk amplified with spices (the sauce without the "e" — tartar — offered with fish at some restaurants is a distant relative).

Word of the machismo of the Tartars spread throughout the world thanks to explorers, including none other than Marco Polo himself. He wrote that "a Tartar can have as many wives as he pleases — 100 if he can afford them." Polo was rhapsodic about the Tartars' agility in battle and commented on the grace of their Mongolian horses, which he said, "can turn as quickly as a dog."

When Polo and other explorers brought word back that these warriors consumed vast amounts of what was to become known as steak tartare, countless men throughout the world took to steak tartare to boost their libido. Subsequently, gastronomes grew to appreciate the dish not for its alleged rejuvenating qualities but for the honesty of its flavor.

THE ULTIMATE STEAK TARTARE

Steak tartare is an acquired taste, like Scotch or sushi. In fact, it wasn't until I sampled Chef Guy Pierre Baumann's rendition of the classic that I came to enjoy it. Baumann, a Certified Master Chef who owns Restaurant Baumann Marboeuf, in Paris, suggests that you have your butcher put his leanest steak through the grinder just once, and that you use the meat as soon as possible. He stresses that you should think *cold*! Not only should the steak be served very cold but it should be *prepared* cold by putting the mixing bowl in a nest of ice. The chef even recommends that you mix the meat with utensils rather than by hand, to avoid warming the meat.

1 egg yolk
1½ teaspoons hot mustard (preferably Dijon)
1 teaspoon Worcestershire sauce
1 teaspoon ketchup
1 teaspoon Tabasco sauce
2 tablespoons peanut oil
½ teaspoon cider vinegar
salt and freshly ground black pepper to taste
1 heaping tablespoon chopped onion
1 tablespoon capers
½ tablespoon chopped fresh parsley
1 pound lean ground steak
⅓ Golden Delicious apple, peeled and diced
parsley sprigs for garnish

In a mixing bowl set on a nest of ice in a larger bowl, combine the egg yolk, mustard, Worcestershire, ketchup, and Tabasco. Whisk in the peanut oil and vinegar. Season with salt and pepper.

Add the onion, capers, and parsley and stir well. Add the meat and apple. Using a fork, gently mix the ingredients together, being careful not to overmix. Transfer to two chilled plates, shape into ovals, garnish each with a sprig of parsley, and serve immediately.

SERVES 2 AS MAIN COURSE, 4 AS APPETIZER

"BAUERBRATEN"

This is my favorite sauerbraten recipe. The reason I call it "Bauerbraten" is that I learned the recipe from my wife, Doris, whose maiden name was Bauer. I've always had a weakness for a good (or even a bad) pun. The recipe works best when you marinate the meat for three days in the refrigerator. The sauce is a "snap" to make—literally. You use ginger snaps to fashion it!

2 cups water
¾ cup vinegar
5 cloves
6 peppercorns
1 large lemon, sliced
3 bay leaves
1 rib celery, cut up
2 large carrots, cut up
2 medium onions, sliced
3–4 pounds top round beef
¼ cup flour, for dusting
¼ cup vegetable shortening
2 ribs celery, coarsely chopped
4 small onions
2 carrots, coarsely chopped
1 parsnip, coarsely chopped
10 ginger snaps, crushed
2 tablespoons all-purpose flour
salt and freshly ground black pepper to taste

To make the marinade, combine the first 9 ingredients in a large pot and bring to a boil; boil for 1 minute and remove from heat. Put the beef into a porcelain or earthenware pot (don't use metal) and pour the marinade over it. Refrigerate, covered, for at least 24 hours (I like to marinate mine for 3 to 4 days).

Remove the beef from the pot, reserving the marinade (remove the lemon and discard). Pat the beef dry and dust on all sides with flour. Put the shortening into a Dutch oven and brown the beef on all sides over medium-high heat (you can add more shortening if it begins to stick). Add the reserved marinade to the pot; lower the heat to a simmer and cook, uncovered, for 2 hours. Add the remaining celery, onions, and carrots, and the parsnips. Cover and simmer for an hour.

Remove the meat to a heated holding platter and strain the marinade into a large saucepan. Add the ginger snaps to the marinade and bring to a boil, slowly adding the flour as you do, stirring all the while. After the sauce comes to a boil, lower the heat and simmer for 3 to 4 minutes (it should become thick), stirring constantly. Season with salt and pepper, strain (if desired), and serve the gravy over the beef, with some on the side.

SERVES 8–10

MARINATED SIRLOIN STEAK

When I'm on the road I often crave a good marinated steak, like this one, which is rich with an assortment of flavors.

¾ cup olive oil
¾ cup soy sauce
¼ cup Worcestershire sauce
½ cup red wine vinegar
¼ cup red wine or ¼ cup fresh orange juice
⅓ cup fresh lemon juice
1 tablespoon fresh lime juice
2 teaspoons dry mustard
2 garlic cloves, minced
1 teaspoon grated fresh ginger
pinch salt and freshly ground black pepper
2–2½ pounds flank steak

In a bowl large enough to hold the steak, combine all the marinade ingredients. Refrigerate, covered, for 24 hours. Broil or grill to desired doneness and serve immediately.

SERVES 4

MOUSSAKA

Here's my favorite recipe for this Greek classic. The flavor intensifies if you make it a day in advance, refrigerate it, and then reheat it before serving.

2 sticks (½ pound) unsalted butter
3 medium eggplant, cut into slices ½ inch thick
3 large onions, finely chopped
2 pounds lean ground beef or lamb
3 tablespoons tomato paste
½ cup red wine
½ cup chopped fresh parsley
¼ teaspoon cinnamon
salt and freshly ground black pepper to taste
6 tablespoons all-purpose flour
1 quart milk
4 eggs, beaten until frothy
dash nutmeg
2 cups ricotta cheese
1 cup freshly grated Parmesan cheese
1 cup unseasoned bread crumbs

Melt 4 tablespoons of the butter in a medium skillet and sauté the eggplant slices on both sides until brown. Remove and set aside. In the same skillet, add 4 more tablespoons of butter and cook the onions until they're golden brown, stirring occasionally. Add the ground meat and cook over medium heat for 10 minutes.

In a small bowl, combine the tomato paste with the wine, parsley, cinnamon, salt, and pepper. Stir the mixture into the skillet with the meat and simmer until all of the liquid has been absorbed, stirring often. Remove from the heat.

Preheat the oven to 375°. Bring the milk to a boil. Meanwhile, in another skillet, melt 8 more tablespoons of the butter over moderate heat; stir in the flour with a wire whisk. Slowly add the milk to the butter-flour mixture, stirring all the while. When the mixture is smooth and has started to thicken, remove from the heat and cool slightly. Stir in the eggs, nutmeg, and ricotta cheese.

Dust the bottom of a greased 11 x 16-inch pan with some of the bread crumbs. Arrange alternate layers of eggplant and meat sauce in the pan. Sprinkle each layer with Parmesan cheese and bread crumbs. Pour the ricotta cheese mixture over the top and

OFF THE EATEN PATH:
The Versatile Eggplant

A native of India, the eggplant turns up in many of the world's cuisines. It is particularly popular in England, where it is known by the swanker name "aubergine." In France, it is an integral part of *ratatouille*. A sister dish from Italy using eggplant is *caponata*. In India, it turns up in curries and deep-fried as snacks. Down Under, they like it baked and stuffed with oysters. In the Far East, it is often paired with chicken or pork. In Greece, besides being fashioned into moussaka, they also make "slippers" out of it by hollowing it out and filling with a combination of cheese, egg, onion, and béchamel sauce.

bake 1 hour, or until the top turns golden. Remove from the oven and cool 20 to 30 minutes before serving. Cut into squares and serve warm.

SERVES 8

STEAK AU POIVRE WITH MUSTARD-CREAM SAUCE

A delicious rendition of medium-cooked steak in the French manner.

3 tablespoons black peppercorns
4 beef fillets (4 ounces each)
2 tablespoons unsalted butter

SAUCE:
$^1/_3$ cup dry white wine
$4^1/_2$ tablespoons Dijon mustard
$^1/_4$ teaspoon paprika
$^1/_2$ cup heavy cream
$1^1/_2$ tablespoons cognac or Armagnac
salt and freshly ground black pepper to taste

Coarsely crack the peppercorns between 2 pieces of waxed paper with a rolling pin, then press them into the fillets. Set aside for 30 minutes.

Melt the butter in a medium-size saucepan over moderate heat and brown the steaks on one side. Turn the meat over, reduce the heat to low, and cook for 3 minutes. Transfer the steaks to a platter, reserving the cooking juices. Cover the steaks with aluminum foil and keep them warm in a low oven while you make the sauce.

Pour the cooking juices into a small saucepan; over medium heat, add the wine, stirring all the while. Slowly add the mustard, then stir in the paprika. Add the cream, raise the heat to high, and bring to a boil. Lower the heat and whisk in the cognac. Cook on low-moderate heat until the sauce reduces by about a quarter; season with salt and pepper. Over moderate heat, warm the steaks in the pan you cooked them in. Transfer the steaks to heated plates and serve them napped with the sauce.

MAKES 4 SERVINGS

TRAVELIN' GOURMET MEAT LOAF

The all-American meat loaf can now be found in restaurants all around the world. I created this recipe to give the American classic an international flair. Use your hands to mix it all together, and make sure it is thoroughly mixed. Also, pack it as tightly into the loaf pan as possible. Although most meat loaf recipes call for regular ground beef, I like to use lean ground round. If you decide to use a fattier meat, pour off the fat periodically while it's cooking.

CHILI GLAZE:

12-ounce jar prepared chili sauce
2 tablespoons red wine
1 teaspoon A-1 Steak Sauce
1 teaspoon dried basil
½ teaspoon celery salt
½ teaspoon cayenne pepper
1 teaspoon fresh lemon juice

MEAT LOAF:

2 tablespoons unsalted butter
2 cups finely chopped onions
3 garlic cloves, minced
3 slices Italian bread, diced
¾ cup milk
2 pounds ground beef
2 eggs, lightly beaten
2 teaspoons salt
½ teaspoon freshly ground black pepper
½ teaspoon Tabasco
½ cup finely chopped walnuts
½ cup Italian-seasoned bread crumbs
½ teaspoon dried thyme
½ teaspoon dried marjoram
2 tablespoons chopped fresh parsley
¼ cup red wine

TO MAKE THE CHILI GLAZE: Combine all of the glaze ingredients in a small bowl and mix well. Refrigerate, covered, until ready to use.

OFF THE EATEN PATH:
Catch Up on Your Ketchup Background

The first mass-produced ketchup product, created by the H. J. Heinz Co., debuted in 1876. By the way, on the cap of most Heinz Ketchup bottles you'll see a code consisting of two letters followed by four numbers, which tell a story. The last digit indicates the year the ketchup was bottled (0 would mean it was bottled in 1990). The three numbers before it indicate the production day of the year in which the ketchup was bottled. Thus, if the last four numbers on the cap are 1450, that means the ketchup was bottled on the 145th day of 1990.

TO MAKE THE MEAT LOAF: Melt the butter in a skillet and add the onions and garlic; sauté until they turn golden (do not brown). Cool. Soak the bread in the milk for 10 minutes; drain in a sieve, pressing down on the bread to remove as much excess milk as possible.

In a large mixing bowl, mix the beef thoroughly with the drained bread and the cooled onions and garlic. Mix in the eggs, salt, pepper, Tabasco, walnuts, bread crumbs, thyme, marjoram, parsley, and wine.

Use a pastry brush to "paint" the bottom and edges of a nonstick 9 × 13-inch loaf pan with some of the chili glaze. Pack the meat mixture into the pan and form it into a loaf, leaving about ¾ inch around the edges of the top to give room for any fat to run off. Firm the loaf by refrigerating for at least 1 hour.

Preheat the oven to 350°. Brush the top of the meat loaf with a layer of chili glaze. Bake on the lowest rack of the oven until the meat is cooked through (about 60 to 70 minutes). About 10 minutes before it is done, brush the top with another layer of chili glaze. Remove from the oven, pour off any fat, and let it rest for 5 minutes. Slice and serve each slice liberally napped with the chili glaze.

SERVES 6–8

TRAVELIN' GOURMET MEATBALLS

These meatballs are meant to be simmered in the Travelin' Gourmet Tomato Sauce and served with pasta. However, you can substitute your favorite spaghetti sauce recipe.

2 pounds lean ground beef
1 teaspoon minced garlic
¾ cup Italian-flavored bread crumbs
½ teaspoon cayenne pepper
1 teaspoon dried basil
½ teaspoon dried oregano
½ teaspoon dried fennel
⅛ teaspoon freshly ground black pepper
¼ teaspoon salt
½ cup grated Parmesan cheese
½ cup diced white onions
2 eggs
olive oil
1 recipe Travelin' Gourmet Tomato Sauce (page 81)

Put all of the ingredients except the olive oil and spaghetti sauce into a medium bowl and mix thoroughly with your hands. Shape into 14 to 18 balls about 1½ inches in diameter. Put a thin layer of olive oil on the bottom of a large skillet, add the meatballs, and brown on all sides over medium heat. Don't crowd them; you may have to cook them in two batches.

Reduce the heat to low and simmer, covered, until the meatballs are nearly cooked through (about 15 minutes), turning several times. Drain on paper towels and transfer to a pot of spaghetti sauce. Simmer until the meatballs are cooked through and have absorbed the sauce (1 hour or more).

You can serve them right away. However, I think they work even better if you let them steep in the sauce overnight (simply put the meatballs in the sauce and store, covered, in the refrigerator). Reheat when ready to use.

MAKES 14–18 MEATBALLS

"Never order a drink that comes with an umbrella or a glass you can keep."

—M.K.

"Hearty" Delicacy

Love-in-disguise was the name of a dish that once was considered a delicacy in England. It's actually a calf heart wrapped in veal force-meat and bacon.

BEEF STROGANOFF

Once this famous Russian dish was quite popular in the United States, but I don't see it on too many menus these days. And occasionally I miss it. When crossing the Atlantic a few years back, it turned up on the menu of the Queen's Grill on Cunard's *QE II*, which is where I got this recipe.

3 tablespoons vegetable oil
2 pounds steak fillet, cut into thin strips (1 by 4 inches)
1 cup beef stock
3 medium onions, finely chopped
½ cup tomato sauce
1 cup sour cream
1 tablespoon chopped chives
1 tablespoon minced fresh parsley
¼ cup dry sherry

In a medium saucepan, heat the oil until it is very hot. Add the steak strips and brown them lightly. Lower the heat, and add the beef stock, onions, and tomato sauce; simmer until sauce thickens (25 to 30 minutes), stirring occasionally. Stir in the sour cream, chives, parsley, and sherry. Heat gently until heated through. Serve with noodles or rice.

SERVES 4–6

FILETTO SORPRESSO

The name of this Italian dish literally translates to "fillet surprise." I think you'll find that the dish packs a surprising amount of flavor. It's from the repertoire of Luigi Adamo, a noted restaurant consultant who works in Florida and Pennsylvania.

4 beef fillets (4 ounces each)
salt, freshly ground black pepper, and garlic salt to taste
1 garlic clove, minced
8 slices prosciutto
4 thin slices mozzarella cheese
2 tablespoons thinly sliced mushrooms
1 teaspoon chopped fresh parsley
1 tablespoon grated Romano cheese
3 eggs, well beaten
¼ cup milk
¾ cup unseasoned bread crumbs
3 tablespoons clarified unsalted butter (page 38)
2 tablespoons olive oil
juice of 1 lemon
¼ cup white wine
¼ cup chicken broth
watercress sprigs, for garnish

Preheat the oven to 375°. Slice each fillet horizontally, butterfly-style, making certain to leave an edge intact so that the fillet is not cut all the way through. Open out the fillets like a book and pound with the heel of your hand to flatten them a bit. Season with salt, pepper, and garlic salt.

Place 2 slices prosciutto, 1 slice mozzarella, and ½ tablespoon of the mushrooms in the center of each opened fillet. Close the halves as you would a sandwich. Press the meat together around the edges to seal.

Mix the parsley and grated cheese into the eggs. Dip the fillets into the milk, then into the bread crumbs, then into the egg mixture, and place on a platter. Heat the butter and oil in a large ovenproof skillet until bubbling hot. Add the fillets, lower the heat to moderate, and cook until lightly browned on both sides.

Drain the cooking fat from the skillet and add the lemon juice, wine, and chicken broth; then place the skillet in the preheated oven for 10 minutes — less time is required for rare; more for well done. Pour a little of the juice in the skillet over each fillet, garnish with watercress sprigs, and serve immediately.

SERVES 4

MARINATED BEEF KABOBS

Here's an easy shish kabob recipe.

*1½ cups plain yogurt
juice of 1 lemon
½ teaspoon fresh lime juice
2 tablespoons red wine
1 onion, finely chopped
3 bay leaves
salt and freshly ground pepper to taste
2 pounds lean beef, cut into 1-inch cubes
8 large mushroom caps, cleaned
2 medium onions, cut into chunks
1 red bell pepper, cored, seeded, and cut into 1-inch squares
1 green bell pepper, cored, seeded, and cut into 1-inch squares*

Make the marinade by blending together in a medium bowl the first 6 ingredients; season with salt and pepper. Add the beef and mix well with the marinade. Cover and refrigerate overnight, turning twice. Remove the beef and reserve the marinade. Thread the beef on 8 skewers, alternating with the vegetables. Grill 10 to 15 minutes (depending on how you want the beef cooked), basting often with the reserved marinade. Serve immediately.

SERVES 4

OFF THE EATEN PATH:
London, a City of Pubs

There are more than 6000 public houses or "pubs" in Greater London. And, yes, it's possible to get cold beer in a pub. Just ask for a lager, which is about the closest thing to American beer you can find in London. Some of the pubs are called "tie houses," meaning they're owned by breweries. The rest are "freehouses," meaning the owners can buy from whomever they please.

One of the most romantic of the big ships that plied the cold, turbulent waters of the Atlantic during the halcyon days of sea travel was the SS *France*. Fine food, of course, was the ship's trademark. In fact, none other than that great gastronomic guru Craig Claiborne once called the ship's Chambord dining room the "best in the world." I almost had the opportunity to see if he was right by booking passage on the ship in the early '70s on her final voyage from New York to Le Havre. I managed to secure the last room available on the ship and counted the days when I would prance across her teakwood decks and savor her fabled cuisine.

Alas, a few days prior to departure my travel agent called me with the sad news that the crew had taken her over in Le Havre in a last-ditch attempt to try to force management not to pull her out of service. They failed. My dream of sailing on her disappeared like a *quenelle* when it hits the tongue.

Since then, the ship has been reincarnated as the SS *Norway*. I visited her in 1988 while she was docked in the Bahamas. It was a depressing sight to see how the grand old lady of the seas has been restored. She looks like a gigantic floating hospital. Incidentally, most of the old SS *France*'s memorabilia was destroyed when the ship was removed from service. However, many of her recipes are still very much alive, including this one from former chef Henri Le Huéudé, which I've varied slightly.

VEAL CHOPS NORMANDE

⅔ *cup unsalted butter*
6 veal chops (8 ounces each), trimmed
salt and white pepper to taste
3 tablespoons fresh lemon juice
2 cups heavy cream
12 Granny Smith apples, peeled, cored, and quartered
4 tablespoons unsalted butter, softened
¼ *cup granulated sugar*
1 tablespoon chopped chives

In a large skillet, heat the ⅔ cup butter until it browns. Season the chops with salt and pepper, then sauté them gently in the butter. Transfer the chops to a very warm platter, cover with

aluminum foil, and place in a low oven to keep warm. Add the lemon juice and cream to the skillet. Simmer for 20 minutes; strain the sauce through a fine sieve into another pan; keep very warm.

Preheat oven to 450°. Put the apples in a shallow, greased ovenproof baking dish, dot with the 4 tablespoons butter and sprinkle with the sugar as evenly as possible. Bake for 10 to 12 minutes. Arrange the chops on a heated serving platter, surround with the apples, coat with the sauce, and sprinkle with the chives. Serve immediately.

SERVES 6

VEAL WITH EGGPLANT

Veal and eggplant are frequently teamed up in Italy.

2 medium eggplant, peeled and sliced
1½ teaspoons salt
½ cup all-purpose flour
½ cup vegetable oil
2 pounds veal steak, cut into thin slices
½ teaspoon freshly ground black pepper
¼ cup unsalted butter, melted
1 cup tomato sauce
1 cup shredded mozzarella cheese

Put the eggplant in a medium bowl and lightly dust with 1 teaspoon of the salt; let the eggplant "sweat" off its bitter juices for about 3 hours. Pat dry with paper towels and dust with ¼ cup of the flour. In a large skillet, heat the oil and sauté the eggplant. Drain on paper towels, then transfer to a warm platter and place in a low oven, covered, to keep warm while you prepare the veal. Clean the skillet in preparation for cooking the veal.

Season the meat with the remaining ½ teaspoon salt and the pepper; dust with the remaining flour. Sauté quickly (2 to 3 minutes) on both sides over moderate-high heat in the melted butter.

Preheat the broiler. In a shallow baking pan, arrange 4 to 6 servings of at least 3 slices eggplant; top with the cooked veal slices. Spoon a little tomato sauce and grated cheese over each serving. Broil just until the cheese melts (about 3 minutes).

SERVES 4–6

VEAL WITH PROSCIUTTO AND CHEESE

In Italy, they call this dish *Cotoletta Imbottita alla Palatino.* I think you'll call it delicious. It's from the culinary repertoire of restaurant consultant/food researcher/friend Byron Bardy.

1½–2 pounds veal
6 ounces freshly grated Parmesan cheese
6 tablespoons unsalted butter, softened
6 eggs, lightly beaten (beat 2 separately)
6 slices prosciutto
6 slices Swiss cheese
2 cups all-purpose flour
2 cups unseasoned bread crumbs
1½ cups olive oil
½ cup dry sherry
½ teaspoon lemon juice
3 tablespoons chopped fresh parsley

Cut the veal into 12 slices, each about 3 x 2 x ½-inch thick. Put the slices between 2 pieces of waxed paper on a pounding surface and flatten until about ⅛ inch thick (if you don't have a pounding mallet, you can use the flat edge of a cleaver to do this; I use a light, narrow rolling pin).

Make a paste by mixing together the Parmesan cheese, 3 tablespoons of the butter, and 2 of the eggs. Line up 6 slices veal and place 1 slice prosciutto and 1 slice cheese on top of each. Spread the egg/cheese mixture on top of the remaining 6 slices veal. Top each of the first 6 slices with a spread slice (spread-side down), which will result in 6 "sandwiches." Press together firmly with your hands, trimming any rough edges to form a smooth cutlet. Chill in the refrigerator.

Dip each "sandwich" into the flour, then into the remaining eggs, and finally into the bread crumbs, making certain all of the seams are coated with the mixture. Heat the olive oil until very hot (you need this much olive oil in order to cook the sides properly). Fry the cutlets in the oil until brown on both sides. Remove from the pan and keep hot.

OFF THE EATEN PATH:
A Man or a Mozzarella?

Wimpy young men are known as *mozzarellas* in some sections of Italy. Why? Apparently because fresh mozzarella is soft and delicate. Soccer fans in Italy also refer to weak teams as *mozzarelle.*

Pour off the excess oil from the pan, then add the sherry, stirring; cook over medium heat until reduced by a third. Add the rest of the butter and cook over high heat until the butter browns. Add the lemon juice and parsley. Pour over the cutlets and serve very hot.

SERVES 6

VEAL IN TUNA SAUCE

This dish, known as Vitello Tonnato in Italy, is a highlight of many of the antipasto bars in Rome. It's a great picnic or party dish because it is served cold or at room temperature.

1 pound veal loin
1 bay leaf
1 small onion, cut into chunks
1 cup dry white wine
1 carrot, peeled and sliced
1 rib celery, sliced
2 anchovy fillets
2 tablespoons capers
7-ounce can water-packed tuna, drained
½ cup mayonnaise
¼ cup brandy
juice of 1 lemon
thin lemon slices and fresh parsley, for garnish

Put the veal into a saucepan large enough to hold it comfortably; add water to cover. Over high heat, add the bay leaf, onion, wine, carrot, and celery. Bring to a boil, reduce the heat to moderate, and cook for about 35 to 40 minutes. Remove from the heat and allow to cool.

Partially desalt the anchovies by running water over them, then wiping them with paper towels. Transfer to a food processor and add the capers and tuna. Add the mayonnaise, brandy, and lemon juice and process until very creamy (sauce shouldn't be too thick; if it is, thin it with some cream). Refrigerate for 30 minutes, then slice the meat thinly and liberally coat with the tuna sauce. Garnish with lemon slices and parsley; refrigerate, covered, until ready to use. Serve cold or at room temperature.

SERVES 4–6

VEAL ROMANO

I know you're going to think I'm chauvinistic, but one of the most spectacular sites in America for a restaurant happens to be in Pittsburgh, at the top of Mt. Washington, overlooking the city's Golden Triangle. Christopher's Restaurant, one of Pittsburgh's finest, is perched high atop the mount with window seats offering some of the most delicious scenery you can imagine. This is one of the restaurant's simpler dishes.

2 eggs
salt and white pepper to taste
1 tablespoon chopped fresh parsley
1 tablespoon grated Romano cheese
8 pieces veal (about 1½ ounces each), flattened to about ⅛
    inch thick between 2 pieces of waxed paper
all-purpose flour, for dredging
1 tablespoon olive oil
½ cup clarified unsalted butter (see page 38)
½ cup Chablis or Chardonnay
1½ tablespoons lemon juice
½ cup chicken broth
chopped fresh parsley, for garnish

In medium bowl, whisk the eggs with salt and pepper; add the parsley and Romano and mix well. Dust the veal lightly with the flour, shaking off any excess. Dip the veal into the egg mixture, draining off the excess.

In a large skillet, heat the oil, then add the butter; when hot, add the veal and sauté until golden brown on each side. Transfer the veal to a heated platter and wipe any excess oil from the skillet. Return the veal to the skillet and add the wine, lemon juice, and broth. Simmer about 3 to 4 minutes, sprinkle with the parsley, and serve immediately.

SERVES 4

VEAL CUTLETS WITH LIME MAYONNAISE

Chef Linda Hagen of Chateau St. Jean Vineyards, Sonoma Valley, California, created this intriguing dish.

MAYONNAISE:

1 egg yolk, at room temperature
1½ tablespoons fresh lime juice
⅓ cup vegetable oil, mixed with ¼ cup olive oil
1 teaspoon grated lime peel (zest)
¼ teaspoon salt

CUTLETS:

6 veal cutlets (about 1¼ pounds total), sliced ¼ inch thick
⅓ cup all-purpose flour
2 eggs, lightly beaten
1½ cups unseasoned bread crumbs
½ cup olive oil
salt and white pepper to taste
lime slices, for garnish

TO MAKE THE MAYONNAISE: With an electric beater, beat the egg yolk with 1 tablespoon of the lime juice in a deep bowl; when it turns pale yellow, start to add the oil blend, drop by drop, while beating the mixture at a moderate speed. After 2 tablespoons of the oil blend have been added, start to add the rest in a thin stream, stopping occasionally to make sure that the oil is incorporating well into the mixture before adding any more. When all of the oil has been added, keep beating until the mayonnaise has thickened; then beat in the remaining lime juice and the zest and salt. Refrigerate, covered, until ready to serve.

TO MAKE THE VEAL CUTLETS: Put the veal cutlets between sheets of waxed paper and pound until about ⅛ inch thick. Dredge the cutlets in the flour, dip into the egg, and then into the bread crumbs, patting to make sure that the crumbs adhere. In a large skillet over moderate-high heat, warm the olive oil until hot but not smoking. Sauté the cutlets until golden brown. Remove, drain on paper towels, and cut into 1-inch strips. Serve at room temperature topped with the mayonnaise and a garnish of lime slices.

SERVES 4–6

There is no people in the world more fascinated with the lowly pig than the Spanish. In fact, Spaniards consume some 25 million of the critters annually. And the Spanish ministry says that figure is growing about 10 percent annually.

It's not all due to appetite, mind you, but to history, too. In fact, after the Moors and Jews were driven from Spain in the late fifteenth century, eating pork became a way of underlining the Spaniards' link to Christianity. Pig season officially begins with the feast of San Martin on November 11, and many families gather together for the ritual slaying of a porker.

The Cadillac of cured hams in Spain is the mouth-watering *jabūgō*, from the city of the same name in the western end of the Sierra Morena Mountain range. It's made from pigs bred only on the Iberian peninsula, whose main diet consists of acorns. It has to be tasted to be believed. Unfortunately, you'll have to venture to Spain to sample the ham's melt-in-the mouth, slightly sweet tenderness because most countries, including the United States, prohibit the importation of Spanish hams.

Here's a recipe based on a pork dish I had in a famous Madrid restaurant called Lhardy.

PERKY PAPRIKA PORK

2 medium-sized onions, chopped
2 tablespoons olive oil
1 pound lean pork, coarsely chopped
½ teaspoon chili powder
2 garlic cloves, minced
1½ tablespoons sweet paprika (preferably Hungarian)
1 tablespoon all-purpose flour
1 cup chicken broth
3 ripe tomatoes, chopped
1 tablespoon tomato puree
1 red pepper, seeded and chopped
¼ pint plain yogurt
salt and freshly ground black pepper to taste

In a medium skillet with a heavy bottom, sauté the onions for 5 to 7 minutes over medium heat in the olive oil. Add the pork and brown it on both sides. Mix in the chili powder, garlic, and paprika; cook for 2 to 3 minutes, scraping up particles that may stick to the bottom. Add the flour a little at a time, stirring all the while; cook 2 to 3 minutes. Slowly stir in the chicken broth and mix well; stir in the tomatoes, puree, and red pepper. Simmer gently, tightly covered, until the meat is cooked through (about 1¼ to 1½ hours), stirring occasionally.

Pour off about ¼ cup of the cooking juices into a small bowl and blend the yogurt into it; mix well. Remove the pork from the heat and stir in the yogurt mixture; season with salt and pepper. Heat on medium until the mixture is heated through (do not boil). Serve immediately with buttered noodles, if desired.

SERVES 4–6

BAVARIAN-STYLE SMOKED PORK LOIN

An easy recipe from Germany often served during *Oktoberfest*.

2 pounds smoked pork loin
freshly ground black pepper to taste
2 medium onions, quartered
1 cup boiling water
1 cup beef broth, mixed with ½ cup sour cream
salt and freshly ground black pepper to taste

Preheat the oven to 350°. Put the pork into a roasting pan and season with pepper; add the onions, then pour the boiling water over both. Roast, uncovered, for an hour, basting often. Pour the beef broth/sour cream mixture over the meat and roast 30 more minutes, basting often with the pan juices. Season with salt and pepper. Let rest for 5 minutes, then carve and serve.

SERVES 4

MERRIMAN'S ROAST PINEAPPLE PORK

One of the most heralded young chefs to make his mark in Hawaii is Peter Merriman of Merriman's Restaurant, Waimea.

½ cup olive oil
2 tablespoons chopped fresh rosemary, or 1 tablespoon dried
2 teaspoons minced garlic
1 teaspoon salt
½ teaspoon freshly ground black pepper
4 pounds fresh pork butt
¼ cup vegetable oil
¼ fresh pineapple, peeled and cut into 1-inch chunks
2 celery ribs, cut into 1-inch pieces
1 medium carrot, peeled and cut into 1-inch pieces
1 leek (white part only), cleaned (see page 182) and coarsely
    chopped
1 small onion, coarsely chopped
14–15 ounces canned chicken stock
1 cup unsweetened pineapple juice
salt and freshly ground black pepper to taste
1 bunch watercress (optional)

Preheat the oven to 350°. In a small bowl, mix together the oil, rosemary, garlic, salt, and pepper; rub the mixture on the pork, making sure to cover all the surfaces. In a large ovenproof skillet over medium heat, brown the pork on all sides in the vegetable oil. Surround the meat with the chopped pineapple, celery, carrot, leek, and onion. Roast for 2 to 2¼ hours, or until the meat is cooked through (if you have a meat thermometer, it should read at least 155°). Every half hour while it's in the oven, give the meat a quarter-turn and stir the vegetables.

Transfer the meat to a carving board and keep warm. With a slotted spoon, remove the vegetables and transfer to a food processor. Remove any excess grease from the roasting pan; add the chicken stock and pineapple juice and cook over medium heat, stirring frequently, until the mixture becomes syrupy (about 20 minutes). Put the liquid into the food processor with the vegetables and puree. Season with salt and pepper if necessary.

Thinly slice the pork and spoon the sauce over the slices; serve immediately, garnished with watercress, if desired.

SERVES 4

BURGUNDY LAMB

A simple recipe based on a more complicated one from the former British Harvest Restaurant in the London International Hotel.

3 pounds lamb breast, trimmed and cut into individual portions
salt and freshly ground black pepper to taste
1 cup Burgundy
¼ cup boiling water
¼ cup currant jelly
3 tablespoons chopped fresh parsley

Preheat the oven to 375°. Place the lamb, fatty-side down, in a shallow pan and season with salt and pepper. Roast until tender (about 90 minutes). In a medium bowl, blend together the Burgundy, water, jelly, and parsley. After the roast has cooked for an hour, remove it from the oven and pour off the excess fat. Pour the Burgundy mixture over the lamb and roast for another 30 minutes, basting every 10 minutes or so with the sauce. Serve immediately.

SERVES 6

"The English have everything in common with the Americans except the language."
—OSCAR WILDE

One of the most spectacular restaurants I've ever visited is Tantris, in Munich. It's a German restaurant with Austrian chefs who serve French food in a Polynesian atmosphere at prices that are, well, out of this world. But the food is so good, it's worth it. In fact, no less a source than the revered Michelin Guide has given it its highest rating.

What more can you say about a restaurant so classy that its flower bill alone is $300,000 a year? The burnt orange and black decor laced with modernistic lights and a bevy of unique, whimsical sculptures is unlike that of any other restaurant I've ever visited.

Although it is brash and bright, the atmosphere of Heinz Winkler's three-star establishment has an air of captivating elegance — glitzy, yes, but glorious. Some locals object to what they call the Hollywood look of Tantris. Perhaps that's one of the reasons why many of its more devoted customers are tourists, including countless affluent traveling Americans, as well as celebrities from around the world.

Needless to say, you won't find dumplings and sauerbraten on the menu of this Munich restaurant, but supernal offerings like the elegant dish that follows. I wish I could say it's easy to make, but it takes some effort. However, the rewards are delicious!

LAMB CHOPS IN PUFF PASTRY

STUFFING:

1 cup finely chopped mushrooms
1 tablespoon unsalted butter
4 ounces veal, cut into chunks
salt and freshly ground black pepper to taste
1/3 cup heavy cream

CHOPS:

4 lamb chops (3 ounces each)
salt and black pepper to taste
oil for frying
1/2 teaspoon dried thyme
1/2 pound large spinach leaves

OFF THE EATEN PATH:
Holding "Mass"

The only beer mug legally allowed at Munich's famed *Oktoberfest* is called a "mass," and holds exactly one liter of beer—a little over a quart. So you don't have to be religious in Munich to hold "mass." By the way, they give a different twist to the dining experience in Munich: giant pretzels are a staple at many Munich restaurants. The word *pretzel* comes from the Latin *pretiole*, which means "little gift."

PASTRY:
½ pound (1 sheet) frozen puff pastry, thawed
1 egg yolk, mixed with 1 teaspoon water

FINAL TOUCH:
Lamb Sauce (recipe on page 148)

TO MAKE THE STUFFING: Gently sauté the mushrooms in the butter until the mushroom liquid has evaporated. Set aside to cool. Salt the veal chunks, transfer to a food processor, and process until finely minced. In a medium bowl, mix the meat with the cream and mushrooms (the mixture should have a creamy consistency). Season with salt and pepper, and place, covered, in the refrigerator to cool.

TO PREPARE THE CHOPS: Remove the fat and gristle from the lamb chops, lightly season with salt, and quickly brown on both sides in a lightly oiled frying pan. Cool on a wire rack set in a pan to catch the drippings. Season the meat with a bit more salt and pepper, and thyme; baste with the captured juices.

Blanch the spinach and transfer to a colander; refresh under cold running water. Press down on the spinach to remove as much liquid as possible. Spread the 4 largest leaves out on a tea towel. Cover with a second cloth and press to dry the leaves. Divide and spread the stuffing over the meaty part of the lamb chops. Wrap the spinach leaves around each chop to make a square envelope, completely covering the meaty part of the chops with the leaves. (If the leaves aren't big enough you can use 2 or more smaller ones).

TO PREPARE THE PASTRY: Roll out the puff pastry dough into a thin sheet; cut into eight 4- to 5-inch squares. Put the 4 spinach-lamb "envelopes" on top of 4 of the pastry squares; cover with the other 4 pastry squares. Moisten the pastry edges with egg wash; press the top and bottom edges of the pastry together tightly to seal (you can trim the edges a little, if necessary). Brush the top of the pastry with the remaining egg wash. In order to prevent the pastry from rising too much in the oven, set aside for at least 30 minutes before baking.

Preheat the oven to 500°. Put the squares in a baking pan and bake until crisp and golden (about 8 minutes); reserve the drippings for the sauce. Let the squares rest at room temperature for 2 minutes before serving with Lamb Sauce (recipe follows).

SERVES 4

Lamb Sauce

3 tablespoons minced onion
1 tablespoon unsalted butter
1 tablespoon all-purpose flour
4 tablespoons red wine
4 tablespoons beef broth
pinch thyme
reserved lamb drippings
3 tablespoons unsalted butter
salt and freshly ground black pepper to taste

Sauté the onions in the butter until they become limp. Stir in the flour and cook slowly over moderate heat until the mixture turns light brown. Remove from the heat; stir in the wine and beef broth. Cook over medium heat for 4 to 5 minutes; stir in a pinch of thyme, reduce heat to low, and whisk in the reserved lamb drippings and the butter, about a tablespoon at a time. Season with salt and pepper and serve immediately over the lamb chops.

CHEESE SOUFFLÉ

This nod to vegetarians is a variation of a recipe from the exclusive Dorchester Hotel in London when the great Anton Mosimann was presiding over the kitchen.

2 tablespoons unsalted butter, softened
2 tablespoons grated Gruyère cheese
1 cup milk
¼ cup unsalted butter
2 tablespoons all-purpose flour
½ teaspoon salt
½ teaspoon white pepper
pinch nutmeg (if freshly grated, ⅓ teaspoon)
3 large egg yolks
¾ cup grated Gruyère cheese
⅛ teaspoon salt
4 egg whites, at room temperature
6 slices Gruyère, cut into triangles

OFF THE EATEN PATH:

On the Lamb...

The Middle-Eastern version of steak tartare is called *kibbeh*. However, rather than making it with ground steak, they use ground lamb and bulgur (or bulghur, actually cracked wheat). They also offer it baked, often with onions, pine nuts, and cinnamon.

Put a baking sheet on the bottom rack of the oven; preheat the oven to 400°. Coat a 4-cup soufflé dish with 2 tablespoons of the butter, then dust with the 2 tablespoons grated Gruyère. Scald the milk. Meanwhile, in a medium saucepan, melt the ¼ cup butter over low heat. Remove from the heat and whisk in the flour. Return to the heat and cook over low heat for 2 minutes. Remove from the heat again and whisk in half of the scalded milk. Continue whisking until the sauce is very smooth. Whisk in the rest of the milk; cook, over low heat, whisking slowly, until it becomes quite thick (about 5 minutes). Stir in the salt, pepper, and nutmeg. Remove from the heat.

Put the egg yolks in a small bowl and beat until blended; stir about ¼ cup of the white sauce into the egg yolks, then quickly reverse the procedure by stirring the yolk mixture into the remaining white sauce. Cook over low heat, stirring all the while, until the mixture starts to boil. Complete the batter by transferring the mixture to a large bowl and stirring in the remaining ¾ cup grated Gruyère.

Add the ⅛ teaspoon salt to the egg whites and beat until stiff but not dry. Fold a quarter of the beaten whites into the batter. Fold in the rest of the beaten egg whites until just blended. Spoon into the prepared soufflé mold, arrange the cheese triangles on top, and gently tap the dish to remove any air bubbles. Put the soufflé dish on the baking sheet, lower the oven to 375°, and bake until nicely puffed and brown. Serve immediately.

SERVES 4

I used to flake out every time I tried to make puff pastry. Then someone brilliant invented frozen puff pastry, which has become a boon to the modern cook. If your local supermarket doesn't carry it, make a request to the manager (get down on your knees if you have to).

The key to working with puff pastry is to keep it cold when rolling it out. If you get a phone call while rolling out the thawed dough, put the dough back in the refrigerator until you are ready to work with it. If possible, roll it out on a chilled surface. Also, after you've finished rolling it out, chill it for about 30 minutes (this will help make it rise evenly).

Don't overhandle the dough when rolling it out because that might hamper the rising process (we're talking about a finicky dough). However, even if it doesn't rise to great heights, it still tastes pretty good, and I'm sure your dinner guests won't complain.

Once you get the knack of working with puff pastry, you can fashion it into fancy shapes. It's fun and makes for an attractive presentation.

SALMON IN PUFF PASTRY

1 box (16–17 ounces) frozen puff pastry, containing 2 sheets, thawed
2 fresh salmon fillets (8–10 ounces each)
salt, freshly ground black pepper, and fresh lemon juice to taste
3 tablespoons cold water, for sealing
1 egg, beaten with 1 teaspoon water
Blender Hollandaise (recipe page 151; optional)

On a floured surface, chilled if possible, roll out 1 sheet puff pastry thinly (refrigerate the other sheet until ready to use); cut it in two, making sure that each layer is large enough to cover the salmon, with about an inch left over around the edges so it can be sealed properly.

Put a salmon fillet on top of the pastry and season with salt, pepper, and lemon juice. Moisten the edges of the pastry all around with cold water; drape the other layer over the fillet; unite the

OFF THE EATEN PATH:
Puff the Magic Pastry

The French name is *pâte feuilletée*, which literally translates to "pastry of leaves." Marie Antoinette was a great fan of puff pastry, and one story is that she was responsible for the invention of the croissant, which simply means "crescent" in French, named for its shape. Incidentally, she didn't say "Let them eat cake." The famous French writer Rousseau is responsible. Perhaps Marie said: "Let them eat croissants!"

bottom layer with the top layer by pulling up and sealing as tightly as possible. Cut a few small slits in the top of the pastry all the way through with a sharp knife and trim the edges, if necessary. Refrigerate for at least 30 minutes. Repeat the procedure with the other fillet and the remaining sheet of puff pastry.

Preheat the oven to 350°. Brush the pastry-coated fish with the egg wash (this will help it brown nicely in the oven). Place on a well-greased baking sheet (or one lined with parchment paper) and bake until the crust has browned (15 to 20 minutes). Serve with Blender Hollandaise on the side, or your favorite sauce, or simply melted butter spiked with lemon juice.

SERVES 2 AS ENTRÉE; 4 AS APPETIZER

Blender Hollandaise

¾ cup clarified unsalted butter (see page 38)
3 egg yolks, at room temperature
1 tablespoon lemon juice
few drops Tabasco (optional)
1 tablespoon boiling water
salt and white pepper to taste

Fill a blender with very hot water and set aside to warm. Bring the clarified butter to a boil in a small saucepan, then remove from the heat. Empty and dry the blender; pour in the egg yolks, lemon juice, Tabasco (if desired), and boiling water and season with salt and pepper. With the motor still running, add the butter in a thin stream. Blend until satiny and thickened. Serve immediately.

MAKES ¾ CUP

TRAVELIN' GOURMET TIP:
Make Hard Butter a Soft Touch!

You can quickly soften cold, hard butter by shredding it with a coarse grater and letting it stand for a minute at room temperature. If you have a microwave, you can soften it by zapping it for 20 to 25 seconds on High.

SNAPPER GIGGI FAZI

Another wonderful recipe from Giggi Fazi in Rome.

1/4 cup olive oil
1 pound red snapper (sea bass or grouper are okay too),
    cleaned
2 small garlic cloves, cut into slivers
1 large piece dried hot red pepper, minced
1/2 cup tomato pulp made from the freshest tomatoes you can
    find*
salt to taste
1/4 cup dry white wine
fresh parsley, for garnish

Put the oil in an iron skillet, add the fish and sprinkle with the garlic. Add the red pepper, tomato pulp, and salt. Cover and cook gently for 15 minutes. Add the white wine, re-cover, and cook gently until the fish is cooked through and is tender (about 15 minutes). Garnish with fresh parsley and serve as hot as possible.

SERVES 2 AS MAIN COURSE; 4–6 AS APPETIZER

*To make the tomato pulp, peel, core, and mash the tomatoes.

It is not really an exaggeration to say that peace and happiness begin, geographically, where garlic is used in cooking.
—MARCEL BOULESTIN

SPICED RED SNAPPER EN PAPILLOTE

Cooking in a bag, or "en papillote," started out as a gimmick to honor man's first ascent in a hot-air balloon. The puffing up of the bag when it was in the oven was supposed to represent the balloon. This unusual recipe is from the gastronomic "bag" of Chef John Dolan of the Al Fahidi Grill in Dubai. It's one of the few spicy snapper dishes I've ever enjoyed. As is characteristic of all dishes prepared in this manner, a burst of aromatic wonders wafts up as you open the packages of flavor.

¼ teaspoon salt
½ teaspoon freshly ground black pepper
½ teaspoon ground cumin
½ teaspoon paprika
¼ teaspoon ground cloves
¼ teaspoon ground cinnamon
¼ teaspoon ground coriander
1 lime
1 tablespoon minced cilantro or basil leaves (optional)
¼ cup minced fresh parsley
4 red snapper fillets with skin on (about 3 ounces each)
4 circles aluminum foil (each 11 inches in diameter)
1 tablespoon olive oil
2 tablespoons unsalted butter, cubed

Preheat the oven to 400°. Combine the salt, pepper, cumin, paprika, cloves, cinnamon, and coriander. Peel the lime, cut the skin into very thin strips, and add about ½ teaspoon of it to the spices. Add the juice from the lime to the spices, along with the cilantro and parsley; stir to combine. Coat the fish with this mixture, dividing it as evenly as possible.

Paint one side of the foil with the oil. Place the fillets, skin-side down, on half of each oiled circle and dot with the butter. Fold the other half as you would a turnover; tightly crimp the edges. Transfer the packets to a baking sheet and place in the lower third of the oven; bake until cooked through (8 to 10 minutes). Serve immediately. The chef suggests you serve the remaining lime zest in a little bowl so each diner can sprinkle it on the fish as he opens his aromatic package.

SERVES 2–4

SAUTÉED SWORDFISH WITH RED WINE SAUCE

One of the finest hotels in Atlanta is the Ritz-Carlton. It also has an excellent restaurant, which tempts with dishes like this one.

4 swordfish steaks (about 6 ounces each)
salt and white pepper
1 tablespoon fresh lemon juice
¼ cup dry white wine
4 tablespoons unsalted butter

RED WINE SAUCE (BEURRE ROUGE):

4 tablespoons chopped shallots
½ cup red wine
½ cup heavy cream
½ pound unsalted butter, softened and cubed
1–2 tablespoons vinegar to taste
1–2 tablespoons fresh lemon juice to taste
pinch salt
pinch cayenne
lime wedges for garnish (optional)

Season the fish with the salt, pepper, lemon juice, and wine. In a medium skillet, sauté over medium heat in the butter until tender (8 to 10 minutes). Transfer to a warm platter, cover with aluminum foil, and keep warm in a low oven while making the sauce.

To the same skillet, add the shallots and sauté over medium heat until light colored. Add the red wine and reduce until almost dry (about 1 to 2 teaspoons). Add the cream and cook until it reduces and thickens, whisking frequently. Add the butter, a few chunks at a time, whisking all the while, until well incorporated (do not allow to boil). Season with vinegar, lemon juice, salt, and cayenne. Strain the sauce, then spoon it onto the center of each serving plate; put the swordfish on top and garnish with lime wedges, if desired.

SERVES 4

ENGLISH FISH 'N' CHIPS

The secret to making authentic English fish (as in "fish 'n' chips") at home is good old-fashioned milk. If you'd like to be authentic, layer some newspapers with waxed paper and serve the fish wrapped up in the paper, just like they do in England. If you have some trendy dinner guests coming over, wrap it in the *Wall Street Journal*!

4–6 fresh cod fillets (about 6–8 ounces each)
1–2 cups whole milk
4 eggs, mixed with 1 cup milk
oil, for deep-frying
all-purpose flour, for dredging
lemon wedges, for garnish

Soak the fillets in milk for about an hour, drain well on paper towels. Dip the fillets into the egg-mixture; drain. Heat the oil in a deep-fryer to 365–375°. Dredge the fillets in flour, shaking off any excess, plunge into the deep-fryer, and cook until golden brown and crispy. Drain and pat dry with paper towels. Serve with "chips" and lemon wedges.

TO MAKE ENGLISH "CHIPS":

3–4 large, unpeeled potatoes, cut into thick strips (about ½
  inch thick)
oil for deep-frying

Put the potatoes into a medium bowl and cover with cold, salted water for about 30 minutes. Just before time is up, heat a deep-fryer partially filled with vegetable oil to 300°. Remove the potatoes and pat dry with paper towels.

Plunge the potatoes into the deep-fryer and cook for 2 minutes. Remove, pat dry with paper towels, and let cool to room temperature (about 5 to 8 minutes).

Increase the temperature of the deep-fryer to 365–375°. Put the chips back into the oil and cook again until they're cooked through and golden brown.

SERVES 4–6

CURRY-RUBBED GRILLED SWORDFISH

This recipe is from the repertoire of the Sea Grill in New York's Rockefeller Center. I love it!

4 8-ounce swordfish steaks
salt and freshly ground black pepper to taste
2 teaspoons curry powder
1 teaspoon unsalted butter
1 tablespoon freshly cut chives

Season the fish on both sides with salt and pepper. Lightly dust both sides of each steak with about a quarter teaspoon of the curry powder. On a very hot, well-oiled grill, sear each side of the fish for 30 seconds.

Transfer to a cooler section of the grill; finish cooking the steaks (approximately 3 to 4 minutes on each side). Sprinkle the fish with chives, and nap with the sauce (recipe follows). You also can serve the fish on top of the sauce, if you want to be trendy.

SERVES 4

SAUCE:

1 cup dry white wine
2 large shallots, finely minced
1 tablespoon curry powder
½ cup heavy cream
4 ounces (½ stick) unsalted butter, cut into 4 pieces
salt and freshly ground black pepper to taste

Pour the wine into a medium saucepan and add the shallots and curry powder. Bring to a boil over high heat and continue cooking until the liquid is reduced by about two thirds, whisking frequently.

Add the heavy cream and return the mixture to a boil; continue cooking until the mixture thickens, whisking frequently. Reduce the heat to low and whisk in the butter, 1 piece at a time, until it is all well incorporated. Season with salt and pepper. Strain through a sieve and keep warm until serving (but not too hot).

SERVES 4

SWORDFISH WITH AVOCADO BUTTER

The avocado turns up in a variety of different dishes in Spain. In this recipe avocado butter can enliven swordfish, and can be used on other fish as well.

⅓ cup light soy sauce
I garlic clove, crushed
I½ teaspoons grated lemon peel
½ cup olive oil
¼ cup fresh lemon juice
I teaspoon minced fresh parsley
8 I-inch-thick swordfish steaks (4 ounces each)

AVOCADO BUTTER

½ cup unsalted butter, softened
½ cup mashed ripe avocado
2 garlic cloves, minced
2½ tablespoons minced fresh parsley
5½ tablespoons fresh lemon juice
pinch salt

Make a marinade by mixing together the first 6 ingredients. With the tip of a sharp knife, cut shallow slits in both sides of the fish, then place the steaks in a baking dish in single layer. Pour the marinade over the fish and refrigerate, covered, 4 to 5 hours, turning twice.

Preheat the broiler while making the avocado butter. Whip the butter with a whisk until very creamy, then beat in the avocado, garlic, parsley, lemon juice, and salt. Drain the fish, reserving the marinade. Broil 9 to 10 minutes, turning once, brushing occasionally with the marinade. Remove to a heated platter, nap each steak with about a tablespoon of avocado butter, and serve immediately.

SERVES 4–8

OFF THE EATEN PATH:
Dishwasher Fish

Most chefs use fancy, costly fish poachers to poach fresh fish. However, you don't have to run out and spend $89 to buy one. Use your dishwasher! It's perfect for poaching fresh fish fillets if you're in a bind. The trick is to seal the fish in aluminum foil (or in a Ziploc plastic bag). Put the fillets on aluminum foil, season to taste with salt, pepper, and lemon juice (or you can include a few thinly cut lemon slices), and seal tightly. Transfer the fish to the top rack of the dishwasher and run it through one full cycle (if you use a fish of Shamu proportions, you may have to run it on two cycles). Hold the soap, of course! You'll be surprised at the results!

GRILLED SALMON WITH RADISH SAUCE

A recipe from Larry Brudy, co-director of the International Culinary Academy in Pittsburgh, of which I am co-founder.

4 boneless, skinless salmon fillets (about 8 ounces each)
3 cups heavy cream
3 cups white wine
2 cups minced radishes
2 cups minced shallots
1 cup grated beet horseradish
¼ pound unsalted butter
fresh dill, for garnish

Preheat the oven to 350°. Grill the salmon on one side only, then transfer to the oven and bake until the fish is done. In a medium saucepan, combine the heavy cream, wine, radishes, and shallots and simmer until the mixture is reduced by half, stirring occasionally. Stir in the horseradish and butter. Top the fillets with the sauce and serve immediately, garnished with fresh dill.

SERVES 4

TROUT WITH ALMOND BUTTER

When I visited Spain, I became acutely aware of the fact that the Spanish are nuts about almonds, which are native to the Mediterranean.

4 cleaned trout (about ½ pound apiece)
salt and white pepper to taste
all-purpose flour for dredging
4½ tablespoons unsalted butter
2 tablespoons peanut oil
⅓ cup blanched, slivered almonds
¾ tablespoon fresh lemon juice
salt to taste

Season the fish on both sides with salt and pepper, then quickly dredge in the flour, shaking off any excess. In a large skillet, heat 2 tablespoons of the butter and all of the peanut oil over moderate-high heat. Add the trout and cook on each side until nicely browned (about 3 to 4 minutes) on each side.

In a small frying pan, heat the rest of the butter. Mix in the lemon juice with the almonds and season with salt. Arrange the trout on warmed plates, spoon the almond sauce over them, and serve immediately.

SERVES 4

CABERNET SALMON

The jury is still out in other parts of the country over whether or not you should serve red wine with fish, but where I come from, a robust red is the usual accompaniment to "Pittsburgh Surf and Turf": Carp and Kielbasa. Red wine also can be called into play in the creation of more subtle, but easy-to-prepare dishes, like this recipe from London, which uses a hearty red wine rather than the more usual white wine sauce.

1 tablespoon unsalted butter
4 salmon fillets* (about 8 ounces each), trimmed
1 shallot, chopped
¾ cup Cabernet Sauvignon (or other robust red wine)
2 teaspoons fresh tarragon, or ¾–1 teaspoon dried
salt and freshly ground black pepper to taste

Melt ½ tablespoon of the butter in a heavy frying pan and add the fillets, skin-side up. Add the shallot and cook gently for 2 minutes. Turn the fish over and cook gently another 2 minutes, or until cooked through (the thicker the fillet, the longer the cooking time).

Remove the fillets to a warm platter and put them into a preheated warm oven. Over high heat, add the wine to the frying pan, bring to a boil, and continue boiling until the alcohol burns off, scraping up the bits that stick to the bottom as you do. When the wine becomes syrupy and reduced by about half, add the tarragon and the remaining butter; whisk until nicely blended into the sauce, then season with salt and pepper.

Remove the fillets from the oven, place on heated serving plates, top with the sauce, and serve immediately.

SERVES 4

*Second choices: Mako shark, swordfish, or tuna fillets.

If any of the Ritz hotels in Europe actually lives up to its name, it's the one at 5 Plaza de la Lealthad, in Madrid, just across from the famed Prado Museum. The first thing you notice when you walk into the hotel is the acres of handmade carpets. No other hotel in the world can match them for quality, design, and character, from the massive ones in the lobby to the ones in your room. The hotel maintains a staff that does nothing but look after the carpets. In addition to cleaning them, each is an expert in the art of reweaving, when that becomes necessary.

The lounge, just off the lobby, is one of the most elegant in Europe, highlighted by a breathtaking ceiling that I found hard to take my eyes off. The plush Ritz Restaurant is adjacent to it — one of the most tastefully appointed dining rooms in Europe. Wing-collared waiters who are fine-tuned in the art of dealing with people of discriminating taste, dispense dishes from the French/Spanish menu to handsome couples poised at tables appointed in linen, silver, and crystal. Even if you can't afford to stay at the Ritz, save up for at least one meal in the Ritz Restaurant. I know of few other places in Europe that so graphically give you an idea of how the other half dines.

Here's a recipe adapted from the Ritz kitchen.

SEA BASS FILLETS WITH CREAM SAUCE

The sauce works equally well with lemon sole, Dover sole or Virginia spots.

12 sea bass fillets (about 3 ounces each)
6 tablespoons clarified unsalted butter (see page 38)
½ teaspoon chopped shallots
¼ teaspoon fresh tarragon (⅛ teaspoon dried)
6 tablespoons dry white wine
juice of ½ lemon
½ cup heavy cream

Sauté the fillets in the butter over low heat for 2 minutes on each side. Add the shallots and tarragon and cook briefly. Drain off the excess butter, then add the wine and cook briefly. Add the lemon juice and cook until the fillets are done. Remove the fillets to warm serving plates and keep warm in a low oven. Over medium heat, add the cream to the liquid left in the sauté pan and cook until it reduces by about a third, stirring constantly. Pour the sauce over the fillets and serve immediately.

SERVES 4

OFF THE EATEN PATH:
Don't Be a Cork-Sniffer!

What do you do with the cork when a waiter presents it to you? Bite it? Sniff it? Neither. Simply move it to one side or put it into an ashtray after feeling if it is moist. In the days before there were wine labels on bottles, corks were presented to diners because all of the information about the wine was written on the cork.

WALNUT-BREADED FLOUNDER

If you're floundering around about what to serve, why not try this dish from Australia?

6 flounder fillets (about 5 ounces each)
all-purpose flour, for dusting
I cup unseasoned bread crumbs
2 cups walnuts: I½ cups chopped finely, ½ cup broken into
    pieces
2 tablespoons chopped fresh parsley
salt and white pepper to taste
6 eggs
½ cup Parmesan cheese
10 tablespoons margarine
¾ cup vegetable oil
2 tablespoons unsalted butter
juice of I lemon
parsley sprigs, for garnish
2 lemons cut into wedges, for garnish

Dust the fillets in the flour, shaking off excess; set aside. Combine the bread crumbs, walnuts, parsley, salt, and pepper. Mix well and set aside. Combine the eggs and cheese in a bowl to make a batter.

Preheat the oven to 350°. Dip the fillets into the batter, then dredge them in the walnut mixture, gently patting the nuts into the fish. In a large skillet, heat the margarine and oil over medium-high heat until it starts to sizzle. Add the fish, reduce the heat to a simmer, and cook about 3 minutes on each side. Transfer the fish to a shallow ovenproof glass baking dish (don't substitute a metal pan).

Drain the oil and margarine from the skillet, then add the butter and lemon juice; cook over medium heat until hot. Pour the lemon-butter sauce over the fillets and bake for 10 minutes. Remove to a heated platter, garnish with parsley and lemon wedges, and serve immediately.

SERVES 6

ROAST MONKFISH IN ORANGE SAUCE

From the culinary repertoire of Olivier de Saint Martin of the Bellevue Hotel, Philadelphia.

1¼ pounds green cabbage, cut into thin strips
juice of 4 oranges
segments of 2 oranges, cut in half
2 pounds monkfish fillets, cleaned and trimmed
salt and white pepper to taste
all-purpose flour, for dredging
2 tablespoons olive oil
4 tablespoons unsalted butter
2 tablespoons olive oil perfumed with vanilla*
4 1-inch chives

Blanch the cabbage in lightly salted water; drain and refresh in cold water; drain again. Put the cabbage in a deep ovenproof casserole with the juice and orange segments.

Preheat the oven to 450°. Season the fish with salt and pepper. Dust in flour and shake off the excess. Sauté in the olive oil until brown on both sides. Put the fish on top of the orange segments, reserving the juices in the sauté pan. Cover the casserole and bake for 10 to 15 minutes, depending on the thickness of the fish. When the fish is slightly firm to the touch, remove the casserole from the oven and transfer the fish to a warmed platter; cover with aluminum foil to keep warm.

Divide the contents of the casserole among 4 serving plates; slice the fish into 4 portions and place on top of the cabbage/orange mixture. Meanwhile, slightly reduce the liquid remaining in the sauté pan over medium heat, then add the butter; bring to a boil and continue boiling, whisking all the while, until the butter is emulsified. Reduce the heat, whisk in the vanilla-infused oil, and incorporate well; season to taste with salt and pepper. Pour the sauce around the fish and decorate each plate with a 1-inch-long chive.

SERVES 4

*Cut a vanilla bean in half and put it into a jar of olive oil for at least 24 hours.

OF TEA I SING
(a.k.a. TEA-COOKED BASS
à la BOUTERIN)

I first had chicken cooked in tea in France and loved it. However, it was not often that I found it on the menus of restaurants in the States. I was discussing this one delicious evening with George Briquet, owner of my favorite restaurant in New York, Le Perigord, when he informed me that his chef, Antoine Bouterin, had a recipe for bass cooked in tea. Here it is.

¾ pound bass fillets, cut into 4 pieces
salt and freshly ground black pepper to taste
1 cup dry white wine
4 plain tea bags
1 quart very hot water
1 small carrot, halved
2 tablespoons fresh lemon juice
½ lemon
¼ cucumber, peeled, seeded, and thinly sliced
1 leek leaf (the green, upper part), washed and sliced crosswise
2 tablespoons frozen peas
4 tablespoons unsalted butter, cubed and softened
2 pinches white pepper

Season both sides of the fillets with salt and pepper. In a medium-sized saucepan over high heat, combine the wine, tea bags, and hot water and boil for 3 to 4 minutes; remove from the heat. Blanch the carrot, then cut it into thin strips lengthwise.

Pour the lemon juice over the fish. Remove the tea bags from the saucepan; add the fish, lemon half, carrot, cucumber, leek leaf, and peas. Cook over medium-high heat, just under a boil, for 5 to 6 minutes.

Ladle 3 tablespoons of the tea mixture into a small saucepan and cook over moderate heat until reduced by half. Add the butter, piece by piece, stirring gently. Season with the white pepper. Serve the fish surrounded by the vegetables and topped with the sauce.

SERVES 2 AS ENTRÉE; 4 AS APPETIZER

GRILLED ASIAN MONKFISH

The marinade enlivens the monkfish marvelously.

4 monkfish steaks* (about 8 ounces each)
3½ tablespoons minced fresh ginger
1 tablespoon dark soy sauce
2 tablespoons light soy sauce
⅛ teaspoon freshly ground black pepper
3 tablespoons red wine
1 tablespoon sesame oil

Place the fish in a single layer in a bowl or casserole. Put the rest of the ingredients into a blender and puree. Spread the mixture over the steaks and marinate, covered, in the refrigerator overnight. Grill the fish over white-hot coals (or broil) until done (about 5 to 7 minutes on each side), basting with the marinade. Serve immediately.

SERVES 4

*You may substitute cod or halibut.

A LA CARTE:
The Magic of Caviar

There are bigger food boutiques in Paris, and there are more famous ones. But none can match the discreet opulence of the one at 18 Blvd. La Tour-Maubourg. Like the caviar it is famous for, Petrossian's is a dream. Everything about it, from the way the tins of Russian caviar are displayed to the dress of the clerks, reflects the influence of owner Christian Petrossian, one of the world's leading purveyors of caviar.

As you enter, a pastiche of delicious sights competes for the eye: More azure tins of beluga caviar than you thought you'd ever see under one roof, each holding a kilo of those "jewels from the Caspian"; smoked salmon resting regally in display cases illuminated as judiciously as some of the monuments of Paris; mounds of fresh *foie gras*, worth its weight in gold; and black truffles as big as plums.

"Like those whose first bottle of champagne happened to be a cheap bottle, those whose first taste of caviar was some discount, salty brand may be turned off for life," said the impeccably tailored Petrossian as he sipped a glass of iced vodka in the dining room of his office above the store.

"One taste of this and you realize that fine caviar is something very special." He delicately inserted a solid-gold paddle into a huge mound of glistening, gray beluga and carefully handed it to me. I put it close to my mouth and shook it slightly so the eggs slipped onto my tongue. After savoring them for a moment, I gently pressed them to my palate, where they exploded in bursts of unforgettable flavor.

"With caviar of this quality," Petrossian said as he watched a look of satisfaction erupt on my face as the eggs went down, "you don't dare present it with, say, chopped eggs, lemon, or onions. It's best delivered to the mouth either on toast points or aboard these gold paddles. Because the 'taste' of gold is neutral, it doesn't intrude with the flavor of the caviar."

Although many visitors to Paris think caviar has long been as much a part of the City of Light as the Arc de Triomphe and the Eiffel Tower, it's a relative newcomer, dating back to 1917, when Petrossian's father and brother fled to Paris from Russia during the revolution.

When they arrived, they were surprised to learn that most Parisians hadn't even heard of caviar. Seeing the potential market, they cabled the new lords of the Kremlin to see if they could import caviar to Paris. "Their prompt reply was, 'Money first!' Capitalists, those Russians!"

They complied and the rest, as they say, is history. Almost. There were some hitches along the way, as well as skepticism. The turning point was when the Petrossian brothers took a booth at the 1929 World Exposition in Paris, where they offered visitors a taste of their delicacy. Many influential food writers were among them, and they subsequently waxed rhapsodic about the joys of caviar, which they thought was pretty *haute* stuff.

It was not long after the Exposition that the Petrossians had almost more business than they could handle, but they managed. In the meantime, they secured, through the Soviet Ministry of Fisheries, exclusive rights to import caviar not only to France but also to Switzerland, the United States, and Canada. That empire has since swelled to include Scandinavia, South America, Africa, Asia, and much of the Middle East. Christian and his partner/brother Armen now purchase about 65 percent of the caviar produced in Russia.

Christian said he makes regular trips to the Caspian Sea. He exhibited photos of himself overseeing the removal of eggs from a sturgeon by a "master," as caviar "surgeons" are called. After the roe is carefully removed, the master sorts it on a cotton sieve, then gently rinses it and treats it with a rare salt.

"This is the critical moment," Petrossian said. "Too much salt destroys the taste; too little causes it to spoil." I was surprised to learn that a typical sturgeon holds about $30,000 worth of caviar.

Next in quality to beluga, which has the largest eggs, is osetra, which has smaller eggs and a more intense flavor. It varies in color from golden yellow to brown. Next in the caviar hierarchy is sevruga, with tiny eggs that are grayish in color.

Another version is pressed caviar, which is just that: caviar that's been pressed into a condensed form. It's usually made with broken eggs, with five pounds of broken eggs yielding one pound of pressed caviar. Petrossian feels that only pressed caviar should be used to garnish, say, blini or baked potatoes.

In addition to selling caviar through his store in Paris, Petrossian's $40 million-a-year caviar conglomerate includes a wholesale operation, with clients all over the world. He also owns the world's only caviar restaurant, Petrossian's, in New York City. It is also the only restaurant I know of with mink-lined walls.

VEGETABLES

One of the greatest food festivals on earth is the Feast of San Gennaro, which takes place every September in New York's Little Italy. Entire blocks are roped off to make room for hundreds of food booths during the ten-day event. The air is seductive with the aroma of homemade sausage dancing on gigantic griddles, *brasciole* roasting over charcoal, pork ribs turning on spits, *calamari* and *scungili* gurgling in deep-fryers, meatballs as big as baseballs resting in heavily seasoned tomato sauce, and gorgeous red and green peppers frying in olive oil. You can wash down the delights with homemade wine sold at many of the stands.

This unique artichoke recipe is from the festival.

SAUTÉED ARTICHOKE HEARTS

This easy Italian dish can be made with canned artichoke hearts, available in most supermarkets.

2 14-ounce cans artichoke hearts, drained
3 tablespoons fresh lemon juice
5–6 tablespoons olive oil
3 garlic cloves, minced
⅓ cup all-purpose flour
salt and freshly ground black pepper to taste
½ cup chicken broth
½ cup chopped fresh parsley

In a small bowl, toss the artichokes with the lemon juice. Heat the olive oil in a medium-sized skilled and sauté the garlic until golden brown. Remove the garlic with a slotted spoon.

Dust the artichokes in flour and sauté them in the garlic oil until they brown. Season with salt and pepper, then add the chicken broth and cover. Cook over medium heat for 4 to 5 minutes. Transfer to a serving dish, dribble some of the cooking juices over the artichokes, dust with the parsley, and serve immediately.

SERVES 6

WALNUT-DILL GREEN BEANS

Although green vegetables are not nearly as popular in Spain as they are here, I found a version of this recipe in a little restaurant outside Madrid. I think you'll like it.

1 pound fresh green beans, ends trimmed
⅔ cup coarsely chopped scallions (including green tops)
½ cup shelled walnuts
2 tablespoons snipped fresh dill
2 tablespoons chopped fresh parsley
3 tablespoons red wine vinegar
⅓ cup olive oil
salt and freshly ground black pepper to taste

"Great food is like great sex—the more you have, the more you want."

—GAEL GREENE

TRAVELIN' GOURMET TIP:
Sour Stuff

If you submerge a lemon in very hot water about 20 minutes before squeezing it, it will yield more juice (often twice as much!).

Steam the beans over boiling water until they're tender (about 10 minutes). Plunge them in ice-cold water to stop them from cooking further; drain and set aside. Put the scallions, walnuts, dill, parsley, vinegar, and olive oil into a food processor or blender and process until the walnuts are in tiny pieces (if it seems dry, add more oil). Season with salt and pepper, then toss the beans in the dressing; refrigerate at least 1 hour. Serve slightly chilled.

SERVES 4

ZUCCHINI COINS PERSILLÉ

A recipe from my friend Byron Bardy.

PERSILLÉ BREAD CRUMBS:

3 baguettes of stale French bread, or 6 long sandwich rolls
    (about 1 pound total)
½ cup chopped fresh parsley
2 garlic cloves, chopped
1½ teaspoons salt
1 teaspoon freshly ground black pepper

ZUCCHINI:

2–3 small-to-medium zucchini, sliced into ¼-inch rounds
all-purpose flour, seasoned with salt and black pepper
2 eggs, mixed with 1 cup milk
peanut oil, for greasing

Make the *persillé* bread crumbs a day before using. Finely chop the bread in a food processor. Add the parsley, garlic, salt, and pepper. Refrigerate in a plastic container.

Preheat the oven to 375°. Dust the zucchini in the seasoned flour, dip into the egg mixture, and then in the persillé bread crumbs. Lightly grease a cookie sheet with peanut oil. Place the breaded "coins" on a cookie sheet and bake until golden brown and tender (8 to 10 minutes). Serve immediately.

SERVES 6–8

When a waiter asked to recommend something says, 'Everything's good,' the opposite may be true.
—M.K.

GRILLED SCALLIONS

Next up is something very easy but good. I first had these in an Indian restaurant in London. They were served with Chicken Tandoor (page 112).

2 dozen scallions
4 tablespoons virgin olive oil
salt

Preheat the grill. Trim the scallions so they're approximately 5 to 6 inches long. Brush them with the olive oil and lay them on the grill pan or aluminum foil. Lightly dust them with salt and put them over the fire. Turn them over with tongs (or a fork) when they are lightly browned; brown the other side. Serve immediately.

SERVES 4–6

ZUCCHINI LASAGNE

This is an interesting variation on traditional lasagne. The cheeses listed are mere suggestions; you can substitute your favorites.

¼ pound unsalted butter, cut into thin pats
3–4 large zucchini, thinly sliced
3–4 tomatoes, thinly sliced
½ pound Cheddar cheese, grated
1 cup freshly grated Parmesan cheese
½ pound mozzarella cheese, sliced
Parmesan cheese, for dusting

Preheat the oven to 350°. Line a meat-loaf pan with half the butter pats. Top it with half of the zucchini, half of the tomatoes, and half each of the cheeses. Make another layer with the rest of the zucchini, tomatoes, and cheese. Top with the remaining butter pats. Bake for 40 to 45 minutes. Serve right away, with a dusting of Parmesan.

SERVES 4–6

OFF THE EATEN PATH:
A Dash of History About Salt

Salt once was so valuable that Roman soldiers were paid their wages with it. And they were more than happy to be paid off in salt, which they could not only include in their diets but also use to barter. Thus, the expression a man "worth his salt." In fact, the word salary comes from the Latin sal—for salt.

A great way to keep salt pouring is to put a few grains of rice in the shaker. Salt is not just for cooking, but is useful for cleaning as well. For example, if you happen to break an egg on the floor, rather than trying to blot it with fifty-four paper towels, coat it with salt and let it set for about a half hour. You can then make a clean sweep of things. You can also use salt to eliminate odors in your kitchen drain or garbage disposal. Just moisten the drain, pour about a quarter cup of salt down it, and let it stand until you use the sink again. It also will soak up red wine spills and can put out flames from splattering oil in a broiler pan.

When a recipe calls for garlic and salt, mince the appropriate amount of garlic on a cutting board sprinkled with the amount of salt that the recipe calls for. This achieves more than killing two birds with the proverbial one stone. The salt helps to draw more juice out of the garlic as well as cutting down garlic odor on the cutting board.

ZUCCHINI TORTE

A robust vegetable concoction from chef Ann Vercelli, of Geyser Park Winery, which was founded more than a century ago in California's Sonoma Valley.

½ cup cooked white rice
1 pound unpeeled zucchini, grated
¼ cup chopped scallions (green tops included)
½ cup grated Cheddar cheese
1 tablespoon freshly minced parsley
2 eggs, well beaten
¼ teaspoon garlic salt
½ teaspoon salt
sweet paprika

Preheat the oven to 350°. Combine all of the ingredients except the paprika in a 9 x 12-inch ovenproof pan. Bake until a toothpick inserted in the center comes out clean (45 to 55 minutes). Dust with the paprika, cut into 3-inch squares, and serve immediately.

SERVES 12

ROAST ONIONS

Some of the Roman recipes are unbelievably simple — like this one for roast onions from Caminetto, in the American quarter in Rome. Be liberal with the olive oil, and use the finest you can get your hands on.

4 large onions
olive oil
salt and freshly ground black pepper to taste

Preheat the oven to 450°. Boil the onions for 5 to 6 minutes, then drain, cool, and peel. Cut each onion in half horizontally; cut the rounded ends off evenly so each onion stands evenly. Cover the bottom of a baking dish with olive oil. Place the onions, cut-side up, on top of the oil. Dribble olive oil over each onion and sprinkle with salt and pepper to taste. Bake until the onions are nicely browned (about 50 to 60 minutes) and serve immediately.

SERVES 4

The famous Four Seasons Restaurant in New York City has been enchanting diners with wonderful food and a grand atmosphere since its auspicious debut in 1959. The next recipe is based on one of its lesser-known dishes. Fennel, an interesting and aromatic vegetable, is not nearly as popular in the United States as it is in Europe, particularly in Italy, where this recipe had its roots. At the Four Seasons, they don't use the powdered cumin, but I think it adds a delightful touch to the dish.

BAKED FENNEL PARMESAN

3 large heads fennel
2 cups milk
1 medium onion, sliced
2 quarts water
salt and freshly ground black pepper to taste
¾ cup Parmesan cheese
1 tablespoon unsalted butter
2 tablespoons unseasoned bread crumbs (freshly made, if possible)
1½ teaspoons powdered cumin
olive oil

Trim the leaves and the root end of the fennel and clean. In a large pot, make a stock by combining the milk, onion, and water and slowly bringing the mixture to a boil. Add the fennel, making sure it is covered with the stock; if not, add enough water to cover. Simmer for 45 minutes, or until the fennel is tender. Remove from the heat and drain all but ¼ cup of the cooking liquid.

Preheat the oven to 425°. Cut each bulb in half vertically and season with salt and pepper. In a buttered baking dish, arrange the six pieces in an overlapping pattern. Dot the fennel with Parmesan cheese mixed with the butter. Scatter the bread crumbs all over, then pour the reserved cooking liquid around the edges of the dish. Sprinkle ¼ teaspoon of cumin over each half and bake until they brown (about 5 minutes). Drizzle olive oil over the fennel and serve immediately.

SERVES 6

OFF THE EATEN PATH:
Paprika

Although it is most often associated with Hungary, paprika hails from the West Indies. It was introduced to Europe by none other than Christopher Columbus, who brought it to Spain after his fabled spice expedition, which resulted in the discovery of America. Today, the best paprika comes from Hungary, where it is available in three types: *edes* (mild), *feledes* (pungent), and *eros* (very hot). Incidentally, there is a significant amount of vitamin C in paprika. Research leading to that conclusion resulted in the award of a Nobel Prize in 1937 to Dr. Albert Szent-Gyorgi, a professor at a university in Szeged, where most Hungarian paprika is produced.

This is one of the most famous French potato dishes, taking its name from Anna Deslions, a noted French actress in the nineteenth century. The dish made its debut about a century ago at the fabled Le Café Anglais, more or less the Spago of Paris in its day. Incidentally, it was considered the ultimate in gastronomic chic in Paris at the time to create dishes in honor of actors and playwrights. About the same time that Pommes Anna was created, Lobster Thermidor was unveiled in honor of Sardou's play *Thermidor*.

The trick to making good Pommes Anna is that the potatoes have as much starch as possible, so don't wash them. After you peel them, simply wipe them with a damp cloth or paper towels before slicing them (I use the thinnest blade on my food processor). The sooner you use the potatoes once you slice them, the better.

"Cooking is a way of giving and making yourself more desirable."

—MICHEL BOURDIN

POMMES ANNA

½ cup clarified unsalted butter (see page 38)
2 pounds peeled potatoes, thinly sliced
freshly ground black pepper
⅜ teaspoon freshly ground black pepper
¾ teaspoon salt

Preheat oven to 425°. Heat half of the butter in a small oven-proof skillet over medium heat until it begins to bubble. Layer 2 cups of the potatoes atop the butter in an overlapping spiral pattern. Dribble 1 to 2 tablespoons of the butter over the potatoes; season with ⅛ teaspoon of pepper and ¼ teaspoon of salt.

Repeat the procedure, making more layers until the potatoes fill the pan. Cover the top with a triple thickness of aluminum foil. Put a heavy pan on top of the aluminum foil and press down hard. With the pan on top, cook over moderate to high heat for 12 to 15 minutes.

Remove the pan and the foil from the top; bake, uncovered, until the potatoes are nicely browned on the top and crisp (35 to 45 minutes). Invert on a platter and serve immediately.

SERVES 6–8

VARIATION: An interesting variation is to cover each layer of potatoes with a thin layer of Swiss cheese slices.

GRATIN DAUPHINOIS

This recipe is from George Perrier, whose Le Bec-Fin Restaurant is one of Philadelphia's finest.

1 garlic clove, peeled and halved
1 teaspoon unsalted butter
6 medium-sized potatoes, peeled and thinly sliced (about 1/8-inch thick)
salt and freshly ground black pepper
1 1/8 cups heavy cream
1/2 cup milk

Preheat the oven to 350°. Rub the bottom and sides of a baking pan with the garlic clove until most of the halves are used up; butter the pan. Season the potato slices with salt and pepper, then layer them in the baking dish, making 3 to 4 layers. Blend together the cream and milk and pour over the potatoes. Put the pan into a larger pan and add enough water to come to about an inch from the top of the smaller pan;* bake until the potatoes are tender and golden (about 2 to 2 1/2 hours) and serve immediately.

SERVES 4–6

SWEET POTATO PATTIES

A Pennsylvania Dutch recipe. Surprisingly, this dish works well with elegant entrées.

2 cups cooked, mashed sweet potatoes
1/2 cup brown sugar
1/2 cup cracker crumbs
1 teaspoon salt
cracker crumbs for coating
3–4 tablespoons unsalted butter

Mix together the potatoes, sugar, cracker crumbs, and salt and shape into balls. Roll in cracker crumbs, shape into patties, and sauté in the butter on both sides until well browned. Serve immediately.

SERVES 4

*This is known as a water bath, or bain-marie.

OFF THE EATEN PATH:
Potato Lore

Potatoes were first used as a food in Europe by monks in Spain in the mid-sixteenth century. They didn't become popular until the mid-1700s in France, and then it was thanks, in large part, to the efforts of a chemist named Antoine Parmentier. He convinced Louis XVI that the potato was a great all-around food.

He also inadvertently started a short-lived fashion fad in France. He sent Louis XVI potato flowers on his birthday and the Queen placed the blossoms in her hair. Before you knew it, potato flowers worn in the hair by women or in the lapel by men were considered the ultimate in chic.

> *All's well that ends with a good meal.*
> —ARNOLD LOBEL

> *To eat is human; to digest, divine.*
> —CHARLES COPELAND

TWICE-BAKED POTATOES

I used to think that the "twice-baked potato" was a U.S. phenomenon, but I've found them on the menus of numerous restaurants overseas, including France.

2 large Idaho baking potatoes
2 tablespoons unsalted butter
2½ tablespoons sour cream
2 egg yolks
¼ teaspoon nutmeg
½ tablespoon chopped chives
½ tablespoon chopped fresh parsley
1–2 tablespoons half-and-half
salt and freshly ground black pepper to taste
½ cup freshly grated Parmesan cheese

Preheat the oven to 400°. Wash the potatoes, then pierce the ends of each with the tines of a fork; bake for 1 hour. Remove the potatoes and cool, but leave the oven on.

When the potatoes are cool enough to handle, slice them in half, and without breaking the skin, scoop out the pulp and place it in a small bowl. Vigorously mix in the butter, sour cream, egg yolks, nutmeg, chives, and parsley. Add enough half-and-half to attain a smooth consistency. Season with salt and pepper. Put the mixture back into the shells using a cake bag (or a spoon), dust the tops with Parmesan cheese, and bake until brown on top (10 to 12 minutes). Serve immediately.

SERVES 4

CLAPSHOT

This famous Scottish concoction is often served with haggis, the national dish of Scotland, which poet Robert Burns helped to make famous. Even though I am a promiscuous eater, haggis is not to my taste. Made with a mixture of suet, spices, onions, oatmeal, and the heart and liver of a sheep and boiled in a sheep's stomach, haggis tasted to me as bad as it sounds, sort of a cross between oatmeal and lead. The following dish, however, is quite palatable and goes nicely with robust beef or game dishes. The meat drippings are an important part of the dish, which you might consider the next time you have a roast. In a pinch you can substitute beef broth or stock.

1 pound turnips, peeled, cubed, and cooked
1 pound potatoes, peeled, cubed, and cooked
2–3 tablespoons meat drippings
1 tablespoon chopped chives
salt and freshly ground black pepper to taste

In a large pot, mash the cooked, drained turnips and potatoes together and beat until smooth. Stir in the drippings and chives, and season with salt and pepper. Stir the mixture vigorously over moderate heat until very hot. Serve immediately.

SERVES 6

ALMOND-POTATO CROQUETTES

This recipe is from LeMont Restaurant, which offers commanding views of Pittsburgh's Golden Triangle.

8 medium-sized potatoes, peeled, cubed, and cooked
salt, freshly ground black pepper, and freshly grated Parmesan cheese
4 eggs, separated
flour, for dusting
1½ cups unsalted slivered almonds
oil, for deep-frying

Preheat the oven to 375°. With an electric beater, whip the drained, cooked potatoes until they're very smooth. Season to

I hate people who are not serious about their meals.
—OSCAR WILDE

taste with salt, pepper, and Parmesan cheese. Mix in the egg whites and allow the mixture to cool.

Beat the egg yolks and set aside. Use a 4-ounce ice cream scoop to scoop out potato, then roll each ball gently between the palms of your hands so that it becomes elongated. Dip each ball first into the flour, then into the beaten yolks, and finally into the almonds. Heat the oil in a deep-fryer to 365–375° and deep-fry the croquettes until almost done; drain, then bake in the oven until golden brown (5 to 10 minutes). Serve immediately.

SERVES 4–6

DANISH POTATO PUFFS

In Denmark this dish in known as *kartoffelboller*. It goes well with dishes with sweet sauces, including pork and duck, or makes a nice party snack. It can also be made with sweet potatoes.

2 pounds potatoes, peeled, cooked, and mashed
salt to taste
1 cup all-purpose flour
1 cup brown sugar
⅓ cup sesame seeds
oil, for deep-frying

Season the cooked, drained potatoes with salt in a large bowl. Add the flour and mix thoroughly with a wooden spoon until the mixture resembles bread dough. Dust your hands with flour and shape the mixture into little balls about an inch in diameter. Partially flatten the balls and put a teaspoon of brown sugar on top of each; reshape each into a ball, then roll in the sesame seeds. Heat the oil in a deep-fryer to 365–375° and deep-fry the puffs until they turn dark brown (3 to 5 minutes). Drain and serve immediately.

SERVES 8–12

TRAVELIN' GOURMET TIP:
A Bag of Tricks

If you don't have a cake bag, you can fashion one out of a Ziploc bag. All you do is put the filling inside the plastic bag, "zip" the top shut, and cut a hole in one bottom end and you're ready to start piping! When you're finished, there's no cleanup—just throw the bag away.

ELIZABETH POTATOES

The combination of potatoes and spinach is rather unorthodox, but it works! The recipe was invented on the old *Queen
Elizabeth*, one of the great ocean liners of yore.

1½ pounds potatoes, peeled, cubed, and cooked
¼ pound spinach, chopped and cooked
½ pint whole milk
½ stick (4 tablespoons) unsalted butter
⅛ teaspoon salt
½ cup sifted flour
3 eggs, lightly beaten for dredging
salt, freshly ground black pepper, and nutmeg to taste
flour and unseasoned bread crumbs, for dredging
oil, for deep-frying

In a large bowl, mash the potatoes. Remove as much moisture
as possible from the cooked spinach, then blend in with the
potatoes; set aside. Put the milk, butter, and salt in a saucepan
and bring to a boil. Stir in the flour with a wooden spoon over
the same heat until it forms a smooth paste.

Remove from the heat and beat in 2 of the eggs, one at a
time, then mix thoroughly with the potato-spinach mixture. Season
to taste with salt, pepper, and nutmeg. Shape the mixture into
croquettes, then dip each into flour, the remaining egg, and bread
crumbs; deep-fry at 365–375° until golden brown. Drain and serve
immediately.

SERVES 6

CURRIED EGGPLANT

This Haitian dish gives a new dimension to eggplant. It's a
real surprise!

7 tablespoons yellow cornmeal
½ teaspoon salt
1 teaspoon curry powder
1½ teaspoons crushed red pepper flakes
1 eggplant (4–5 ounces), peeled and cubed
2 egg whites, lightly beaten
salt
oil, for deep-frying

Mix together the cornmeal, salt, curry powder, and red pepper flakes. Dip the eggplant slices into the egg whites, then roll into the cornmeal mixture. Heat the oil in a deep-fryer to 375–385° and deep-fry the eggplant until it's golden brown (1 to 2 minutes). Drain on paper towels, dust with salt, and serve immediately.

SERVES 4–6

PECAN-CAULIFLOWER CASSEROLE

The pecans add a delightful crunch to the proceedings in this dish which I first enjoyed in a pub in Dublin that was not too far from the jewel of a hotel I was based in, the Shelbourne.

½ teaspoon salt
1 cup water
1¾–2 pounds cauliflower, broken into flowerets
4 ounces Cheddar cheese
1 cup sour cream
1 tablespoon all-purpose flour
2 teaspoons chicken broth
1 teaspoon dry mustard
½ cup chopped pecans
¼ cup seasoned bread crumbs
1 tablespoon unsalted butter, melted
1 teaspoon dried marjoram
½ teaspoon minced garlic

Mix the salt and water in a Dutch oven and bring to a boil over high heat. Add the cauliflower and continue cooking on high until the water returns to a boil. Lower the heat and simmer until the cauliflower is tender (12 to 15 minutes). Drain in a colander, then place in a baking dish.

Preheat the oven to 400°. Mix together the Cheddar cheese, sour cream, flour, chicken broth, and dry mustard and pour over the cauliflower. Toss the pecans with the bread crumbs, butter, marjoram, and garlic and sprinkle on the cauliflower. Bake in the center of the oven until the casserole starts to bubble (12 to 15 minutes). Let rest for 5 minutes, then serve.

SERVES 6

OFF THE EATEN PATH:

Marjoram

Marjoram, a close relative of oregano, is a member of the mint family. Historically, the herb has been associated with good things. Brides in England often put marjoram into their wedding wreaths.

Leeks, which look like scallions on steroids, are quite common in Europe, where they're often referred to as "the poor man's asparagus." The leek is wildly popular in Wales, where it is the national vegetable. On March 1 of every year, the Welsh wear leek leaves in their hatbands or on their lapels. The national affinity for this vegetable stems back to the days when Welshmen embroiled in battle for their country distinguished themselves from the enemy by wearing leeks in their helmets.

Leeks are among the mildest and sweetest members of the onion family, and are available in many U.S. supermarkets year-round. Select leeks that have crisp, bright-green tops and unblemished bulbs that are approximately 1½ but not more than 2 inches in diameter (fatter bulbs may have a tough inner core). To prepare a leek for cooking, trim off the green tops about 2 inches from the white base. Carefully slice the leek lengthwise to about an inch from the end. Hold the leek under rapidly running water and fan out the sections so you can clean out the dirt and sand. (By the way, if you don't plan to use them right away, store them in a plastic bag in your refrigerator's vegetable crisper, where they'll usually keep for a week or so, depending on the condition they were in when you bought them. Don't wash or trim them until you're ready to use them.)

In Wales, real men *do* eat quiche, providing it's made with leeks. I've never been much of a quiche fan, but this rendition changed my mind.

LEEK QUICHE

3 tablespoons unsalted butter
1½ pounds leeks (white part only), cleaned and cut into small
    rounds (see page 182)
⅔ cup whipping cream
3 large egg yolks
salt, white pepper, and freshly grated nutmeg to taste
9-inch pie shell, unbaked

Preheat the oven to 400°. Over low heat, melt the butter, add the leeks, and simmer until tender, turning several times; remove

TRAVELIN' GOURMET TIP:
"Revive" Vegetables

If your vegetables look tired and are on the withered side, you can breathe new life into them by letting them stand in cold salted water for an hour before using.

from the heat. Whisk the cream and the egg yolks together, seasoning to taste with salt, white pepper, and nutmeg. Add to the leeks and mix thoroughly. Pour the mixture into the pie shell and bake until the quiche sets (30 to 40 minutes). Let rest for about 5 minutes before serving.

SERVES 4–6

LEEKS AU GRATIN

This is one way the French prepare leeks. By the way, *au gratin* means "cooked brown."

8 leeks, tops and bottoms trimmed, split lengthwise, cleaned
    and cut into 3-inch pieces (see page 182)
garlic salt
1 cup plain bread crumbs
3 tablespoons unsalted butter
1 tablespoon olive oil
1 tablespoon all-purpose flour
2 tablespoons unsalted butter, melted
1 cup half-and-half
salt and freshly ground black pepper
unseasoned bread crumbs, for topping
¼ cup grated Swiss cheese
4 teaspoons cognac or brandy

Simmer leeks in lightly salted water until they're tender (about 10 to 12 minutes). Drain, pat dry with paper towels, and place in a buttered 2-quart casserole lightly sprinkled with garlic salt.

Preheat the oven to 400°. Brown the bread crumbs in the butter and oil. Stir the flour into the bread crumb mixture, then whisk in the half-and-half; season with salt and pepper to taste. Cook over medium heat for 3 to 4 minutes to reduce, stirring occasionally, then pour over the leeks. Dust the top with the additional bread crumbs and the cheese and cognac or brandy Bake for 12 to 15 minutes. Serve immediately.

SERVES 4–6

"A good eater must be a good man; for a good eater must have a good digestion, and a good digestion depends upon a good conscience."
—BENJAMIN DISRAELI

VEGETABLE CASSEROLE WITH DIJON MUSTARD

The Dijon region of France is world-renowned for having the finest mustard seeds. Dijon mustard has become very popular in the United States, but I have rarely found it in recipes for vegetables, with this notable exception from Joe Parrotto, co-director of the International Culinary Academy, Pittsburgh.

2 cups broccoli flowerets
2 cups cauliflower flowerets
2 cups onions, sliced
1 cup grated Cheddar cheese
1 cup mayonnaise
4 tablespoons Dijon mustard
½ teaspoon salt
½ teaspoon freshly ground black pepper
3 garlic cloves, minced
2 teaspoons freshly minced parsley

Steam the broccoli, cauliflower, and onions separately. In a 2-quart buttered casserole dish, make two layers with the vegetables and two with the cheese, alternating. Preheat the oven to 350°. In a small bowl, blend the mayonnaise, mustard, salt, pepper, garlic, and parsley and spread it on the vegetable-cheese mixture. Bake for 20 minutes. Serve immediately.

SERVES 6

ASPARAGUS TART

10 asparagus spears, steamed
½ pound frozen puff pastry (1 sheet), thawed
unsalted butter, for greasing
2 eggs
freshly grated nutmeg
2 pinches salt
pinch pepper
1 cup heavy cream
1 tablespoon chopped fresh parsley

“There is no spectacle on earth more appealing than that of a woman in the act of cooking dinner for someone she loves.”
—THOMAS WOLFE

Preheat the oven to 375°. Cut off the tips of the asparagus and slice each tip in half vertically. Cut the asparagus stalks into 1-inch pieces. Discard the tough bottom ends. Lightly butter an 8-inch tart pan with scalloped edges. Roll out the pastry to a shape slightly larger than the pan. With your hand, fit the pastry into the pan, filling in all the scalloped indentations, and cut the pastry edges by rolling a rolling pin over the top of the pan. Prick the pastry with a fork.

Beat the eggs in a bowl with the nutmeg, salt, and pepper, then beat in the cream and parsley. Cover the pastry with the cut asparagus stalks. Pour the egg and cream mixture over the asparagus stalks, then arrange the asparagus tips like the spokes of a wheel on top. Place the tart on a cookie sheet and bake for 20 minutes. Let rest for 5 minutes, then serve.

SERVES 6

ASPARAGUS WITH ASIAN SAUCE

This is a delicious departure from asparagus with hollandaise sauce or lemon-butter. It's even better if you make the sauce a day ahead.

2 garlic cloves, minced
¾ teaspoon minced fresh ginger
pinch salt
3–4 tablespoons soy sauce
½ teaspoon sugar
½ teaspoon sesame oil
1 tablespoon white wine vinegar
⅛ teaspoon freshly ground black pepper
4 teaspoons chopped scallions (white parts only)
1 pound asparagus, steamed

In a small bowl, mix together the garlic, ginger, and salt. Add the soy sauce, sugar, sesame oil, vinegar, pepper, and scallions, and mix vigorously. Pour over the steamed asparagus or serve on the side in small bowls.

SERVES 4

TRAVELIN' GOURMET TIP:
Nothing Like a Good Pot of Asparagus!

I've found that the electric coffee percolator works nicely as an asparagus cooker. Make sure it's clean, then fill it partially with water, add the asparagus upright leaving the tips exposed, plug it in, put on the lid, and let the machine go to work. In about 15 minutes or so the asparagus will be ready.

SWEET POTATO SOUFFLÉ

They enjoy this dish during the holidays in many cities in the Deep South. As the degree of sweetness of the potatoes varies considerably, the sugar should be added to taste. I have given approximate guidelines.

2 pounds sweet potatoes, washed
1/3 cup regular cream
3–5 tablespoons granulated sugar
4 1/2 tablespoons unsalted butter
2 eggs, lightly beaten
1/4 teaspoon cinnamon

Preheat the oven to 350°. Cook the potatoes in boiling, lightly salted water until soft (about 1 hour). Drain, peel, place in a large bowl, and mash. Mix in the cream, sugar (to taste), butter, eggs, and cinnamon. Transfer to a buttered, 1-quart baking dish and bake until it sets (35 to 45 minutes). Let rest for a few minutes, then serve.

SERVES 4–6

RISI E BISI (PEAS AND RICE)

This is a traditional Italian dish that, simple as it seems, was once served at banquets in Venice.

2 tablespoons chopped onion
3 1/2 tablespoons olive oil
1 garlic clove, minced
1 cup uncooked rice
2 cups chicken stock
salt and freshly ground black pepper to taste
1/2 cup cooked ham, diced
1 cup cooked peas
1/2 cup pimientos, finely diced

Preheat oven to 350°. In a medium-sized, ovenproof saucepan, sauté the onion in the olive oil over medium heat until light golden

A true gastronome should always be ready to eat, as a soldier should always be ready to fight.
—CHARLES MONSELET

in color. Add the garlic and sauté 1 to 2 minutes. Stir in the rice and sauté until the rice is light brown in color (3 to 4 minutes).

Stir in the chicken stock, season with salt and pepper, and slowly bring to a boil. Let it boil for 2 minutes, then cover and bake in the oven until most of the remaining liquid has almost all been absorbed (5 to 10 minutes). Remove from the oven and stir in the ham, peas, and pimientos; re-cover, return to the oven, and cook until the last 3 ingredients are heated through (3 to 5 minutes). Serve immediately.

SERVES 6

THARKARI (MIXED VEGETABLES)

The recipe for this pastiche of vegetables is from India.

2 teaspoons vegetable oil
1/2 teaspoon mustard seeds
1 medium onion, chopped
1/2 teaspoon cayenne pepper
1/8 teaspoon freshly ground black pepper
1 teaspoon salt
1/2 teaspoon fresh ginger, chopped
1/2 cup carrots, diced
1/2 cup frozen peas, thawed
1/2 cup frozen lima beans, thawed
3/4 cup water
1 tablespoon fresh mint leaves, minced
1 1/2 teaspoons fresh lemon juice

In a medium skillet over moderate-high heat, heat the oil; add the mustard seeds and cover (the seeds will start to pop). When the seeds are all popped, lower the heat to medium and add the onion; sauté for 3 to 4 minutes. Stir in the cayenne, black pepper, salt, and ginger.

Add the carrots, peas, and lima beans and mix well. Add the water, cover, and cook on medium for 10 to 12 minutes. Remove from the heat and stir in the mint leaves and lemon juice. Serve immediately.

SERVES 4–6

SAUTÉED CABBAGE

A lot of my neighbors are Eastern European. This is one way they prepare cabbage. They don't use a wok, but I think it's easier if you do.

½ cup unsalted butter
¾ pound cabbage, thinly sliced
⅛ teaspoon salt
¼ teaspoon freshly ground black pepper
5–6 strips bacon, fried and crumbled

Heat the butter in the wok until very hot; add the cabbage and stir-fry until *al dente* (3 to 5 minutes). Add the salt, pepper, and bacon and toss well. Serve immediately.

SERVES 4–6

SPINACH WITH PEANUTS AND COCONUT MILK

The original recipe for this soul-food dish called for a grating of fresh coconut. However, the fact that many Asian grocers now carry canned coconut milk makes this delicious dish a lot easier.

1 large onion, chopped
1½ teaspoons chili powder
1 tablespoon olive oil
1 cup unsweetened coconut milk
½ cup unsalted peanuts, coarsely chopped
¾ pound fresh spinach, chopped
salt and freshly ground black pepper to taste

In a medium skillet, sauté the onion and chili powder in the olive oil until the onion is transparent. Over medium-high heat, stir in the coconut milk and peanuts and bring to a boil. Add the spinach; season with salt and pepper. Lower the heat and simmer until spinach is cooked (12 to 15 minutes). Serve immediately.

SERVES 4–6

"Some of the best meals come out of the smallest kitchens.**"**
—M.K.

SHERRY-SAUTÉED MUSHROOMS

This is one of the many ways that the French prepare mushrooms.

3½ tablespoons unsalted butter
1 pound mushrooms, cleaned and sliced
salt and freshly ground black pepper to taste
½ cup sherry

Melt the butter in a medium skillet; add the mushrooms and season with salt and pepper. Sauté over medium heat for 3 to 4 minutes, then pour the sherry over the mushrooms. Raise the heat slightly and cook for 2 to 3 more minutes. Serve immediately.

SERVES 4–6

SQUASH TART

This makes not only an interesting side dish but a great first course. The recipe is based on one from Harrod's in London.

2 cups acorn squash puree (fresh, frozen, or canned)
2 eggs
1 cup ricotta cheese, drained
⅓ cup freshly grated Parmesan cheese
1½ teaspoons dried thyme
¼ cup minced onion
9-inch deep dish pie shell, baked
1 small acorn squash, peeled and seeded

Preheat the oven to 350°. In a medium bowl, beat together the squash puree, eggs, ricotta, Parmesan, thyme, and onion; transfer into the pie shell. Slice the squash into paper-thin half-moon shapes and arrange in an overlapping pattern on top. Bake for 30 to 35 minutes. Let rest for 5 minutes before serving.

SERVES 4

GRILLED MARINATED VEGETABLES

This delightful vegetable recipe is from Chef Stefano Battistini of the Sea Grill Restaurant in New York's Rockefeller Plaza.

MARINADE:

1 cup olive oil
2 tablespoons Balsamic vinegar
1 garlic clove, minced
¼ cup chopped onions
½ teaspoon thyme
1 sprig rosemary
1 teaspoon kosher salt
½ teaspoon coarsely cracked black pepper

VEGETABLES:

3 zucchini, cut into ⅜-inch thick diagonal slices
3 yellow squash, cut into ⅜-inch-thick diagonal slices
12 shiitake mushrooms, caps only
2 carrots, scraped and thinly sliced lengthwise
2 tomatoes, sliced

Mix all of the marinade ingredients together in a medium bowl and let stand for at least 1 hour before using.

Grill the vegetables until they're slightly softened but still crisp (5 to 10 minutes). Remove from the grill and place them in the marinade for 10 to 15 minutes, keeping them warm, then serve immediately.

SERVES 6–8

INDONESIAN CORN FRITTERS

Amsterdam is where I learned to love Indonesian dishes like these fritters, which have even more spark than those I sampled on my excursions through the U.S. South.

17-ounce can corn, drained
2 garlic cloves, minced
3 large eggs
6 scallions (including green tops), minced
¼ teaspoon each salt and freshly ground black pepper
vegetable oil

Mix the first five ingredients thoroughly and shape by the teaspoonful into little balls. In a medium-sized skillet, heat about an inch of vegetable oil to high (365–375°); drop the balls, a few at a time, into the oil and fry until golden brown (3 to 4 minutes). Drain on paper towels and serve immediately.

SERVES 8

A LA CARTE:
A Taste of Paris' Oldest Restaurant

One thing you instantly get from a trip to Europe is a sense of the past, not only in the museums and architecture, but also in the restaurants. Imagine a restaurant so old that it was where the fork made its first dining-out appearance. Prior to the introduction of that great complement to the dining experience, one ate with the fingers or with knives.

Civility in dining got its start at Paris's oldest restaurant, La Tour d'Argent, on the top floor of an ancient building on the Left Bank in one of the most gorgeous settings on earth: Paris is at your feet, the waters of the Seine ripple tantalizingly below, and looming in the distance like a giant jewel is the fabled cathedral of Notre Dame.

The way owner Claude Terrail tells it, the fork was introduced at his restaurant on March 4, 1582, when King Henry III, dining at La Tour, noticed three Italian tourists using a fork instead of their fingers. The unusual-looking device, which was invented in Italy, immediately caught his fancy and the owner saw to it that forks became a fixture of La Tour.

La Tour also was where covered dishes were first introduced to the world, but not, at first, to keep food warm. Said Terrail: "Catherine de Medici, who was a regular here, was terribly frightened that someone would poison her food. So it was always delivered under a cloche."

One of my favorite tales of La Tour is the story about a grand larceny orchestrated by one of the world's richest men, industrialist J. P. Morgan, who had several cohorts snatch a prized bottle of 1788 Napoleon cognac from the restaurant's esteemed *cave.* As Terrail tells it:

"Not a month would go by without some enlightened nabob or wealthy collector offering a fortune for that bottle. The most relentless was Morgan, who returned ten times, each time bettering the offer and signing blank checks. Ten times my father refused. It became almost like a game. André Terrail was more stubborn, but Pierpont Morgan, it turned out, was the slyer. One fine day, three clients of innocuous appearance, whom Morgan had bribed, made off with the coveted prize. In its place they left a letter of apology and a blank check, which André cleverly sent back. But J. P. Morgan never returned the bottle."

Although La Tour's cellar may be missing that precious bottle of cognac, there are some 250,000 other bottles of wines and cognacs in one of the best collections in Paris, if not the world.

"Whenever I get some extra money, I spend it on wine," Terrail told me. He not only prides himself on the vastness of his collection but also on his cellar which, he told me, "is the most technically perfect cellar in Paris." It also is one of the most expensive. As French food critic Christian

Millau put it: "The wine tabs [at La Tour] fly higher than the angels. . . ."

The restaurant's specialty is duck. Raised on a farm in Challans, the ducks, which have a genealogy dating back to Philip IV of Spain, are sacrificed for gastronomy at the age of six weeks, when they've grown to about five pounds. They meet their maker by being smothered to prevent loss of blood, which is used in the sauce.

At one time, La Tour featured fourteen different renditions of duck, including the classic, *canard pressé*. That number has since been trimmed to four. What hasn't changed is the tradition started by owner/chef Frederic Delair in 1890 of numbering each duck. On my last visit, I consumed #664,121, as indicated on a postcard presented to me at table.

The duck is roasted to a rare condition, then its carcass is put into a silver press; a captain slowly turns the screw to extract the blood, euphemistically called the "juice." After the blood is captured in a silver container; it's used to create a sensational sauce in which the underdone meat of the duck is cooked. (The sauce is enhanced with 3 tablespoons of Madeira, 4 tablespoons of cognac, and the juice of half a lemon.)

Terrail not only is the owner of one of the world's greatest restaurants, which he operates like a diplomat, he also has a reputation of being a *bon vivant* of the highest order. He used to live with Ava Gardner in the '50s (after "she left the *singer*," his reference to Francis Albert Sinatra). Through the years he has been a favorite of Parisian *paparazzi*, who have photographed him squiring countless beauties around Paris, including Marilyn Monroe and Jayne Mansfield. And he once was married to the daughter of the late movie mogul Jack Warner. Now in his seventies, however, he is finally settling down.

"Today, the restaurant is my mistress," he noted with a smile.

DESSERTS

Parisians are so passionate about chocolate that it helps to usher in practically every holiday of the year. Even on April Fool's Day, or *Poisson d'Avril*, the city's candy shops jump with large chocolate fish chasing schools of milk-chocolate minnows and sardines. Chocolate flowers symbolize the advent of Mother's Day, and, as in the United States, chocolate hearts are the edible icons for Valentine's Day and chocolate bunnies for Easter. The first day of May is symbolized by chocolate lilies of the valley.

When summertime approaches, the windows of the city's chocolate shops burst with every symbol of the season imaginable — from miniature chocolate beach umbrellas to milk-chocolate representations of beaming Mr. Suns. Fall is the season for chocolate truffles, sweet representations of the pricey subterranean fungi revered by master chefs for their uncanny ability to bring a touch of gastronomic magic to their dishes. The popularity of chocolate truffles spread to the United States in the 1980s, and they've since become not just a seasonal treat but are enjoyed year-round. Christmas is symbolized in chocolate by *bûche de Noël*, a cake richer than Donald

Trump used to be. It's fashioned in the shape of a log to represent the days when it was a fashion for Christmas guests to offer a log to keep the home fire burning, as it were.

Chocolate desserts are also wildly popular in Parisian restaurants. One of my favorites is the Chocolate Marquise offered at Taillevent, which many critics consider the finest restaurant in Paris. Opened in 1946, the restaurant's name pays tribute to a fabled chef to French royalty in the fourteenth century, who invented the miniature cream puffs called *profiteroles*.

I have Americanized the dessert a bit with the addition of a butterscotch sauce, which lives up to its name (it's actually laced with Scotch). I think it works better with the marquise than the pistachio sauce they serve at Taillevent. It's also a lot easier to make. If you'd rather, you can serve it with raspberry or strawberry puree — or simply a dollop of whipped cream. It also can stand alone.

TAILLEVENT CHOCOLATE MARQUISE WITH BUTTERSCOTCH SAUCE

½ pound semisweet baking chocolate
⅔ cup confectioners' sugar
¾ cup unsalted butter, softened and cubed (1½ sticks)
5 egg yolks, at room temperature
pinch salt
5 egg whites, at room temperature
Butterscotch Sauce (page 197; optional)

Melt the chocolate in the top of a double boiler. Add the sugar and mix thoroughly until well incorporated. Beat in the butter a little at a time. Stir in the egg yolks, one at a time. Add a pinch of salt to the egg whites and beat until stiff. Remove the chocolate from the heat and slowly fold in the egg whites, about a third at a time. Rinse a loaf pan (approximately 10 x 5 x 2½ inches) with very cold water and fill it with the chocolate mixture; chill overnight.

To serve, run a knife along the edges, then loosen the cake from the pan by putting the bottom in hot water for about 30 seconds. Put a platter on top, invert the pan, and nudge the cake out carefully onto the platter. Serve it in slices, about ½ inch thick, atop Butterscotch Sauce, or the sauce of your choice.

SERVES ABOUT 12 NORMAL PEOPLE—OR 4 CHOCAHOLICS

Butterscotch Sauce

This sauce also is great on ice cream.

½ cup brown sugar, softened
6 tablespoons light corn syrup
3 tablespoons unsalted butter
2 tablespoons water
2 tablespoons heavy cream
1 teaspoon Scotch

Bring the sugar, corn syrup, butter, and water slowly to a boil in a heavy saucepan. Let boil for 1 minute. Remove from the heat and cool slightly. Slowly add the cream and stir until smooth. Stir in the Scotch. Cool to room temperature and serve underneath servings of the marquise.

MAKES A LITTLE OVER 1 CUP OF SAUCE

OFF THE EATEN PATH:
How Sweet It Is!

Chocolate originated in Mexico; in fact, the word comes from the Indian word *xocolatl*, or "bitter water." It was introduced to France by the Spaniards in the seventeenth century and was first popular as a beverage. The first commercially produced candy bar in the United States was the Hershey Bar, manufactured in 1894 by Milton S. Hershey in Lancaster, Pa.

ITALIAN CHEESECAKE

The cheesecake has been around since the halcyon days of ancient Rome. This recipe from Italy is light, delicious, and easy to make. If you like a more traditional cheesecake try the recipe on the facing page.

1½ pounds ricotta cheese
1 pound cream cheese, softened
1½ cups granulated sugar
6 eggs
6 tablespoons all-purpose flour
1 pint sour cream
1 tablespoon vanilla extract
1 tablespoon lemon juice

Preheat the oven to 325°. Put the ricotta and cream cheese into a large bowl and beat until smooth. Add the sugar and the eggs, one at a time, beating well after each. Add the remaining ingredients and mix well. Pour into a greased and lightly floured 9-inch springform pan; bake for 1 hour. Turn off the heat, but leave the cake in the oven for an additional 2 hours. Remove from the oven and refrigerate. Serve cold.

SERVES 6–8

BANANAS FOSTER

This renowned dessert was invented at Brennan's Restaurant in New Orleans back in the early 1950s. I like this variation better than the original.

2 tablespoons unsalted butter
3 ripe bananas, quartered
1 teaspoon ground cinnamon
¼ cup brown sugar
2 tablespoons banana liqueur
2 tablespoons brandy
4 scoops each vanilla and chocolate ice cream

In a medium-sized skillet, melt the butter and sauté the bananas until they're soft (don't overcook or they'll become mushy).

OFF THE EATEN PATH:
Ricotta Vita

Ricotta is more or less the Italian version of cottage cheese, except it's smoother and made with whole milk rather than skim. Ricotta, which means "recooked," is made with whey that comes from the manufacture of other cheeses. Incidentally, once upon a time an entrepreneur thought the Italians would take to American cottage cheese since they were so in love with its "relative," ricotta. Wrong. It was practically an instant bomb. Market analysts said the Italians apparently didn't like the lumpier texture of cottage cheese. So a possible cottage industry was spiked from the start.

Sprinkle the cinnamon and brown sugar over the bananas and turn to coat them with the sugar mixture. Add the liqueur and brandy (if the dish flames up, let the alcohol burn off). Take the ice cream scoops from the freezer and place a scoop of each flavor in 4 dishes, top with the hot bananas and some of the sauce, and serve immediately.

SERVES 4

SMILE AND SAY CHEESECAKE

My favorite cheesecake recipe. It is reminiscent of the famous cheesecake that was served at the old Lindy's Restaurant in New York City.

CRUST:

1 cup finely chopped blanched almonds
2 tablespoons granulated sugar
2 tablespoons unsalted butter, softened

CHEESECAKE:

2½ pounds cream cheese, softened
1½ cups granulated sugar
3 tablespoons all-purpose flour
zest from ½ lemon and ½ orange
5 large eggs
2 egg yolks
½ teaspoon vanilla
½ cup heavy cream
⅓ cup confectioners' sugar for dusting

Preheat the oven to 400°. In a small mixing bowl, blend all of the crust ingredients thoroughly and press into a well-greased 9- to 10-inch springform pan. Bake until the crust turns golden in color (5 to 6 minutes). Cool.

Raise the oven to 500°.

Use an electric mixer to blend the cream cheese, sugar, flour, and zest. Add the eggs and yolks, one at a time, then the vanilla; mix thoroughly. Add the heavy cream and mix well. Transfer to the springform pan; bake for 12 minutes; reduce heat to 200° and bake 1 hour more. Remove from the oven; cool. Dust with confectioners' sugar and serve.

SERVES 12

FRIED MILK

Yes, fried milk—it's a specialty of Spain. This recipe is from Posada de la Villa, in Madrid.

3½ cups milk
1 vanilla bean
5½ tablespoons granulated sugar
1 egg
4½ tablespoons all-purpose flour
4½ tablespoons cornstarch
1 cup all-purpose flour
3 eggs, beaten
2–3 tablespoons vegetable oil, for frying
ground cinnamon and confectioners' sugar, for dusting

In a large pot with a heavy bottom, heat the milk with the vanilla bean just until it starts to boil. Remove from the heat and set aside. In a medium bowl, beat the sugar and 1 egg with a wooden spoon until well blended. Add the 4½ tablespoons flour and the cornstarch; mix well. Remove the vanilla bean from the milk and bring to a boil. Remove from the heat and slowly add the milk to the flour mixture, stirring all the while. Pour the mixture back into the pot and bring to a boil again; stir constantly as you let it boil until it begins to thicken a bit (about 6 to 8 minutes). Watch it carefully so it doesn't burn.

Pour onto a small greased baking dish or metal tray. The mixture should be about ¾ inch deep. Cool in the refrigerator. Cut into 3-inch squares. Put 1 cup flour into a shallow bowl, and the 3 eggs into another. Pass the squares through the remaining flour, shake off the excess, then pass through the beaten eggs; gently fry on both sides in vegetable oil until golden. Place in the middle of a metal dish, sprinkle with cinnamon and confectioners' sugar, and serve warm.

SERVES 4–6

OFF THE EATEN PATH:
The Spice Is Nice!

One of the few naturally sweet spices, cinnamon also is the oldest known. Available in powdered or stick form, cinnamon is used in many of the world's cuisines. It is most popular in Mexico, however, where it turns up in sauces, confections, and drinks. Cinnamon actually is the dried bark of trees. We can thank the Dutch for discovering the spice in Ceylon, where a refined and subtle form of it is found. The stronger version, the kind we use in our cooking, is grown in the East Indies and China.

APPLE STRUDEL

My favorite version of the Bavarian classic.

¾ cup granulated sugar
½ cup toasted walnuts, coarsely chopped
1½ cups toasted almonds
½ cup golden raisins, steeped in white wine for 1 hour
1½ teaspoons ground cinnamon
6 Granny Smith apples, peeled, cored, and coarsely chopped
2 tablespoons lemon juice
½ pound phyllo pastry (about 6–8 sheets)
4 sticks (1 pound) unsalted butter, melted
confectioners' sugar, for dusting

Combine the sugar, walnuts, almonds, raisins, and cinnamon in small bowl and set aside. Put the apples into a large bowl, sprinkle with lemon juice, and toss to mix. Add the nut/raisin mixture to the apples and combine gently. Taste, and add more sugar if the apples are too tart. Refrigerate the mixture as you prepare the pastry.

Preheat the oven to 375°. Stack the phyllo leaves on a slightly damp towel, and fold in half. Keep the leaves in their folded stack; open the first sheet out to full length; brush the exposed portion with melted butter. Open the second sheet to full length and repeat the process. Continue until you reach the final sheet, which you may brush all over with the butter, as it will be totally exposed. Sprinkle the apple/nut mixture on the lower end of the pastry leaves and carefully roll it up into the shape of a log; brush the top with some melted butter and bake on a cookie sheet for 10 minutes. Remove from the oven and pour off the accumulated juices.

Cut the pastry into 1½-inch diagonal slices, and brush again with melted butter. Push the slices together to reshape the log, brush the top with melted butter; return the strudel to the oven and bake until it's crisp and golden brown (30 to 35 minutes), brushing every 10 minutes or so with the remaining butter. Let cool a bit and serve warm, dusted with confectioners' sugar.

SERVES 8–12

One of my favorite pursuits in Paris is cruising for pastries. A regular stop is Poilane, 8 Rue du Cherche-Midi. When you're within a three-block area of it, you can smell the magnificent aromas wafting from the shop operated by Paris's best bread baker, Lionel Poilane, who looks like the French version of Roman Polanski.

The apple tarts made at Poilane's are my favorite; fresh from the oven, they are extraordinary. The buttery crust shatters sensuously as it hits the tongue, making way for the sweet, hot apple slices to bring further joy to the palate.

A tart is actually any pastry filled with fruit, jam, custard, or other ingredients. Fillings don't have to be sweet, either. Leek tarts and onion tarts are quite popular, too, particularly in Europe. A dessert tart differs from a pie in that it has no top crust. In addition to layering tarts creatively with fruit, you also can decorate the outer rim attractively with leftover pastry. For instance, you can make a leaf border by cutting out leaf shapes from pastry, then use the back of a knife to etch in rib lines. Brush each ''leaf'' with cold water and affix it to the rim of the crust.

FRENCH APPLE TART

This recipe was inspired by my visits to Poilane's.

CRUST:

2½ cups all-purpose flour
3 tablespoons granulated sugar
2 sticks (½ pound) unsalted butter, chilled and cubed
2 eggs, beaten
2 teaspoons vanilla extract
3–4 tablespoons cold water

TART:

1 cup apricot preserves
2 tablespoons brandy
2 teaspoons granulated sugar
6–7 Granny Smith apples
½ stick (⅛ pound) unsalted butter, cubed
4 tablespoons granulated sugar
confectioners' sugar, for dusting (optional)

Put the flour into a food processor and pulse a few times; add the sugar. With the motor running, start adding the butter, a little bit at a time, then the eggs and the vanilla extract. Start adding the water, a little at a time, until the dough starts to form a ball. Only add as much water as you need, or it may get too moist (if it does, add a little flour).

Remove the dough from the food processor (be careful not to cut yourself on the blade, which I have done on occasion) and put it on a floured pastry board. Divide in half; tightly wrap half of the dough and freeze for future use. Shape the rest into a ball, then flatten it out on the floured surface. Push the edges out firmly, using the heel of your hand. Reshape it into a ball again and repeat the procedure a few more times. Wrap it in waxed paper or foil and chill in the refrigerator for about 30 minutes.

While it's chilling, push the apricot preserves through a fine sieve into a small saucepan over low heat. Stir in the brandy and the 2 teaspoons sugar until the mixture becomes smooth. Remove from heat.

Roll out the crust onto a floured pastry board in a circle about ⅛ inch thick and large enough to fill a 9- or 10-inch greased tart pan. Place it into the pan and make sure that it is tight on the bottom and the sides. Chill for another 30 minutes.

Preheat the oven to 400°. Prick the bottom of the crust with the tines of a fork. Layer the crust with aluminum foil and top with pie weights, which can be bought in gourmet stores (or you can use dried beans, which can be reused time and time again). Prebake the crust until it is lightly browned (10 to 12 minutes). While it's baking, peel and core the apples and cut them into half-moon shapes.

Take the crust from the oven and remove the aluminum foil and pie weights. Put the crust back into the oven for 2 to 3 more minutes. Remove from the oven and cool. Meanwhile, gently reheat the apricot mixture and stir it well. After the crust has cooled, layer it with a light though thorough coating of the apricot mixture, using a pastry brush (or spoon). Top the crust with the apples in an overlapping circular pattern. Distribute the cubed butter around the apples, then dust the top with the 4 tablespoons sugar. Bake at 400° for 12 to 15 minutes, or until the top has carmelized and the crust is crisp. Dot the top with some of the remaining apricot puree. Cool to room temperature and serve with the top dusted with confectioners' sugar, if desired.

SERVES 8

PECAN TART

An easy one from the Windsor Court Hotel in New Orleans.

2 sticks (½ pound) unsalted butter
1⅓ cups dark brown sugar
¼ cup granulated sugar
¾ cup honey
¼ cup heavy cream
1 pound pecan halves
9- or 10-inch prebaked pie crust

In a heavy saucepan, bring the butter, brown sugar, white sugar, and honey to a boil over medium-high heat, stirring occasionally. Let the mixture boil for exactly 3 minutes. Remove from the heat and add the heavy cream, stirring all the while. Slowly add the pecan halves and stir until well mixed. Pour the mixture into the prebaked pie shell; cool to room temperature and serve.

SERVES 8

PUMPKIN MOUSSE

Although Chef Dave Watson of the International Culinary Academy created this great option to pumpkin pie to serve around the holidays, it's a sweet delight any time of the year.

2 cups milk
⅓ cup brown sugar
2 egg yolks
2 whole eggs
4 tablespoons plus 1 teaspoon cornstarch
¼ cup granulated sugar
4¼ teaspoons ground cinnamon
3½ teaspoons ground nutmeg
2 tablespoons honey
2 tablespoons molasses
½ cup pumpkin puree
2 tablespoons unsalted butter
½ tablespoon vanilla extract
½ tablespoon gelatin
¼ cup water
¾ cup egg whites (3–4 eggs)

OFF THE EATEN PATH:
Just Desserts

The word *dessert* comes from the French *desservir*, which means to "clear away"; i.e., prior to enjoying the sweet finale to your meal, the table generally is cleared away for the final course.

Bring the milk and brown sugar to a boil. Meanwhile, in a large bowl mix together the next 9 ingredients. Over high heat, slowly stir in the milk mixture and bring to a boil, stirring all the while. When it starts to boil, remove from the heat and stir in the butter and vanilla. Dissolve the gelatin in the water, then add it to the pumpkin mixture. Stir until it's well incorporated. Cool to room temperature. Whip the egg whites to soft peaks and fold into the cooled mixture. Chill until set. Transfer to dessert cups or champagne glasses and serve.

SERVES 8–12

DRAMBUIE PEARS

Drambuie is a sweet liqueur made of Scotch laced with honey and a variety of herbs. Here's a recipe in which it plays an important role.

6 firm ripe pears
1¼ cups water
½ cup firmly packed brown sugar
1 orange
2 teaspoons arrowroot
4½ tablespoons Drambuie

Remove the skin of the pears with a potato peeler or sharp knife. Remove as much of the core as possible, but leave the stem intact. Put the water and sugar in a pan just deep enough to hold the pears upright; dissolve the sugar over low heat, stirring frequently.

Pare the rind from the orange with the potato peeler and add it to the pan; squeeze in the juice from the orange. When the sugar has all melted, bring the syrup to a boil. Reduce the heat and add the pears; cover and simmer gently for about 35 to 45 minutes, or until they're tender.

Transfer the pears to a serving dish. Remove the orange rind and cut half of it into tiny strips to use as a garnish. Add the arrowroot to the Drambuie and whisk gently until it becomes very smooth. Over low heat, stir the mixture into the syrup; when it's all incorporated, raise the heat slightly and bring it to a boil, stirring all the while. Spoon the sauce over the pears and scatter with the strips of orange zest and serve.

SERVES 6

I've enjoyed many a dessert soufflé on my various excursions to Europe and often wondered if there were an easy way to create one at home without going through the hassle of doing it the traditional way. I found the answer in this recipe from Elsie Hillman, of Pittsburgh. The dessert is sort of a cross between a soufflé and a lemon pie. The top portion browns beautifully in the oven, and when you're ready to present it, the top half of the dessert, which is spongelike, separates from a custard that forms on the bottom. The result is like a lemon soufflé with its own built-in custard. If you want it to be a bit more tart, add grated lemon rind and fresh lemon juice to taste.

LEMON FANTASY

½ stick unsalted butter, softened
¾ cup granulated sugar
3 large eggs (at room temperature), separated
⅓ cup fresh lemon juice
⅓ cup all-purpose flour
1½ tablespoons grated lemon rind
¼ teaspoon salt
1½ cups whole milk
pinch cream of tartar
boiling water
confectioners' sugar, for dusting

In a large bowl, cream the butter and sugar; add the egg yolks, one at a time, beating well after adding each yolk. Beat in the lemon juice, flour, zest, and salt. In a steady stream, add the milk, beating well as you do until it all is well incorporated.

Preheat the oven to 350°. Whip the egg whites with a pinch of cream of tartar until stiff peaks start to form. Add about a quarter of the whipped whites to the lemon mixture; stir until well incorporated. Gently fold in the remaining whites, then transfer to a 1½-quart soufflé dish. Put it inside a deep pan, and add enough boiling water to come halfway up the sides. Bake 45 to 55 minutes, or until the top has puffed and browned nicely. Crown with a light dusting of confectioners' sugar. Chill before serving.

SERVES 4–6

OFF THE EATEN PATH:
"Slaving" in the Kitchen

In ancient Italy, chefs were slaves; nonetheless, some of them still lived pretty well. In fact, Mark Antony gave a whole town to his chef after a particularly successful banquet. However, chefs that weren't up to snuff were spanked in public.

These next two recipes were developed for my cooking classes by Patricia Tascarella, my former assistant and sweet-fanatic beyond compare. She is a former winner of the Silver Spoon Award for *Women's Day* Magazine.

CHOCOLATE HAZELNUT TORTE

Use an electric mixer to stir things up properly.

TORTE:
6 ounces semisweet chocolate
¾ cup unsalted butter (1½ sticks)
¾ cup granulated sugar
1 teaspoon vanilla extract
6 eggs (at room temperature), separated
¾ cup ground hazelnuts

FROSTING:
6 ounces sweet chocolate
¾ cup heavy cream

Preheat the oven to 375°. Melt the chocolate in the top of a double boiler over simmering water. Meanwhile, mix together the butter and sugar; mix in the vanilla, then the egg yolks, one at a time. When the eggs are well incorporated, stir in the ground nuts and melted chocolate; mix well. Beat the egg whites until stiff peaks form; fold into the chocolate mixture. Turn the batter into a buttered 9-inch springform cake pan. Bake for 20 minutes; then lower heat to 350° and bake an additional 50 minutes; remove from oven and cool.

Meanwhile, make the frosting by melting the sweet chocolate in the top of a double boiler over simmering water. Stir in the cream and cook over the simmering water for 10 minutes. Cool, then slather on top of the cooled cake and serve.

SERVES 8

PATTY'S PEACHES AND CREAM

1 sheet frozen puff pastry, thawed (½ pound)
2 tablespoons unsalted butter
3 cups fresh peaches, thinly sliced (about 8 slices per peach)
2 tablespoons brown sugar
1 teaspoon vanilla extract
¼ teaspoon almond extract
1 pint peach ice cream
½ cup toasted slivered almonds

Preheat the oven to 350°. On a floured surface, chilled if possible, roll out the puff pastry sheet so it will cover a standard-sized cookie sheet. Line the cookie sheet with parchment paper, transfer the pastry sheet to it, and mist with water (this will help it puff more). Bake until nicely browned and puffed (15 to 20 minutes). Cool.

Meanwhile, over medium heat, melt the butter in a medium skillet, and cook the peaches for 7 minutes, turning once or twice. Add the brown sugar and cook 3 more minutes. Sprinkle with the vanilla and almond extracts, stirring well to incorporate.

Spread the peaches on the cooled pastry, and cut into 8 wedges. Top each portion with a scoop of peach ice cream and some toasted almonds and serve immediately.

SERVES 8

Cookery is as old as the world, but it must also remain, always, as modern as fashion.

—PHILEAS GILBERT

MILOSTI

The name of this Czechoslovakian delicacy literally translates to "celestial crusts."

½ cup egg yolks
½ cup heavy cream
1 tablespoon unsalted butter, melted
½ cup granulated sugar
1 teaspoon brandy
dash salt
dash mace (or ground nutmeg)
¼ teaspoon grated lemon rind
2½–3 cups all-purpose flour
confectioners' sugar, for dusting

Beat together the egg yolks, cream, melted butter, sugar, and brandy. Add 2½ cups of the flour and the salt, mace, and lemon rind; mix thoroughly. At this stage, the mixture should be firm enough to roll like a pie crust. If not, add enough flour to make the dough the proper texture to be rolled.

Divide the dough into 4 parts; store 3 in a covered bowl until ready to use as you roll out the first. On a floured surface, roll out the first batch of dough until it's ⅛ inch thick. Cut into 3-inch squares; cover with a towel as you repeat the procedure with the remaining dough.

Fry the squares in deep, hot vegetable shortening (or in a deep-fryer heated to 365–375°) until golden brown. Remove with a slotted spoon and drain on paper towels. Dust with confectioners' sugar, and serve hot.

SERVES 8–12

When my buddy Arnie from Aliquippa was at my house for an English dinner while I was testing recipes, I asked him if he wanted Yorkshire pudding with his roast beef. He said he wasn't ready for dessert yet!

Yorkshire pudding, as Arnie now knows, is not a dessert but the English version of the crouton and a popular accompaniment to beef dishes. In merry olde England, Yorkshire pudding was used to catch the juices while meat turned on a spit. I would have loved to bite into it after it was saturated with juice. Today, however, it's usually made separately and served on the side—dry and boring.

But what about making it into a dessert? Here's a recipe that gives a sweet twist to an old British favorite. Topped with confectioners' sugar, it makes an interesting dessert, but it also goes well as a side dish with poultry and game (in that case, eliminate the dusting of sugar).

ARNIE'S YORKSHIRE PUDDING

2 large eggs
½ cup all-purpose flour
pinch salt
½ cup milk
1 teaspoon apple schnapps
2 baking apples, peeled, cored, and thinly sliced
5 tablespoons unsalted butter, melted
confectioners' sugar, for dusting
½ cup toasted slivered almonds (optional)

Whip the eggs with an electric mixer until they're thick and light in color. In another bowl, combine the flour, salt, and half the milk; beat until the flour is well moistened. Add the egg mixture, the rest of the milk, and the apple schnapps. Beat until smooth, then fold in the apples.

Preheat the oven to 425°. Layer the bottom of a well-greased 8- or 9-inch diameter baking dish with the melted butter, then top with the batter. Bake for about 30 to 35 minutes. Serve hot with a dusting of confectioners' sugar, and the toasted almonds if desired.

SERVES 6–8

ISRAELI APPLE CAKE

A wonderfully textured and flavorful cake from Israel.

4 eggs
2 cups granulated sugar
I cup cooking oil
¼ cup fresh orange juice
3 teaspoons vanilla extract
3 cups all-purpose flour
3 teaspoons baking powder
¼ teaspoon salt
I cup chopped walnuts
2 cups Granny Smith apples, peeled, cored, and thinly sliced
1½ teaspoons ground cinnamon
3 teaspoons granulated sugar
confectioners' sugar, for dusting

In a medium bowl, beat the eggs, the 2 cups sugar, and the oil, juice, and vanilla with an electric mixer on high speed for 10 minutes. Sift together the flour, baking powder, and salt, then blend it, a little at a time, into the egg mixture; stir in the walnuts.

Preheat the oven to 350°. Grease a large bundt pan (9 × 3½ inches) and pour in about a third of the batter. Layer the top with half of the apples; sprinkle with I teaspoon of the remaining sugar and ½ teaspoon of the cinnamon. Pour another third of the batter on top and cover with the remaining apples; sprinkle the top with the rest of the sugar and cinnamon. Cover with the remaining third of the batter. Bake until done (75 to 85 minutes); remove from the oven and immediately dust with confectioners' sugar. Let cool. Run a knife along the outside and inside edges and lift cake out by the funnel, if it is removable. If not, run a knife along the outside and inside edges, invert onto a large platter, rap the pan gently and carefully remove the cake. Serve immediately.

SERVES ABOUT 16

Cooking is like love. It should be entered into with abandon or not at all.
—HARRIET VAN HORNE

KAHLÚA MOUSSE

This easy dessert is from El Torito Restaurant and Cantina.

2 cups Cool Whip, plus more for serving
½ cup heavy cream
2 tablespoons unsweetened cocoa powder
1 tablespoon instant coffee
3 tablespoons granulated sugar
6 tablespoons Kahlúa
chocolate sprinkles
wafer cookies

In a medium bowl, whip the Cool Whip with the heavy cream until stiff peaks form. With a rubber spatula, stir in the cocoa powder, instant coffee, and sugar; blend well. Add the Kahlúa and stir thoroughly with the spatula. Put into 6 to 8 dessert cups and chill in the refrigerator. When ready to serve, dust the top of each serving with chocolate sprinkles and crown with a dollop of Cool Whip. Serve with wafer cookies.

SERVES 6–8

> **"**Statistics show that of those who contract the habit of eating, very few ever survive.**"**
>
> —WILLIAM WALLACE IRWIN

SABAYON AU CHOCOLAT

My friend Byron Bardy developed this velvety recipe for a culinary competition. It takes a little elbow grease, but the end result is well worth it. It can be served either hot or cold. By the way, *sabayon* is what the dessert is known as in France. In Italy, it's called *zabaglione*.

12 egg yolks
⅓ cup dry sherry
2 tablespoons Kirsch or Triple Sec
½ teaspoon vanilla extract
dash salt
dash ground nutmeg
¾ cup confectioners' sugar, sifted
1 cup milk chocolate chips, melted

GARNISHES (if serving cold):
shaved chocolate
whipped cream
cherries (optional)

In a medium mixing bowl, use a whisk to combine the yolks with the sherry, kirsch, and vanilla. Add the salt, nutmeg, and sugar. Place the bowl over simmering water and beat the mixture steadily in the same direction until it becomes thick and fluffy. Remove from heat and continue beating until the bowl cools. Fold in the melted chocolate. Transfer to dessert glasses and serve hot or chilled. If serving chilled, garnish with whipped cream, shaved chocolate, and a cherry, if desired.

SERVES 8

LEMON TART

An easy recipe from the Windsor Court Hotel in New Orleans. Serve chilled with a dollop of whipped cream, fresh fruit, or raspberry or strawberry puree, if desired.

5 whole eggs
5 egg yolks
1½ cups granulated sugar
juice of 5 lemons and zest of 2
6 tablespoons unsalted butter, melted
11-inch prebaked tart shell*

Fill a large, deep saucepan three-quarters to the top with water and bring it to a boil. Meanwhile, place the eggs, yolks, sugar, lemon juice, and zest in a large bowl and mix together. Put the bowl just above the boiling water and whisk the mixture vigorously, as if making a hollandaise sauce. Continue whipping until when you draw the whisk through the mixture it forms a ridge that stays in place (about 8 to 10 minutes).

Preheat the broiler. Remove the mixture from the heat and whip in the butter. Pour into the prebaked tart shell, cover the edges with aluminum foil, and brown under the broiler. Remove the foil and chill the tart in the refrigerator before serving.

SERVES 8

*You can also substitute a store-bought pie crust. As it probably will be smaller than 11 inches in diameter, you will have some filling left over.

OFF THE EATEN PATH:
Lemon and Lime Sailors

Although British sailors of yore were nicknamed "limeys" because of the lime juice that they consumed to ward off scurvy, they could have just as easily been dubbed "lemonys." The sailors also were required by the Merchant Shipping Act of 1894 to consume an ounce of lemon juice after they had been at sea for ten days, which was also the amount of lime juice required.

FRENCH STRAWBERRY TART

If you're in a hurry, you can buy a premade crust in your local supermarket. However, this recipe works best with the crust recipe offered. It's a sweet, buttery, rich one that the French call *pâte sablé*. It actually tastes like a giant cookie and is good enough to eat even without the toppings. But with them, it's great!

PÂTE SABLÉ:

½ cup granulated sugar plus 4 teaspoons confectioners' sugar
1 cup all-purpose flour
1 stick unsalted butter, chilled and cut into chunks
1 egg yolk, mixed with 2 teaspoons cold water

PASTRY CREAM:

3 egg yolks
¼ cup granulated sugar plus 1 teaspoon confectioners' sugar
2½ tablespoons all-purpose flour
1 cup milk
¼ stick unsalted butter, chilled and cut into chunks
1½ teaspoons vanilla or almond extract
2 pints fresh strawberries, hulled

FINAL TOUCHES:

¼ cup unsalted butter, melted
½ cup toasted slivered almonds or toasted pine nuts
confectioners' sugar, for dusting

TO MAKE THE "COOKIE": Butter the sides of a 10- or 11-inch loose-bottom tart pan, and line the bottom with parchment paper. Store in the refrigerator until ready to use. Put the sugar, flour, and butter into a food processor and process for 5 seconds. Lift the yolk-water mixture to the opening of the feed tube, turn on the machine, and slowly add in a steady stream until the mixture starts to form a ball. Transfer the dough to a lightly floured surface and knead for a few minutes, then shape it into a smooth ball. Chill in a lightly greased bowl, covered, for about 30 minutes.

Preheat the oven to 350°. Put the chilled dough between two pieces of waxed paper and roll out into a circle about an inch larger than the tart pan. Remove the top paper and invert the dough into the pan. Press evenly along the sides and bottom so you have a nice fit. Prick the bottom liberally with the tines of a fork. Bake until golden brown (about 15 to 20 minutes). Be careful not to overbrown.

TO MAKE THE PASTRY CREAM: In a small bowl, combine the yolks and sugar; blend thoroughly with a whisk. Whisk in the flour and continue whisking until it's well incorporated.

In a medium saucepan, bring the milk to a boil over medium heat. Pour about a third of the milk into the yolk mixture and blend with a whisk. Pour the new mixture back into the saucepan and let it come to a boil over medium heat, whisking all the while. Reduce the heat and whisk until the mixture has thickened. Remove from the heat and blend in the butter until it melts; stir in the vanilla or almond extract. Transfer to a small bowl and chill, covered, until firm (about an hour).

THE FINAL TOUCH: Using a pastry brush, paint the bottom and sides of the "cookie" with the melted butter. Stir the pastry cream until spreadable. Spread it evenly over the bottom of the "cookie." Decorate creatively with the strawberries. Top with the toasted almonds or pine nuts and dust with the confectioners' sugar. Refrigerate until ready to serve.

SERVES 8

PINEAPPLE RHAPSODY

Something easy and festive from Hawaii.

2 ripe pineapples
green crème de menthe to taste
confectioners' sugar to taste

Cut the pineapples in half lengthwise, then halve crosswise. Cut the pulp from the rind by carefully cutting along the length between the pulp and the rind. Cut out the fibrous core and discard. Cut the pulp into bite-size pieces, arrange on the rind, splash with crème de menthe, dust with confectioners' sugar, and serve.

SERVES 6

SOUFFLÉ GLACÉ WITH CARIBBEAN RUM AND COFFEE

The Caribbean isn't known for its food, but there are a few delicious exceptions. One can be found at Les Pitons, the superb restaurant at Cunard's La Toc Suites in St. Lucia where Chef René Kerdranvat, a two-star Michelin man from France, reigns. He calls his cooking style *"cuisine évolutive"* because it combines nouvelle and classic French techniques. Here's one of his most popular desserts. Although the chef suggests you use a casserole dish filled with hot water to whip the egg whites over, you can place the whipping bowl over simmering water.

4 tablespoons instant coffee
4 tablespoons Caribbean rum
4 tablespoons heavy cream, very cold
8 egg whites, at room temperature
1 cup granulated sugar
4 tablespoons unsweetened cocoa powder

Line the outside of 4 coffee cups with aluminum foil, beginning halfway down the cup and extending 1½ inches above the lip (this is to hold the soufflé as it rises from the cup). Store in the freezer until ready to use. In a small bowl, mix the coffee and rum together. In another bowl, whip the cream until soft peaks form. Fold the coffee-rum mixture into the whipped cream and store in the refrigerator.

Bring a casserole dish two-thirds filled with water to a boil. Meanwhile, use an electric beater to whip the egg whites until fluffy. Mix in the sugar a little at a time. When the water comes to a boil in the casserole, remove from the heat and place the bowl with the egg whites over it. Whip the eggs for 5 minutes; remove the bowl from the casserole dish and continue whipping until the mixture reaches approximately room temperature (incidentally, this is known as an "Italian meringue," and is stickier and thicker than a traditional meringue, because it is partially cooked).

Remove the whipped cream from the refrigerator and fold into the meringue, a little at a time, turning gently with a wooden

> **"**When my mother had to get dinner for eight, she'd just make enough for sixteen and serve half.**"**
>
> —GRACIE ALLEN

spatula. Ladle the mixture into the aluminum-lined coffee cups (8 to 9 ounces) and place in the freezer for at least 6 hours. Dust the top with cocoa powder, remove the aluminum foil, and serve.

SERVES 4

ICE CREAM PIE WITH RUM-RAISIN SAUCE

One of the easiest desserts I know, but singing with flavor nonetheless! The sauce also is great as a topping for plain ice cream.

1 pint good-quality vanilla ice cream, slightly softened
9-inch graham cracker crust (available in supermarkets)

RUM-RAISIN SAUCE:
⅔ cup golden California raisins
½ cup plus 1 tablespoon water
1 cup firmly packed brown sugar
pinch salt
½ teaspoon fresh lemon juice
¼ cup dark rum

Spread the ice cream into the prepared pie crust. Store it in the freezer while you prepare the sauce.

TO MAKE THE SAUCE: Simmer the raisins in the water until soft (10 to 12 minutes). Stir in the brown sugar and salt; continue stirring, over low heat, until it dissolves; simmer for 8 to 10 minutes. Stir in the lemon juice; remove from the heat and stir in the rum. Serve half of the sauce right away over the ice cream pie and store the rest in a covered container in the refrigerator, where it will thicken. When ready to use again, thin it with water and some lemon juice.

SERVES 6–8

TUILES

These "tulips," which are actually U-shaped cookies, are great for holding your favorite mousse, ice cream, sabayon, or fresh fruit. This is how George Perrier makes them at Le Bec-Fin in Philadelphia. The knack is to remove the cookies as quickly as possible and shape them over a rolling pin before they start to harden. I work in threes, leaving the rest to warm in the oven.

½ cup granulated sugar
¾ cup ground plain almonds
¾ cup all-purpose flour
½ cup egg whites

Preheat the oven to 350°.

In a medium bowl, mix together the sugar, almonds, and flour; stir in the egg whites and blend well. Let rest at room temperature for 30 minutes. On a well-buttered cookie sheet drop tablespoons of the mixture, then spread each dollop into a thin, 3-inch circle using a wet fork. Bake for 10 to 12 minutes, or until the cookies have browned nicely.

Remove about three cookies at a time with a spatula, leaving the rest warming in the oven. Mold, in threes, over a rolling pin in order to make them curve. Let them cool about 30 seconds on the pin, then set them on a tray to cool further. Repeat the procedure until all the cookies have been shaped over the rolling pin and transferred to a cooling tray where they will harden into crisp cookies.

MAKES 12–15

Note: If you don't use them right away, store in an airtight container at room temperature.

TRAVELIN' GOURMET TIP:
Sweet "Angel Hair"

It's not as delicate as spun sugar, but for thin strands of sweet "angel hair," press caramels through a garlic press. It's a lovely garnish for baked apples and dresses up ornate gingerbread ladies. Use a new press and keep it solely for this purpose.

APPLE WALNUT PIE

Although The Old Original Bookbinder's Restaurant in Philadelphia is most famous for its marvelous seafood offerings, its desserts are enough to FAX home about, too. This is one of the restaurant's most popular desserts. Incidentally, the restaurant was established in 1865, making it one of America's oldest.

6 large Granny Smith apples, peeled and sliced
2 cups sour cream
2 eggs
1 cup granulated sugar
2 teaspoons vanilla extract
½ cup all-purpose flour
pinch salt
9–10-inch pie crust (uncooked)

TOPPING:

½ cup brown sugar
½ cup granulated sugar
½ cup all-purpose flour
1 teaspoon powdered cinnamon
1 cup chopped walnuts
¼ pound (1 stick) unsalted butter

Preheat the oven to 450°. In a large bowl, thoroughly mix the apples, sour cream, eggs, sugar, vanilla, flour, and salt. Pour into the prepared pie shell and bake for 10 minutes. Reduce the heat to 350°; bake for 35 minutes more; remove and gently stir the filling.

Blend together the topping ingredients and spread on top of the pie filling; bake for another 15 minutes at 350°. Serve hot, at room temperature, or cold.

SERVES 8

STRAWBERRY PITHIVIER

This dessert takes its name from a town in France of the same name (but with an *s* on the end), where the dessert was invented. However, they don't make it over there with strawberries. This creation is the handiwork of one of the brightest young chefs in America, Olivier de Saint Martin, head of the food operation at the Bellevue Hotel in Philadelphia. While it's okay to use frozen, whole, unsweetened strawberries, fresh are better.

1 box (1 pound) frozen puff pastry, thawed
1 cup strawberry puree (either freshly made or store-bought)
3 egg yolks
½ pound ground almonds (either ground in a food processor or store-bought)
6 tablespoons granulated sugar
6 tablespoons unsalted butter, softened
4 tablespoons fresh strawberries, hulled and quartered
1 egg yolk, lightly beaten with 1 tablespoon milk
¼ cup confectioners' sugar
½ cup crème fraîche (see page 96), mixed with 2 tablespoons granulated sugar (optional)

On a floured surface, chilled if possible, roll out 1 sheet of puff pastry (chill the other until ready to use). Shape it into a circle about 9 inches in diameter and ⅛ inch thick; store in the refrigerator. Roll out the other sheet to a diameter of about 10 inches in diameter and ⅛ inch thick; store in the refrigerator.

In a medium bowl, mix together the strawberry puree, egg yolks, ground almonds, sugar, and butter. Spoon half of the mixture onto the smaller pastry round and smooth it with a metal spatula to within 1 inch of the edge of the pastry. Layer the mixture with the quartered strawberries; put the other half of the puree mixture on top and smooth with the spatula to within an inch of the edge. Glaze the edges of the pastry with some of the yolk mixture. Place the large pastry circle on top; firmly press the edges of the top circle onto the edges of the bottom to seal well. Chill for 30 minutes before serving.

Preheat the oven to 475°. Remove the pastry from the refrigerator and place a 9-inch flan ring or shallow plate on top of it. With a small, sharp knife, trim the overhanging dough and discard (or freeze for later use). Glaze the *pithivier* with the remaining yolk mixture; with a small, sharp knife mark out faint lines from the center of the cake to the edges, like a sun ray, into the shape of a rosette (try not to pierce the pastry).

Bake for 10 minutes; lower the heat to 400° and bake for 25 minutes more. Remove from the oven and dust the top with confectioners' sugar; return to the oven and bake 5 minutes more. Serve warm, with the crème fraîche mixture on the side, or simply with a dollop of whipped cream or with your favorite ice cream.

SERVES 8

ORANGE VALENCIA

This unique Italian dessert from Ron Herbinko of the International Culinary Academy makes a pretty presentation. You can use your favorite ice cream, but I think that spumoni works the best.

4 large oranges
1–2 pints spumoni ice cream, softened slightly
Galliano (to taste)
whipped cream
crème de cacao to taste

Cut off the top and bottom of each orange to a thickness of ¼ inch and reserve. Run a sharp paring knife along the edges of the orange, then scoop out the pulp and discard (or reserve for later use). Replace the bottom rind disk through top opening so that the hollowed rind will hold the filling. Fill with spumoni and smooth the ice cream with the back of a spoon.

Using a spoon handle or other kitchen tool, make a deep hole in the center of the ice cream about the width of a finger, and fill with Galliano. Top with about 2 inches of whipped cream. Sprinkle the whipped cream with crème de cacao. Cap with the reserved rind top and serve immediately.

SERVES 4

CARTER CUSTARD

In 1988, I was selected to be the food critic for the Democratic National Convention in Atlanta, with my daily reviews appearing on closed-circuit television in all of the delegates' rooms on Convention Network. One of my favorite spots was Mary Mac's Tea Room, an Atlanta landmark. This easy dessert is named after former President Jimmy Carter. It was called Jimmy Carter Custard when Carter was running for the presidency. Then it was changed to President's Pudding after he won. Today it's simply called Carter Custard at Mary Mac's.

6 ounces cream cheese, softened
¾ cup milk
½ cup plain peanut butter
1 cup confectioners' sugar
1 cup heavy cream
9-inch graham-cracker crust (available in supermarkets)
¾ cup chopped dry roasted peanuts

Beat together the cream cheese, milk, peanut butter, and sugar; set aside. In another bowl, beat the cream until firm, then fold it into the cheese mixture. Pour the custard into the graham-cracker crust, sprinkle the chopped peanuts on top, and freeze. When ready to serve, thaw at least 30 minutes and serve cold or at room temperature.

SERVES 6–8

KEY LIME PIE

This dessert is from the repertoire of the American Festival Cafe in New York City, and of all the versions of this dessert I've tried, this is my favorite.

2 egg yolks
2 14-ounce cans sweetened condensed milk
zest of 4 limes, finely grated
½ cup fresh lime juice
9–10-inch graham cracker crust (available in supermarkets)
1 cup heavy cream
2 tablespoons confectioners' sugar
8 thin slices of lime

"At a dinner party, one should eat wisely but not too well, and talk well but not too wisely."
—W. SOMERSET MAUGHAM

Preheat the oven to 400°.

Beat the egg yolks until they are thick and light in color. Gradually mix in the condensed milk. Add the zest and lime juice and mix well. Pour into the graham cracker crust; bake for 10 minutes; cool.

Beat the cream until almost stiff; add the sugar and continue beating until stiff. Reserve ¾ cup of the whipped cream and spread the remainder over the top of the pie and serve.

If you'd like to get a bit fancy, place the reserved cream in a pastry bag fitting with a star tip and make 8 rosettes, one for each slice of pie (optional). Place a lime slice upright in the middle of each rosette.

MAKES 8 SERVINGS

KEY ORANGE PIE

This very easy dessert is as pert as Key Lime Pie and similar in other ways, except it's made with orange, instead. That's why I've dubbed it Key Orange Pie.

1 cup heavy cream
¼ cup cold water
1 packet unflavored gelatin
6-ounce can frozen orange juice concentrate
8 ounces cream cheese, softened
¾ cup confectioners' sugar
2 teaspoons vanilla extract
2 tablespoons Grand Marnier
9–10-inch graham cracker crust (available in supermarkets)
orange slices, for garnish

Put the cream into a small saucepan over high heat. Just before it comes to a boil, put the cold water into a blender and sprinkle in the gelatin, where it should stand for a minute or so. Add the boiling cream to the blender, process on low until all of the gelatin has dissolved (2 to 3 minutes). Add the concentrated orange juice, cream cheese, sugar, vanilla, and Grand Marnier; process until it is all well blended. Chill for 15 to 20 minutes; pour into the crust and chill until it firms up. Garnish with orange slices or whole raspberries, strawberries, or blackberries and serve.

SERVES 6–8

MOM'S HOMEMADE APPLE PIE

Let's not forget that great comfort dessert that many moms are known for, including the late Elizabeth Zelesko, who created this rendition of the American classic.

CRUST:
2 cups all-purpose flour
1 teaspoon salt
¾ cup vegetable shortening
4–5 tablespoons ice water

PIE:
5 cups thinly sliced, peeled, and cored Granny Smith apples
½ cup granulated sugar
2 teaspoons ground cinnamon
2 teaspoons fresh lemon juice
2 tablespoons unsalted butter, cut into tiny cubes
1 egg yolk, well-beaten

TO MAKE THE CRUST: Put the flour and the salt into a food processor and pulse a few times. Add the shortening and process until it has the texture of coarse meal. Put the lid on the machine and slowly add the ice water in a steady stream through the feed tube. Add only enough to allow the mixture to start to form a ball. The dough should be moist but not wet (if it gets too wet, add a little more flour). Remove and shape into a ball.

Cut the ball in half; on a floured surface, roll out the crust into a 9-inch circle and place on the bottom of a greased 9-inch pie pan. Roll out the other half about a half inch larger than the bottom crust; refrigerate until ready to use.

TO MAKE THE PIE: Preheat the oven to 450°. In a medium bowl, combine the apples, sugar, and cinnamon; sprinkle with the lemon juice and toss well.* Put the apples in the crust-lined pie pan and dot with the butter. Place the remaining pastry circle on top and crimp the edges with the tines of a fork. Cut vents in the top for the steam to escape.

*An interesting option is to layer the crust with a few slices of Cheddar cheese before putting the filling into it. That way the cheese bakes along with the apples.

OFF THE EATEN PATH:
The Tower of Butter

The Normans loved butter so much that they couldn't do without it—even during Lent. So they struck a deal with the church to pay for a Lenten dispensation. The monies that subsequently were raised went to build the tower of St. Romain, which is part of the Cathedral of Notre Dame in Rouen. It was nicknamed "The Tower of Butter."

Incidentally, the inexpensive substitute for butter, margarine, was invented in France. It came about as the result of a contest launched in 1868 by none other than Napoleon III. He sponsored the contest in an effort to come up with an "edible fat product that would keep longer than butter." He wanted an inexpensive imitation that could be used to supply the crews of the French fleet. About a year later, a French chemist named Hippolyte Mege-Mouries registered the product. He called it margarine, after the margaric acid it contained. After being tested successfully in France, it spread throughout the world.

Although an American patent for margarine was registered in 1873, American dairy farmers lobbied against its use as a butter substitute. It didn't come into widespread use here until some seventy years later. Margarine, incidentally, has about the same caloric content as butter, but, unlike butter, comes in a no-cholesterol version.

Bake for 15 minutes; reduce the heat to 350°, and bake until the crust is light golden in color (about 15 to 20 minutes). Remove from the oven and brush the top with the egg wash. Bake until the crust is golden brown (about 10 minutes). Serve warm.

SERVES 6

ANGEL CHEEKS

Many Brazilian children find these angel cheeks simply heavenly!

2 egg whites
6 egg yolks
1 teaspoon baking powder
2 teaspoons all-purpose flour
4 tablespoons unsalted butter
2¼ cups granulated sugar
1 quart water
1 teaspoon vanilla extract

Preheat the oven to 350°. In a medium bowl, beat the egg whites until frothy; beat in the yolks, one at a time, until all are well incorporated. Add the baking powder and flour; beat until the mixture becomes thick and creamy. Butter 12 cupcake molds and fill each three-quarters full with the cream; bake until they are light golden in color (about 20 minutes). Remove from the molds and place in a deep plate.

Make a syrup by heating the sugar and water over medium heat until the sugar has dissolved. Stir in the vanilla extract, then pour the mixture over the angel cheeks. Let the syrup soak into the muffins until nearly all is absorbed, then turn them over, and serve.

SERVES 12

HEAVENLY HOTS

This easy recipe from Clark Race, who operates the Sewickley Bed and Breakfast in Sewickley, Pa., took top honors in a recipe contest I helped judge. If you'd rather have it for breakfast, simply eliminate the chocolate-raspberry sauce and serve the ''hots'' with your favorite syrup or fruit after dusting with confectioners' sugar.

BATTER:

4 eggs
½ teaspoon salt
1 teaspoon baking soda
5 tablespoons cake flour
4 tablespoons granulated sugar
2 cups sour cream
vegetable oil (for frying)

CHOCOLATE-RASPBERRY SAUCE (optional):

8 ounces semisweet baking chocolate
½ cup milk
½ cup raspberry syrup (available in most supermarkets or
　　specialty stores)

TO MAKE THE HOTS: To the container of a blender, add the eggs, salt, baking soda, flour, sugar, and sour cream. Process until smooth and set aside.

Heat a griddle over medium-high heat, then add enough vegetable oil to lightly coat it (2 to 3 tablespoons). Ladle enough of the batter onto the griddle to make 2½-inch rounds (about ¾ tablespoon). Cook until a few bubbles appear on the top; turn and cook on the other side until golden brown. (Mr. Race funnels the batter into a clean flip-top squeeze bottle, then squeezes the batter onto the griddle). Serve with chocolate-raspberry sauce if desired.

MAKES ABOUT 50 ''HOTS''

TO MAKE THE CHOCOLATE-RASPBERRY SAUCE: In a heavy saucepan over medium heat, melt the chocolate with the milk and raspberry sauce and stir until smooth. Serve atop the ''hots.''

MAKES 2 CUPS

COEUR À LA CRÈME

This dessert, which literally means "heart of cream," derives its name from the heart-shaped baskets that the French cheese fromage blanc is drained in after it sours.

¾ pound ricotta cheese, drained
½ pound cream cheese
3 tablespoons confectioners' sugar
½ teaspoon vanilla extract
dash ground cinnamon
1 cup heavy cream
½ pound fresh raspberries
3 tablespoons Kirsch
1 pint fresh strawberries, thinly sliced

Cut a piece of cheesecloth about 2½ times the size of a 3-cup heart-shaped mold. Soak it in lemon juice, then wring it dry. Layer it in the mold so that it covers the bottom and sides and there is enough left over to cover the top. In a medium bowl, blend together the cheeses. Add the sugar, vanilla, and cinnamon. Whip the heavy cream until stiff and fold it into the cheese mixture. Pour the mixture into the prepared mold, cover the top with the cheesecloth, and refrigerate.

To unmold the cream heart, pull away the cheesecloth from the top, place a plate on top, invert the heart onto the plate, and remove the cheesecloth. Put the raspberries and Kirsch into a blender and puree. Pour the puree over the cheese mold, garnish with the strawberries, and serve.

SERVES 4–6

A LA CARTE:
The Ultimate Flight of Fancy

My father used to say, "If you can't go first class — go tourist!" And tourist is the way I used to go, if at all. It was only after I became a travel writer and was blessed with that great American institution known as the expense account (and access to countless freebies) that I realized what I'd been missing by flying in the bleacher seats in the sky all those years.

I've become so spoiled by being a regular in first class that if I can't jet in that eminently suitable manner I'll probably reject the free-lance assignment. Unless you've experienced it, it's hard to explain just how special it is to sit in a wide seat in the front of a 747 nibbling Beluga caviar or wiping Camembert from your lips with a steaming towel.

Needless to say, I always felt that first-class flying was the most sophisticated way to get from Point A to Point B, that is, until I flew on the Concorde, that sleek, needle-nosed marvel of engineering that slices through the sound barrier like a hot knife through Brie. Quite frankly, it's heaven above earth — hedonism at 60,000 feet up. It also will instantly change your attitude about airline food.

My British Airways Concorde experience began in the first-class Concorde lounge at Kennedy Airport in New York. Rather than the finger sandwiches, peanuts, and cheese assortments they offer in the first-class lounge, the nibbles included *pâté de foie gras* topped with slivers of truffles, caviar, cold chunks of lobster on hearts of palm wedges, and sticking out of ice buckets, the biggest crab claws I'd ever seen.

And if you'd like to knock back a drink while checking over your stock portfolio, you can choose everything from Dom Perignon champagne to Montrachet wine. Not to mention cognacs, armagnacs, and a host of liqueurs, all of which you were free to pour at your discretion.

I sailed through those appetizers and washed them down with as much Dom Perignon as my body could hold. When the boarding call was made (in genteel tones, I might add), it was the first time I actually was distressed to learn my plane was leaving on schedule!

The inside of the Concorde had more room than you might expect after gazing at the thermometer-with-wings from a window seat in the lounge. The interior is awash in soft tones of gray, with gray leather seats that look and feel like high-tech dental chairs.

After we reached the safe cruising altitude of 10 miles — yes, *10* — a stewardess smothered my "table" with linen and dressed it with real silverware and bone china plates, edged in platinum and black. After presenting tidbits of caviar in tiny, delicate envelopes of pastry, lunch opened with the presentation of canapés: smoked salmon, shrimp with seafood mousse, and a satiny *foie gras* pâté.

For my entrée, I was torn between the

tournedoes grillé au cognac et au poivre vert (beef fillets filled with green peppercorns and brandy butter), and *medallion de turbot poele* (pan-fried turbot medallions in a cider sauce served with wild mushrooms, snow peas, and baby squash).

When the stewardess realized I was perplexed, she asked if she could help solve my airborne dilemma. I said, "I'm tossed between the beef and the turbot. I've already discounted the Maine lobster garnished with tomatoes and barquettes of Sevruga and red American caviar, as well as the cold plate of duckling, veal galantine, and baked ham."

"Sir, if you'd like the turbot *and* the beef, I'll prepare both."

The perfect solution! I said that would be just fine, and she went on her merry way to fetch this upscale rendition of surf and turf. When she returned with the plump tournedos and thick slices of turbot, I eyed them lustily and told her not to go too far with the remaining halves of both orders, because all that fast flying had made me very hungry.

She looked at me, smiled, then said nonchalantly: "Sir, if you're still hungry after you've completed your entrées, I'll prepare you a new order." In other words, she wouldn't be so déclassé as to reheat an order that already had been served. If I wanted more, she'd start from scratch. I mean, I'm used to stewardesses lobbing boxes of "snacks" at me on local flights.

I began to get with it. Having polished off a few glasses of *Cuvée de René Laou Millesime* champagne, I moved on to a Premier Cru Chablis (1983), which worked admirably with the turbot and tournedos. I thought that the other option, a '76 St. Julien Talbot, would have been a bit too assertive with my unorthodox combination.

The entrée was followed by a salad of designer lettuce enhanced with endive, grapefruit, and radish segments tossed with a lime-flavored vinaigrette of yogurt and mint. Next came a savory selection of cheeses, including Stilton, double Gloucester, and Camembert. Because I was en route to England, I opted for the Stilton and a glass of Taylor's vintage port.

This wonderful airborne feast concluded with the presentation of chocolate truffles and coffee, after which a stewardess talked me into a glass of Rémy Martin Napoleon cognac. As I sipped it and admired the glorious sight of the curve of the earth through my window, I asked myself how I could ever go back to flying coach after this.

POTPOURRI

Good things, they say, come to those who wait. I certainly think that's the case with these flavored vinegars, which I first learned about in my gastronomic gallivanting. In countless kitchens I visited around the world I'd often spot attractive bottles filled with herbs resting on shelves like sentinels. I subsequently learned that these were herbed vinegars, which could give a plain green salad an enticing accent or be used to vitalize a marinade. Sprinkled on deep-fried onion rings, shrimp, or chicken breast chunks, they can help to make a snack sublime.

I've also included some interesting flavored whiskeys and vodkas. And just in case you don't have a month or two to wait, I also offer a few flavored sugars, butters, and some of my favorite spreads, which don't have to rest as long before they're ready.

With the exception of the butters, which should be refrigerated, everything else should be stored in a cool, dark place. I've found cleaned wine bottles are great for storing vinegars.

HERBED CIDER VINEGAR

1 cup fresh herbs (rosemary, sage, thyme, basil, or tarragon, or
a combination of all)
1 quart cider vinegar

Put the herbs you choose in a large bottle and add the vinegar. Cork the bottle and store it for at least a month before using.

ITALIAN-STYLE HERBED WINE VINEGAR

1 cup fresh oregano or basil (or a combination of both)
4 garlic cloves
1 quart red wine vinegar

Put the herbs and the garlic cloves in a bottle and add the vinegar. Cork the bottle and store it for at least a month before using.

SOUTHWEST-STYLE VINEGAR

4 jalapeño peppers
4 garlic cloves
1 quart red wine vinegar

If you're using a traditional wine bottle, either pick peppers that are small enough to slide down the neck, or quarter the peppers. Put the peppers and garlic cloves in the bottle and add the vinegar. Cork the bottle and store it for at least a month before using.

❝Life is so brief that we should not glance either too far backwards or forwards in order to be happy. Let us therefore study how to fix our happiness in our glass and on our plate.❞

—GRIMOD DE LA REYNIÈRE

FRENCH-STYLE HERBED WINE VINEGAR

1 cup fresh tarragon
2 garlic cloves
1 quart white wine vinegar

Put the herbs and garlic cloves in a bottle and add the vinegar. Cork the bottle and store it for at least a month before using.

DRIED HERB VINEGAR

With this method the vinegar absorbs the herb flavor quicker but it's not as attractive visually as fresh herb vinegars. Be sure to use herbs with branches—not herbs in flakes.

1 quart cider vinegar
½ cup dried herbs of your choice

Bring the vinegar to a boil, then remove it from the heat. Place the herbs in a bottle and pour in the hot vinegar. Cork the bottle and store it for at least a week before using.

FRUIT VINEGAR

For best results, use raspberries, cranberries, cherries, blueberries, pomegranate seeds, apricots, or blackberries. The fruit can be whole if it will fit into the bottle; if not, cut it to fit.

1 cup fruit
1 quart cider vinegar

Put the fruit and vinegar in a large, wide-mouthed jar with a tight cover. Store it for at least a month before using. Decant the vinegar into decorative bottles and, if you like, throw in a few pieces or slices of fruit for identification's sake.

❝I never worry about diets. The only carrots that interest me are the number you get in a diamond.❞

—MAE WEST

ROSE PETAL VINEGAR

Pick petals from bushes that have not been treated with pesticides. I think that the old-fashioned variety of fragrant roses are the best. Color isn't important, but remember that reds and deep pinks will bleed, tinting the vinegar. This vinegar has a very delicate flavor and should be allowed to "shine" (i.e., as a dressing for plain green salads).

3 cups rose petals
1 quart white wine vinegar

Put the petals and vinegar into a jar, cap and store it for at least a month before using.

Strain the vinegar and pour it into a bottle, discarding the petals. You can place a few buds in the bottle of vinegar, if you like.

These flavored sugars add depth to desserts. You can use them when baking or to sprinkle on fresh fruit.

VANILLA SUGAR

1 vanilla bean, split
2 cups sugar

Bury the vanilla bean in sugar placed in a covered container. Let it sit for about two weeks before using it so that the sugar can absorb the vanilla flavor. By the way, the vanilla bean may be re-used.

CINNAMON SUGAR

This takes a while but it's worth it to get that great cinnamon flavor without the telltale brown coloring.

6 cinnamon sticks
2 cups sugar

Snap or cut the cinnamon sticks in half. Bury the sticks in sugar placed in a covered container. Let it sit for at least a month

OFF THE EATEN PATH:
A Short Course in Vinegars

• *Balsamic Vinegar:* One of the trendiest vinegars of them all. It's made from lambrusco, spergola, or trebbiano grapes and the finest grades are aged in wooden casks for more than a decade.

• *Cider Vinegar:* This all-purpose vinegar is one of the most popular. It's used in everything from soups to sauces.

• *Chive Vinegar:* Wonderful with steamed vegetables and as a flavor-enhancer to dips and soups.

• *Garlic Vinegar:* A great base for sautéeing shellfish, chicken, and vegetables.

• *Rice Wine Vinegar:* Popular in Asian dishes, particularly sweet-and-sour ones.

• *Sherry Vinegar:* The best comes from Spain and it pairs nicely with Spanish olive oil. It is not as sour as other vinegars owing to the sherry base and the long aging process.

• *Tarragon Vinegar:* Another trendy vinegar, it's used to enliven salad dressing, seafood marinades, and chowders.

before using so that the sugar will absorb the cinnamon flavor. The cinnamon sticks may be re-used in cider or in applesauce.

BOURBON VANILLA

Making your own vanillas and other liqueur-based flavorings adds a special personalized touch to compotes and baked goods.

4 vanilla beans
1 pint bourbon

Slash the vanilla beans lengthwise, place in a covered jar, and cover with the bourbon. Store for at least two months before using. Discard the beans before using.

COGNAC VANILLA

A great substitute for commercial vanilla extract.

4 vanilla beans
1 pint cognac

Slash the vanilla beans lengthwise, place in a jar, pour in the cognac and cover. Store for at least two months before using. Discard the beans before using.

LEMON WHISKEY

This can be used to spark up desserts or even to enliven a soup.

peel from 4 lemons
1 pint whiskey

Use only the yellow part of the lemon peel and not the pith. Place it in a jar, pour in the whiskey and cover. Store for at least two months before using. Discard the peels before using.

You can purchase flavored vodkas, but it's fun and easy to make them at home. They're not only great in Bloody Marys or to give a screwdriver a different twist, but you can also use them to spark up stews, soups, and sauces.

MINT VODKA

Try this one on the rocks!

2 cups fresh mint leaves
1 quart vodka

Put the mint into a large jar and pour in the vodka. Cap and store for at least a month before using. Discard the mint before serving.

DILL VODKA

This is outstanding in Bloody Marys.

1 bunch (about 2 cups) fresh dill
1 teaspoon whole black peppercorns
1 quart vodka

Put the dill and the peppercorns into a large jar and pour the vodka over the dill. Cap and store for at least a month before using. Discard the dill and peppercorns before serving.

JALAPEÑO VODKA

I splash a little of this into my chili. However, I have a friend who makes an incendiary Bloody Mary with it.

6 canned jalapeño peppers
1 teaspoon black peppercorns
1 quart vodka

Put the peppers, peppercorns, and vodka into a large jar. Cap and store it for at least a month before using. Discard the peppers and the peppercorns before serving.

RED PEPPER VODKA

I often use this to spark up a tomato sauce or to enliven a barbecue sauce. You can also lace stews and soups with it if you're in a spicy mood.

2 tablespoons plus 1 teaspoon red pepper flakes
1 quart vodka

Put the red pepper flakes into the bottle of vodka. Cap it and store for at least a month before using.

The following spreads can be used on grilled meats or seafood, roasted chicken, breads, green vegetables, or even to toss with pasta. These special spreads should be made ahead to give the flavors a chance to meld.

GARLIC SPREAD

Garlic spread is wonderfully mellow mixed with mayonnaise as a spread or dip or used to season omelettes, pasta dishes, or mashed potatoes.

4 heads garlic, peeled, separated into cloves
½ cup olive oil

Place the garlic and the oil into a pan or soufflé dish. Roast at 250° for 40 minutes. Let cool to room temperature. Pour the oil into a small jar or bottle for later use (e.g.; to brush on meats and poultry or to use as a salad dressing). Puree the garlic cloves in the container of a food processor. Pack garlic puree into a small jar and pour fresh olive oil on the top. Garlic puree will last about a month.

OFF THE EATEN PATH:
Vodka Lore

Vodka, which is made from potatoes or grain, comes from the Russian word "voda," or "little water." It was brought to the United States by a Russian emigré shortly after the end of World War I but wasn't commercially manufactured until 1934 when the Smirnoff people, who had distilleries in Europe, set up shop in Bethel, Connecticut. Poor sales, however, resulted in the sale of the Smirnoff operation to G. H. Heublein & Brothers five years later. Today vodka is one of the top-selling spirits in the United States. Less than 5 percent of it is imported.

PESTO BUTTER

This is good on roasted or grilled meats or fish, or slathered on home-baked breads or Italian-style vegetables. You can also float a tiny scoop on top of hot vegetable soup. Need a quick snack? Spread it on lightly toasted walnut halves.

1 cup unsalted butter, softened
½ cup prepared pesto sauce (your own, commercial, or see
  recipe, page 78
2 tablespoons chopped fresh basil (if available; parsley if not)

   Whip the butter, then slowly beat in the pesto until it's well incorporated. Pack into a container and top with chopped herb leaves. Cover the container and freeze. It will keep in the freezer about two months if undisturbed; however, if thawed, make certain that you use it within a week.

LEMON-GARLIC BUTTER

This works nicely on roasted or grilled poultry and seafood. You can also toss it into rice or on hot roasted almonds.

1 cup unsalted butter, softened
grated rinds of 2 lemons
¼ cup fresh lemon juice
¼ cup minced fresh parsley
4 garlic cloves, minced or pressed

   Whip the butter then slowly beat in the other ingredients until well incorporated. Pack into a container, cover and freeze. It will keep in the freezer about two months if undisturbed. If thawed, use it within a week.

More Tips to Make Life Easier When You're Home on the Range

BASIL: If you're lucky enough to have an abundance of fresh basil, chop it fine, put it into a jar, cover it with oil, and freeze it until ready to use. The oil will help prevent discoloration.

BERRIES: To stop berries or cherries from sinking to the bottom of a cake, put the fruit into a bag, add enough flour to cover the berries, and shake until they're all coated.

BREAD: You can save money by buying day-old bread. All you do is freeze it and use it for toast or making grilled sandwiches.

CARROT CAKE: Bored with plain old cake? You can substitute an equal portion of shredded sweet potatoes for the carrots. It's more voluptuous. Be forewarned, however: it's far higher in calories (but go ahead, live a little).

COFFEE: The best way to store coffee is to put it into an airtight jar and store it in the freezer. Ground coffee will keep about a month; beans about three months. If you don't have a jar handy, you can wrap the coffee bag tightly in a plastic bag and freeze it to get the same results. Vacuum-packed coffee will keep for about three weeks once you open it. Unopened it'll stay fresh in your pantry for about six months.

One way to tell if beans are fresh is to check the shine. The shinier the bean, the fresher it is. And don't overgrind the beans. The finer the grind, the longer it takes the water to penetrate, and the result more often than not will be bitter coffee.

There's no need to have the beans ground in the store or spend $50 or so for a designer coffee-grinder. You can grind fresh beans at home in your blender.

Always use cold water (even better, use cold distilled water) when making a cup of coffee. Because hot water extracts too many of the metals and chemicals embedded in the pipes, it taints the taste of coffee.

The best way to clean a drip coffeemaker is to add ½ cup of vinegar to the pot and then fill the rest of the pot with water. Run the vinegar-water combination through the machine once.

COLESLAW STRETCHERS: If you need to stretch your coleslaw for some unexpected guests, simply add shredded carrots, peppers, and/or spinach.

CONDIMENTS: Those plastic pill boxes with snap-on lids are great for holding everything from mayonnaise to mustard if you're brown-bagging it.

COOKIES: You can dress up plain butter cookies by dipping them partway into melted milk chocolate or semisweet chocolate. You can also spread the chocolate on top of the cookies and swirl it decoratively with a fork.

If you don't have the time to make drop cookies, smooth the dough into a buttered cake pan and bake according to your recipe. Simply slice it into bars to serve.

If you don't have a cookie cutter, roll out the dough into a cylinder, freeze it, then slice it into ¼-inch rounds, and bake as directed.

If you line your cookie sheet with parchment paper, you won't have a sticky situation when you remove cookies from the oven.

CROUTONS: If you're in a hurry, crushed flavored croutons can take the place of bread crumbs, salt, and herbs in a meatloaf recipe.

"CRUMBY" SOLUTION: If you're out of seasoned crumbs to crown a casserole, you can create a pretty good substitute by mixing a teaspoon of powdered garlic with a cup of any *one* of the following pulverized cereals: Shredded Wheat, Rice Krispies, or Wheat, Corn, or Rice Chex.

CUPCAKES: Instead of baking cupcakes in paper liners, try flat-bottomed ice cream cones. Fit each one into a muffin tin, fill ⅔ with cake batter, and bake in a preheated 350° oven for 15–20 minutes (or as your cupcake recipe suggests). The cones taste great with the cupcakes.

FISH: To get the most freshness for your dollar, look for fish with a clear eye and shiny flesh, which should be firm to the touch (if you press it and it stays pressed, throw it back).

FOR THE KIDS: Sandwiches can be even more appetizing when cut in interesting shapes with a cookie cutter. Cut the bread first with the cutters, and save the leftover outlines for crumbs or croutons.

FOR THE HEALTH OF IT!: Pulverize oatmeal in your food processor and save it for the next time you make corn muffins. Just substitute the oat flour for half the total amount of white flour that the recipe calls for (use half oat flour and half white). It adds a nutty flavor and more fiber than regular flour.

• A great way to trim calories in your meatballs is simply to substitute ground turkey for the ground beef.

• For a healthy milkshake, puree 1 cup of frozen fruit (i.e., blueberries, peaches, or strawberries) with 1 cup of skim milk. Season with a dash of vanilla. You won't miss the calories.

• You can cut the calories in a three-egg omelette by using a whole egg and two egg whites. You save about 120 calories, not to mention a substantial amount of cholesterol. Use the same formula (substituting 1 egg and two egg whites for every 3 eggs) with hard-boiled eggs when you're making potato salad.

• Low-fat cottage cheese, with all of the curds smoothed out in a food processor, can be substituted for ricotta in lasagna recipes. Also use it instead of sour cream on your baked potato.

• The next time you're having borscht, top it with a dollop of no-fat yogurt rather than sour cream. Substitute plain yogurt for half of the mayonnaise in chicken, tuna, or egg salad sandwiches.

• Is macaroni and cheese a favorite comfort good, but you're counting calories? Try substituting cooked green beans for the macaroni. We used to call them "Cheese-Whizzed" beans.

GARLIC: To save the mess and chore of cleaning a garlic press, you can press garlic by putting it between two pieces of waxed paper and mashing it with a spoon.

MELONS: To ripen unripe melons, avocados, or mangoes, place them in a paper bag in a dry, warm place.

MERINGUE: If you want a towering meringue, you can whip egg whites to new heights by making sure the egg whites are at room temperature and that you whip them in a copper bowl. A chemical reaction between the protein of the egg white and the copper keeps meringue light and fluffy.

NUTS TO YOU: You have probably made green beans *amandine* (or almondine) but did you know that toasted pecans, cashews, or hazelnuts also are great with buttered green vegetables?

OVERCOOKED VEGETABLES: Overcooking vegetables happens to the best of us. One solution is to puree them with a combination of butter and milk until the vegetables (broccoli, carrots, beets, etc.) have the consistency of mashed potatoes.

PEPPERS: Bell peppers can be seeded, thinly sliced, then frozen. When you're ready to use them, you don't even have to wait until they thaw. Just add them to the frying pan when you start to sauté steaks or hamburgers.

QUICK DESSERTS: In a pinch for an easy dessert? Make ice cream sandwiches with pizzelle cookies. To serve four, set aside eight pizzelles. Peel the paper carton off a hard frozen pint of ice cream and slice the ice cream cylinder into four rounds. Sandwich each round between two of the cookies. You can roll the exposed ice cream surface in chopped nuts or shaved chocolate if you want. Serve immediately or wrap in plastic and freeze until later.

Or roll scoops of ice cream in toasted coconut and nap with pureed fruit or hot fudge sauce (see Quick Fruit Sauce).

QUICK FRUIT SAUCE: For a quick fruit sauce, puree I cup of fruit (peaches, raspberries, or strawberries) with I to 2 tablespoons of sugar. That makes about enough to serve 4.

QUICK GLAZE: For a quick chocolate glaze for cakes, cookies, or brownies, use packaged hot fudge topping.

SALADS: In order to make a good salad, you have to start with fresh lettuce that is completely dry. If not, you'll end up with a wilted mess, and the dressing will roll off it like water off a duck's back. Some people dry their greens with a towel. But I've found a hair dryer does the job a lot faster. Also very good is a salad-spinner, a clever plastic device that costs under $10. All you do is put the lettuce inside, pop on the lid, and give it a few twirls. The water is thrown into the outer bowl and you end up with dry lettuce.

Greens then should be chilled in the fridge, covered. I've found new shower caps make great salad-bowl coverings. Always add your onions just before you're ready to serve the salad. Otherwise their flavor will overpower the entire salad and the onions' acidity will help wilt the lettuce (this is known as the "Lettuce Alone Theory").

In making your classic oil/vinegar dressing, the proper ratio is 2 parts oil to I part vinegar. Exactly. Always add the salad oil first.

Cover the leaves until they glisten. Then add the vinegar. If you hit the greens with the vinegar first, it'll be wilt city. If you're using fresh herbs, put them right in with the greens. If you're using dried ones, incorporate them into the salad dressing.

SALTY SOUP: Soup wouldn't be soup without salt. But what do you do if you've added too much and the guests are about to arrive? Pop in a few peeled potatoes and they'll suck up a sufficient amount of it. A little sugar or vinegar will also hide a salty taste.

SANDWICHES: There's nothing worse than a soggy sandwich. Rather than coating the bread with a condiment like mayonnaise or mustard, try putting it between the slices of meat or cheese. The result is a less soggy sandwich at lunchtime. Even better is to put condiments on just before you're ready to eat the sandwich.

A plant mister filled with vinegar and oil dressing makes a great spritzer for salads and sandwiches.

SPRINGFORM PANS: An easy way to clean up springform pans is to line the bottom with foil before snapping into place. An added bonus is that once the cake cools, you can simply slip the bottom away from the foil, and you won't have to wait to finish the cake to use the pan again.

STRINGS ATTACHED: Out of baker's twine when you're about to truss a bird? Dental floss is a great substitute. It's also good when stitching up a galantine. However, don't use the peppermint- or cinnamon-flavored floss. Only the unflavored version is recommended.

WATERMELON: I've found that the easiest way to carve a watermelon decoratively is to draw the pattern on first with a magic marker.

INDEX

Q

R